AF861587

To Ira M. Schwartz

Thank you for enabling me to come to the Center and to the School of Social Work.

Yours

Ivan Fidand

The Welfare Paradox

Ivar Lødemel

The Welfare Paradox

Income Maintenance and Personal Social Services in Norway and Britain, 1946–1966

SCANDINAVIAN UNIVERSITY PRESS

Oslo - Stockholm - Copenhagen - Oxford - Boston

Scandinavian University Press (Universitetsforlaget AS)
P.O. Box 2959 Tøyen, N-0608 Oslo, Norway
Fax +47 22 57 53 53
URL: http://www.scup.no

Stockholm office
SCUP, Scandinavian University Press
P.O. Box 3255, S-103 65 Stockholm, Sweden

Copenhagen office
Scandinavian University Press AS
P.O. Box 54, DK-1002 København K, Denmark

Oxford office
Scandinavian University Press (UK) Ltd.
60 St. Aldates, Oxford OX1 1ST, England

Boston office
Scandinavian University Press North America
875 Massachusetts Ave., Ste. 84, Cambridge MA 02139, USA
Fax +1 617 354 6875

ISBN 82-00-21242-4

Published with a grant from The Research Council of Norway

Design: Astrid E. Jørgensen
Cover illustration: © Image Bank/Jay Belmore
Typeset in 9.25 on 13 point Photina by Formatvisual Ltd
Printed on Carat Offset 90gsm by Østfold Trykkeri, Norway

Contents

List of Tables and Figures viii
Foreword ix
Preface xiii

Part One: Theoretical Framework

1 *Theoretical Framework* 3
The theme of the study 3
Dimensions of social assistance variation 6
Towards a conceptual and explanatory framework 11
The case studies 22
Method and data 24
Plan of the book 27

Part Two: The Evolution of Institutional Welfare

Introduction: Social Insurance: The Foundation of the Modern Welfare State 31
Financing 33
Coverage 35
Levels of benefits 35
Explanatory factors 36

2 *Towards the Norwegian Model of Social Insurance* 38
Security in old age 38
Alternative schemes 52

Towards an early consensus 58
Summary and conclusions..... 62

3 *Norwegian Social Insurance, 1940–1967: From Pragmatic Selectivity towards Institutional Universality* 64
Social policy and the war..... 64
Priority conflict and compromises, 1948–1957 68
Rising benefit rates, 1957–1966 71
The National Insurance Act 73
Extensions to cover new groups 77
Summary and conclusions..... 86

4 *British Labour and Contributory Pensions: From Rejection to Acceptance and Implementation* 88
The Labour Party and contributory OAPs before the Second World War 90
Discussions in the labour movement, 1940–1943 100
The parliamentary debate, 16–19 February 1943 105
The 1943 non-decision: Possible explanations 108
Conclusions 113

5 *Residual Universality and Increasing Selectivity: Social Insurance in Britain, 1946–1966* 116
The Beveridge Plan 118
Subsistence through supplementation 122
Further limitations to comprehensiveness 131
Renewed debate on the contributory flat-rate system 134
Summary 137

Summary of Part Two: The Unequal Development of Social Insurance 138
Similar ambitions, different methods and means 138
Social insurance, 1946–1966 141

Part Three: Residual Welfare in the Expanding Welfare State

Introduction: Unequal Beginnings: The Poor Law Heritage 149

6 *From Social Assistance to Social Care in Norway: A Study of a Legislative Process* 152
The 1953 proposal 154
The 1963 departmental response 159
The politics of social policy 180
Conclusions 190

7 *Cash and Care in the Norwegian Social Services* 192
Social assistance: From poor relief to social care 192
The 1964 Social Care Act: A fillip to and course-setter for Norwegian social work 199
Conclusions 203

8 *British Social Assistance, 1948–1966* 205
The 1948 National Assistance Act 206
The 1966 Social Security Act 225
Conclusions 227

9 *British Personal Social Services: From Specialisation to Unification* 228
The creation of specialised services to replace the welfare element of the Poor Law 228
Emphasis on the need for co-ordination in the 1950s 233
Money and social work in the 1960s 236
Towards a unified personal social service 240
Summary 243

Part Four: Conclusion

10 *Conclusion* 247
Summary of main findings: The contrasting developments of British and Norwegian residual services 247
Degrees of residuality 249
Towards an understanding of divergence 251
The welfare paradox 261

References 275
Index 281

List of Tables and Figures

Tables

1.1. Index of social assistance and personal social service characteristics 23
1.2. Index of social insurance characteristics 23

5.1. National Assistance grants, 1953 127
5.2. Assistance allowances according to category of recipient 130

Figures

1.1. Development of social security expenditure 5

3.1. Development of old age pensions for married couples 72
3.2. Development in the number of pensions under national insurance schemes during the period 1900–1966 79

5.1. Indexes for NI benefits, NA allowances, retail prices, and average earnings, 1948–1966. Single people 125
5.2. Numbers of National Assistance grants in supplementation of retirement pensions 126

6.1. Heads of families receiving public assistance, 1946–1964 .. 163
6.2. New claimants in relation to total numbers receiving assistance 165
6.3. Numbers with right of citizenship in a municipality other than that where help was provided, as percentage of numbers receiving aid in their own community 165
6.4. Gross decreases in relation to total numbers of claimants 167

Foreword

Ivar Lødemel has written a challenging and highly original study of the growth of Norwegian social assistance services. He sets his inquiry within a wide-ranging institutional and comparative framework. He explores the changing and interactive relationship between social assistance and social insurance. He compares the historical progress of policy developments in Norway and Britain, and he does so in a manner that enables him to make an impressive contribution to the current debates about the institutional and normative dynamics of welfare regimes.

It is clear from Lødemel's research that the Beveridge Report has had little influence on the making of the modern Norwegian welfare state. In 1945 the officials of King Haakon's wartime cabinet may well have gone home with copies of the Beveridge Report in their diplomatic bags, but, if they did so, they certainly did not feel the need to unpack them on arrival.

Lødemel draws attention to some of the striking differences relating to the sequence, the momentum, and the outcomes of policy development in these two countries. After the Second World War Norway gave priority to the urgent tasks of economic reconstruction before moving on to replace its residual Poor Law with new schemes of social security. In Britain, by contrast, the rate of change was far more rapid. As a consequence of the political momentum generated by the publication and adoption of the Beveridge Report, an entirely new and comprehensive social security system was devised and implemented within the space of three years.

Nevertheless, the momentum of change in Britain was not sustained. Within the new universalist framework of social security, the level of insurance benefits as of right was fixed below even Beveridge's stringent subsistence criteria. Thereafter, as the number of insurance beneficiaries grew over time, an increasing proportion of claimants had to seek supplementary assistance through submission to a test of means. In Norway the reform of social security occurred later, but when it came the levels of benefits were more generous and the range of coverage sufficiently broad to leave only a residuum of targeted citizens dependent on social assistance.

Lødemel also casts new light on the key differences between the unilateral character of assistance-based transfers and the reciprocal character of insurance-based exchange relationships. As he reminds us, Richard Titmuss once described the unilateral transfer, or 'gift relationship', as the institutional hallmark of welfare altruism. In doing so, he used the blood transfusion service of the British National Health Service to illustrate his thesis. The voluntary giving of blood, however, has little in common with the statutory giving of money in the form of assistance. Policy analysts often remind us that the taxes we pay for social assistance are levied from the poor as well as the rich. Nevertheless, the persisting variations in the rates of assistance take-up are mute but compelling reminders that many eligible citizens are either unaware of, or not greatly impressed by, such arguments. In any event, the richest and the poorest of blood donors share an absolute equality of status in their common altruism. No such relationship exists in the field of social assistance.

Titmuss, I think, was well aware of these differences. His answer to the problems of stigma that arise in the provision of social assistance was that it is less likely to be experienced when assistance is provided within an overarching framework of universalist services. Universality, he argued, reaffirmed the positive links between the status of citizenship and the usage of all social services.

Social insurance encompasses both the individualist values of the economic market and the collectivist values of the social market. It is essentially a pluralist concept. The links between personal contributions and entitlements express the values and virtues of self-help and independence. At the same time, the provisions made for non-contributory forms of subsidy and an element of redistribution in some social insurance schemes express the collectivist values and virtues of solidarity and mutual aid, as well as a commitment to reducing inequality.

In his comparison of the Norwegian and British social security systems, Lødemel gives special attention to the different nature of the two assistance schemes and the composition of their clientele with particular reference to the needs of elderly and disabled people. In Britain the relatively low level of insurance benefits available to all eligible recipients leads to a greater and more widespread reliance on supplementary forms of assistance. As a consequence, it is very difficult to draw clear-cut distinctions between the clientele of the two systems of social security support. In Norway, with its more generous levels of insurance benefits, the targeting of assistance provision is more sharply focused, and the recipients are more clearly defined as a residualised need group. As Lødemel observes, the Norwegian model of social insurance displays stronger institutional features, while its model of social assistance displays residual features that are stronger than their British counterparts.

Lødemel's analysis is rich in original insights, and it is characterised by a keen awareness of the many paradoxes implicit in the ends and means of modern social security systems. He explores the continuities and discontinuities of policy change in the transition from Poor Law to assistance-based forms of provision. He analyses the implications of the gradual transfer of powers and duties from local to national agencies and from lay to professional and other expert forms of administration. He rightly gives special attention to such issues as the strategic timing of key changes in social security legislation and the successes and failures of the various interest groups and individuals that sought to shape the course and outcomes of events.

There is one further paradox, to which Lødemel makes no reference. At a time when the prospects for continuing progress in social welfare reform have never been bleaker, the quality of comparative social policy research has never been better. Lødemel has been able to draw on a rich and varied range of theoretical and conceptual literature that simply did not exist twenty years ago. In doing so he has made a distinctive contribution of his own to that literature.

The Welfare Paradox offers many new insights into the role of anti-poverty policies with reference to the broader contexts of welfare state regimes and the various typologies used in their comparison. British readers, in particular, will be able to contrast their own social assistance schemes with those of Norway. Lødemel's analysis of the end and means of social assistance provisions will be especially useful at a time when so many Western nations – and influential organisations such as the World Bank – are showing renewed interest in the possibility of developing more effective ways of targeting the delivery of social assistance at high-priority need groups.

Lødemel began his research in 1984, when comparative social assistance was a largely unresearched subject. In the meantime, like Isak in Knut Hamsun's famous novel *The Toil of the Earth*, he has cleared and cultivated new fields in the landscape of social policy studies. His pioneering work has opened up new paths and possibilities for scholarly prospectors to explore.

Robert Pinker
Professor of Social Administration
London School of Economics and Political Science

Preface

The theme of this book grew out of my experiences as a social worker in the Norwegian social services. In my professional training, I was encouraged to develop a relationship to the client based on mutual respect and trust which would lead to a shared understanding of the problems facing the client. As a practicing caseworker, however, my main function was to allocate cash benefits to those who, in my discretion, were eligible for those benefits. I found that my primary role as keeper of the purse undermined my ability to act as a social worker since clients in the first instance were rightfully more concerned with convincing me of their need rather than establishing a relationship of trust and confidence. Often rational but destitute human beings, clients would present themselves in a way designed to unleash the maximum cash benefit. This focus on eligibility on both parts, mine and the clients', thus served to hinder the openness and honesty required for effective social casework.

The resulting frustration and tension I felt between my ideals as a social worker and my job as distributor of cash benefits, made me think about other ways of organising the relationship between cash and care. Britain presented itself as a unique and interesting case for contrast and comparison. I discovered that Britain was the only European country to have separated social work from the allocation of cash benefits. This occurred as early as 1948 when Britain dismantled its Poor Law and established a National Assistance Board to allocate benefits, while maintaining local social service departments to provide care. This separation of cash and care resulted in a very different role for social workers in their work with the poor. Instead of acting as agents of monetary control, social workers were free to serve as advocates for their clients in their dealings with the National Assistance Board and other agencies.

My growing interest in this area led me to pursue a doctorate at the London School of Economics. Ahltough I did not ultimately carry out a comparison of the social worker–client relationship in the two national settings (somebody still ought to do so), my exposure to social policy at the LSE inspired me to seek a greater understanding of why the two welfare states, Norway and Britain, took such different paths and what these divergent developments could tell me about how different welfare states treat their most vulnerable group of citizens: the poor who lack socially or politically acceptable reason for their plight.

The resulting doctoral thesis, from which this book is hewn, was completed in 1989. After venturing into studies of current European social assistance variation, I decided to return to my historical study with a view to making a contribution to what has now become an increasing interest in the comparative study of social assistance.

Both the initial work and this later revision, carried out mainly in the evenings and during vacations alongside my work as a researcher and administrator, has been a lonely task. Still, there are many people who have been with me on this journey, contributing with ideas, encouragement and criticism thereby enabling me to complete the book.

Robert Pinker, my doctoral adviser at the LSE, opened my eyes to the sociological study of social policy. Throughout my four years in London he was a source of inspiration, insightful criticism and friendly support. Also at the LSE, Lutz Leisering and Tor Jacob Klette offered invaluable support and friendship. My colleagues at the Centre for Public Policy Studies at Fafo have inspired me through fruitful cooperation in ongoing research in related fields. Among these, Axel West Pedersen, Jon Hippe and Kåre Hagen have been major sources of inspiration. Aksel Hatland, Jürgen Kohl, Stein Kuhnle, and Steinar Stjernø have all helped me develop the ideas for the book. The leading scholar of Norwegian social assistance, Lars Inge Terum, has endured endless discussions on the topics covered here, as well as provided detailed comments on the theoretical and concluding chapters.

Through research grants and fellowships, several institutions have enabled me to pursue this study. In chronological order, The British Council, The Norwegian State College of Social Work, The Research Council of Norway, and The Humbolt Foundation have generously contributed. My (present) employer, Fafo Institute of Applied Social Research has offered respite from the constraints contract research. I wish to take this opportunity to thank them all. I would also like to thank Glenn Martin for his great editorial work.

My parents gave me the confidence to reach out for the unknown, in parts of the world very far from and foreign to my native fjord. My wife, Susan I. Clark, has sacrified time and provided immense support in enabling me to finish this book. Through encouragement and by offering editorial help and the insights of a scholar of social law, she has pushed me over many of the hurdles of the final leg. In doing so she saved me from the all-too-frequent belated regrets of missed time with children. Still, I look forward to spending more time with her and our son, Benjamin.

Ivar Lødemel

Part One
Theoretical Framework

Chapter 1
Theoretical Framework

The theme of the study

The focus of this study is the development of social protection targeted at the poor in Norway and Britain in the first two decades after the Second World War. During this period both countries greatly expanded their social insurance programmes, replaced their respective Poor Laws with social assistance schemes, and established the structure of their modern welfare states. Similar developments can be found in most other Western European welfare states. These were, therefore, the formative years for the interrelationship between social insurance and social assistance programmes as we see them in Europe today.

In studying Norway and Britain I strived to strike a balance in the tightrope walk of comparative studies: to find countries different enough to make a comparison interesting, while at the same time similar enough to make it meaningful and relevant. During the period under study the expressed objective in both nations was to replace the Poor Law with social insurance, leaving only a small, last-resort social assistance scheme. But while the goals were similar, the methods chosen were quite different. Norway continued the shared pre-war practice of breaking down the Poor Law 'from without' through the gradual extension of social insurance programmes. Britain, by contrast, attempted a more immediate transition through the creation of a universal National Insurance and a nationalised assistance scheme.

The unequal approaches brought about very different developments. An initial picture of the divergence can be pieced together from the relative spending on social insurance and assistance in the period of analysis. The earlier post-war launch of major insurance schemes in the United

Kingdom is reflected in the fact that while Britain spent 10% of GNP on social security in 1950, the corresponding figure in Norway was only 5.7%. In 1966, however, the British proportion had increased to only 12.5%, compared with a near doubling, to 11%, in Norway (see Figure 1.1A).[1] If we look at the spending on assistance as a percentage of total social security spending, a different picture emerges. In 1950 Britain spent 11% on assistance. This proportion remained stable in the following years, and in 1966 it was still 11.1%. In Norway a similar proportion, 12.3%, was spent in 1949. This figure decreased, however, and in 1966 was only 6.2% (see Figure 1.1B).[2]

In the field of social insurance, my emphasis will be on pensions. The proportion of spending on this area of social security increased in Norway from a modest 15.6% in 1949 to 38.7% in 1966. In Britain the same area accounted for 30.8% of total expenditure in 1959, increasing to only 34.1% in 1966 (see Figure 1.1C).[3] This shows that Norway experienced a greater overall expansion of social security during the post-war years. This increase is largely due to more spending on pensions, while the objective of a reduced assistance appears to have been largely fulfilled in Norway. By contrast, assistance continues to constitute an expanding area within British social security. A major objective of this study will be to cast light on the 'hows' and 'whys' of this divergence.

These divergent paths resulted in very different developments in the descendant systems of the cash–care multifunctional Poor Law in the two countries. Today the two countries find themselves at opposite ends of the European social assistance continuum.[4]

Perhaps the most important distinction between the modern welfare state and earlier forms of public provision is the demarcation of the target clientele. Under the Poor Law systems, only those who could document severe economic need were found eligible for support. By contrast, the modern welfare state covers a much larger proportion of the population,

---

1. Flora 1983, p. 456.

2. Ibid., pp. 526, 527 for Norway and pp. 546, 547 for the United Kingdom. By 1974 the number for the United Kingdom had risen to 17.4%, while it had remained stable in Norway.

3. Ibid. Unfortunately, no statistics are available for the United Kingdom before 1959. That year the percentage in Norway was 24.7. Again the divergence continued after 1966, and in 1974 Britain still spent only 34.4% on pensions, compared with 41.6% in Norway.

4. Lødemel and Schulte 1992.

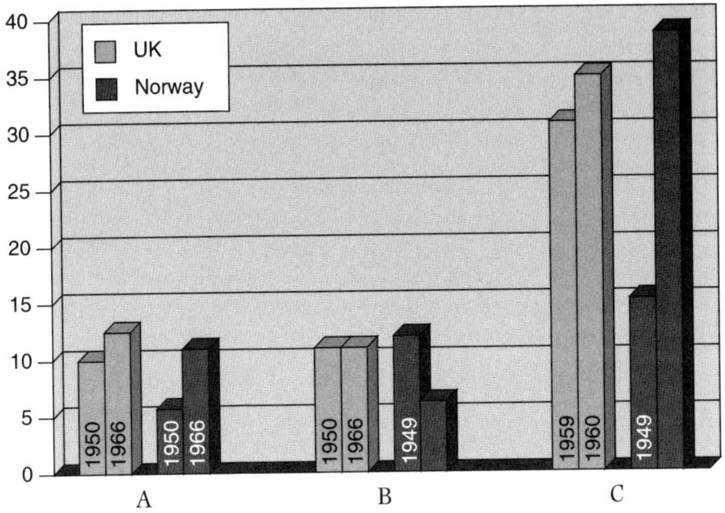

Figure 1.1. Development of social security expenditure. A: Social security as percentage of gross national product. B: Social assistance as percentage of social security. C: Social insurance as percentage of social security.

and typically aid is provided regardless of a person's means. Thus, the transition from the social service state to the welfare state[5] was another extension of the state's responsibility for its citizens. The creation of new programmes also brought about a differentiation of public provision. Whereas the Poor Law was the only form of income maintenance until the end of the 19th century in most European states, the 20th century has seen the growth of alternative schemes, mainly in the form of social insurance and demogrants.[6]

Poverty did not disappear with the abolition of the Poor Laws, and the need for an underpinning safety net for the poor prevailed after the expansion of the welfare state through social insurance. The emergence of the welfare state has been described as an extension of 'social citizenship',[7] but perhaps the best test of the extent of social citizenship through welfare is the way in which a country caters for its most vulnerable

5. 'Social service state' is Asa Briggs's term (Briggs 1961).

6. There are three forms of social security: demogrants, social insurance, and social assistance.

7. Marshall [1965] 1985.

groups. Success in covering the needs of the economically active with good income replacement benefits does not necessarily equate with a strong departure from the harsh tenets of the Poor Law for those with little or no entitlement to social insurance. By tracing the history of two countries, this study aims to describe how and discuss why the services targeted at the poor developed in divergent ways. My overall objective is to contribute to the understanding of the different poverty regimes of modern welfare states as we see them today.

Dimensions of social assistance variation

In order to study social assistance variation, we first need to define the term and to distinguish this system from other income maintenance programmes. Although the term is widely used and appears in some form in the name of the welfare scheme of most countries,[8] there is no internationally recognised definition of social assistance. This lack stands in contrast to social insurance, which is defined by the social risks covered[9] and by the contributory element. Social assistance, on the other hand, usually covers no defined risks, but rather addresses the existence of need regardless of its cause. This lumps together a wide variety of social problems, the composition of and the solutions for which are met by different programmes in different nations. This variety makes it difficult to delineate assistance.

---

8. A few examples of the names of European assistance schemes:
Austria: Sozialhilfe
Belgium: minimum of existence (minimum of subsistence needs)
Denmark: social bistand
Finland: utkomststöd
France: aide sociale; revenue minimum d'insertion
Germany: Sozialhilfe
Ireland: supplementary welfare allowance
Liechtenstein: Fürsorge
Luxembourg: revenue minimum garanti
Netherlands: bijstand
Norway: sosialhjelp
Sweden: socialbidrag
Switzerland: Fürsorge
United Kingdom: income support and family credit
(Source: Lødemel and Schulte 1992)

9. Illness, old age, maternity, unemployment, invalidity, occupational accidents, family charges.

In the 1990s the community of social policy researchers have started to study assistance across national borders. The comparative study of social assistance is still in its infancy, however, and focuses on the mapping of differences. The literature features two main approaches in the attempt to define social assistance and to distinguish it from other forms of income maintenance. One is to define it in relation to social insurance, and the other takes the preceding Poor Law as its starting point. Providing an example of the first approach, Eardley et al. define assistance as 'benefits and services available to guarantee a minimum (however defined) level of subsistence to people in need, based on a test of resources.'[10] The definition thus combines two factors, means-testing and subsistence level benefits. Both factors distinguish assistance from insurance today and are helpful in finding a definition that can be used to map and compare many countries.[11]

Nevertheless, I find the approach of Eardley et al. to be problematic and not fruitful for my study. While all assistance schemes are based on a test of resources, their approach leads to the inclusion of programmes which I would not include in a comparison of assistance. For example, housing benefits are means-tested, but are usually administered outside of social assistance. The problems of using the means-test as the key dimension in defining social assistance is further compounded if it is to be applied to studies with a historical perspective: many means-tested categorical programmes in the build-up period of social security cannot be uniformly referred to as social assistance. As we will see, categorical programmes are often precursors of non-contributory pension schemes.

This study goes beyond mapping of services and programmes and aims to discuss the historical development of assistance. For this reason I will follow the second approach: to define assistance as the modern heir of earlier Poor Law arrangements, which in most countries preceded assistance.[12]

Because this study focuses on the period when social assistance replaced existing Poor Law arrangements, the key comparative theme is the extent to which the new scheme departed from the preceding Poor

10. Eardley et al. 1996.

11. Ibid. This study of assistance covers the entire OECD area.

12. Jones 1985; Lødemel 1989; Lødemel and Schulte 1992; Stjernø 1994. Eardley et al. (1996) found that in all but two of the countries they studied, the existing scheme had a Poor Law antecedent.

Law. In the following pages, I will present the main institutional characteristics of Poor Law systems and discuss how these may be incorporated into, or departed from, in modern social assistance.

From the Poor Law to social assistance

The British New Poor Law of 1834 may serve as a beginning for an outline of the main institutional characteristics of 19th-century Poor Law arrangements. England, the cradle of the liberal tradition in welfare, also went the furthest in legislating the principles behind the tradition. Furthermore, this law served as a guiding example for many European countries.[13]

The two main principles of the 1834 Poor Law were 'less eligibility' and 'the workhouse test'. Less eligibility refers to the level of benefits; benefits should always be set lower than the lowest wage in the labour market, thereby forcing people to take even the least rewarding employment. With the workhouse test, the state made benefits conditional upon the paupers' giving up their freedom by moving into the workhouse and agreeing to work in exchange for their maintenance there. The nature of the workhouse also ensured that this dwelling was the 'least eligible' alternative for the pauper. The implementation of these principles found their expression in specific institutional characteristics.[14]

The nature of the aid provided

Under the Poor Laws, the preferred form of aid was in-kind benefits rather than cash. While there was a less cash-oriented economy in the 19th century as compared with today, the provision of in-kind benefits must

---

13. Diffusion in social policy is therefore no new invention. See De Swaan 1988, p. 46, on the spread of the workhouse institution in the 16th and 17th centuries.

14. Lødemel 1989; Stjernø 1994. The institutional characteristics found in most social assistance schemes today are the following:
1) benefits are subsidiary to income from work and are made available only after a proof of need;
2) benefits are provided as a right;
3) the schemes are mainly universal, that is, available to all citizens;
4) they are financed by general taxation; and
5) benefits are not reimbursable.
(Source: Lødemel and Schulte 1992)

also be understood as a means to control the pauper in two ways: 1) by ensuring that the aid was spent in accordance with the intentions of the provider, and 2) by limiting the freedom of choice for the recipient. In addition to this, other measures were employed with the ambition to change the behaviour of the recipient, with a positive view to furthering self-reliance and a corresponding negative view to discouraging people from approaching the authorities for support. The extensive use of visits to the home of the pauper, either by Poor Law officers or by laypeople, as in the Elberfeld system in Germany, was designed to serve this dual function of control and advice.

In modern assistance schemes, aid is more often provided in the form of cash than in-kind benefits. The US Food Stamp Program, however, is an example of a system which has retained the Poor Law system in this respect. Countries differ substantially with regard to programmes designed to directly influence the behaviour of the recipient. The French system of *revenue minimum d'insertion* stresses this aspect clearly by making attempts to integrate the recipient in society a condition for the receipt of aid. Similar, albeit less stringent, systems have prevailed in the Nordic countries and Germany, among others. The recent upsurge in European workfare programmes, inspired by the US experience, can be viewed as a step in the same direction. Given the variation that we see in today's developed welfare states, it is relevant to make a distinction between countries which continue to offer a cash–care multifunctional service and those which have separated these two functions so that assistance becomes synonymous with material aid. Because some countries have retained the provision of services and social treatment within their assistance scheme, a comparison must also include the new personal social services.

The division of responsibility between the state and local authorities

Poor relief preceded the (central) state's responsibility for welfare provision. Dating back to the Middle Ages, provisions for the poor were financed, organised, and implemented at the parish level. Where the state took a role, it was limited to establishing the responsibility of the local authority through the enactment of framework legislation. Whereas the state took responsibility for social insurance towards the end of the 19th century, the provision of poor relief, and later assistance, remained locally based in most countries. Modern assistance schemes vary, however, and today we find variations with regard to both financial and administrative responsibility.[15]

The nature of the legislation

The Poor Laws gave, as a rule, wide powers to the local authorities in organising and providing poor relief. While such 'framework' legislation governs modern assistance in the Nordic countries, other countries have legalised and codified social assistance to a much greater degree (e.g. United Kingdom, Germany). This has bearing on the extent to which entitlements can be established. Framework laws will tend to allow for more discretion in determining entitlement.

The nature of the personnel in charge of implementation

With few exceptions, laypeople played the dominant role in the day-to-day provision of poor relief. Often, charitable organisations were involved as partners of the local government. Today, these traditions prevail in some countries, while professional staff carry out the work in most countries. Among the latter, the training and professional orientation of the staff vary. Where assistance remains local and cash–care multifunctional, social workers tend to continue to play a central role in the provision of aid. This is often supplemented by a lay influence through politically elected boards. Today these boards typically play a limited role in individual cases; increasingly, they focus on wider policy issues. The difference between discretionary and entitlement-based schemes is closely correlated to this issue. Discretionary schemes often employ social workers rather than administrative officers to assess applications.

The nature of the target group

By definition, the target group of the Poor Laws were the very poor. While some assistance schemes continue in this tradition, others have wider target groups, either by choice or by default (in the latter case, through

15. Lødemel and Schulte 1992, p. 525.

the failure of social insurance to include these groups). The size and the composition of the target group will have bearing on the way in which assistance develops.

The differences outlined above constitute the dependent variables in this study. In addition to analysing each dimension, I will also focus on the relationship between the different variables and discuss the relative importance of each in relation to what constitutes the changing institutional characteristics of social assistance.[16]

Towards a conceptual and explanatory framework

Comparative studies of social assistance are still in their infancy. When I embarked on this study, there were no previous mappings of the terrain which could guide me in the search for tools for the comparison. My first task was therefore to identify the theoretical concepts that could be applied to make sense of the differences, both within each welfare state and from a cross-national perspective. Second, I discuss possible factors which may influence the divergent developments of social assistance. Third, since the development of the welfare state has taken place in a particular historical setting, the key political actors will be highlighted and the relationship between the programmes of the welfare state and non-public alternatives discussed. Finally, the research theme is narrowed and the hypothesis for the comparison is outlined within the framework of the theoretical concepts.

Models of welfare

For the purpose of this study, the typologies developed by Richard Titmuss in the mid-1960s still provide the best analytical tools.[17] My starting point is Titmuss's distinction between 'three contrasting models

16. Regardless of which dimensions are included, the problem of how to weigh their relative importance remains (Gough et al. 1997; Nervik 1993). Although some initial choices must be made also in a historical study, this approach allows me to discuss the importance of the chosen dimensions as the story unfolds.

17. The term currently in vogue, 'welfare state regimes' (Esping-Andersen 1990), is an application of these models to particular aspects of the practical world and is therefore not a competing model as such.

or functions of social policy'.[18] These were developed to analyse differences in welfare state provision and the underlying ideas of the proper role of the state. First, 'the Residual Model of Welfare' sees the function of social services as one of dealing only with people who are unable to help themselves. Social services form a safety net under the economic system, and only when the 'natural' channels of welfare – the private market and the family – break down 'should social welfare come into play, and then only temporarily'. Second, 'the Handmaiden Model' rests on the view that social services are functional to other institutions. According to this model, 'social needs should be met on the basis of merit, work performance and productivity.' Third, 'the Institutional Redistributive Model' 'sees social welfare as a major integrated institution in society, providing universalist services outside the market on the principle of need.'[19]

While the Poor Laws clearly expressed the tenets of the residual model, the departure from this system through the development of social insurance may be seen as a representation of a gradual transition to the handmaiden model, or as a true sign of the Welfare State, the institutional model. The picture is, however, more complex, and elements of the different models can be found in the different forms of income maintenance.

A distinction can be made with reference to the difference between *selective* and *universal* services. While universality is made an explicit feature of the institutional model, selectivity of the role of the social services is an implicit assumption in the residual model. Although the models had strong normative connotations for Titmuss (the matured welfare state was the embodiment of the institutional model), he remarks elsewhere that universality could not be seen as an end in itself:

> The challenge that faces us is not the choice between universalist and selective social services. The real challenge resides in the question: what particular infrastructure of universalist services is needed in order to provide a framework of values and opportunity bases within and around which can be

18. Titmuss 1974, p. 30.

19. The 'residual' and the 'institutional' model were first developed by Wilensky and Lebaux (1965). They used the models to categorise different approaches to social work. It is the wider usage of the terms that is usually associated with the work of Richard Titmuss. While Titmuss wrote only a few pages outlining the models, they have later been applied and elaborated by, for example, Pinker (1971) and Mishra (1977).

> developed socially acceptable services aiming to discriminate positively, with the minimum risk of stigma, in favour of those whose needs are greatest.[20]

Yet it becomes apparent from Titmuss's writing that 'acceptable selectivity' is achievable only in an (as yet non-existent) ideal type of welfare state: in this situation the hierarchy of universal and selective services that currently exists would be eradicated. It is therefore tempting to make an analogy to the Marxist acceptance of greater diversity in society once communism has been achieved. Recognising the stigma that is still associated with selective social services through association with the deliberately stigmatising services of the selective Poor Law, I realise that although the intentions of policy-makers may change, 'the subjective perception of ordinary people', which according to Pinker offers the only real test of a service's stigmatising potential, is a quality much more resistant to change.[21] But, recognising that such changes can be induced to a certain extent through the reform of services, I compare the selective services in the two countries according to the existence of such a 'universalist infrastructure'.

While the Poor Law was unilateral, with the public as the provider and the pauper as the recipient, social insurance brought a new form of reciprocity into public welfare. A notion of entitlement was introduced through the individual's own contributions towards his or her future income maintenance. This change also involved a new rationale in public welfare. Whereas the Poor Laws and social assistance are based on social market values, social insurance incorporates elements of the economic market. This distinction can be useful to better understand the relationship between, on the one hand, universal and selective services and, on the other, the models of welfare outlined above.

Titmuss made a sharp distinction between the social and the economic markets: 'The grant, or the gift or unilateral transfer – whether it takes the form of cash, time, energy, satisfaction, blood or even life itself – is the distinguishing mark of the social (in policy and administration) just as exchange or bilateral transfer is a mark of the economic.'[22] The 'gift relationship' in welfare is thus the mark of the social market, and the relationship between the two markets becomes that of 'warring social

20. Titmuss [1968] 1979, p. 135.
21. Pinker 1971, p. 136.
22. Ibid., p. 22.

principles'.[23] It can, however, be argued that the two markets can and should be combined and accommodated as a means of achieving a high degree of institutional welfare. Titmuss's assessment is perhaps based on the particular British experience in which, in the case of pensions, the two markets have indeed been treated as incompatible entities. By introducing the distinction between the 'differentiated welfare state' and the 'integrated welfare state', Mishra provides a conceptual framework within which such a reconciliation can be understood. In this model, the British 'Keynes–Beveridge' approach is used to exemplify the differentiated or pluralist model. This was 'based on the idea of "correcting" the tendencies of a market economy, through judicious state intervention and limited forms of social policy'.[24] The integrated, or corporatist, model 'recognises the need to harmonise the economic and the social within society as a whole.'

The understanding of a dichotomy between the economic and the social market underlies Titmuss's distinction between the different models of welfare. Both the residual and the handmaiden model are based on a subordination of the social to the economic market. From this perspective, the residual model represents the minimalist approach, while the handmaiden model allows for greater public welfare activity, but only on the condition that it serves the interests of the economic market.[25] Only the institutional model, therefore, represents a true victory of social over economic market values. In income maintenance the distinction between economic and social markets is particularly relevant in the field of social insurance. Pinker argues that the 'insurance principle was based on the ethic of an economic rather than a social market.'[26] (Conversely, the demogrant, as a form of social insurance, is based on the social market values.)

In addition to providing a framework, Titmuss's models are used because of their central position in welfare studies. I will therefore include a discussion of their usefulness with particular reference to assumptions

23. Mishra 1984, p. 106.

24. Ibid., p. 104.

25. Spicker (1983b, p. 190) argues that elements of the handmaiden model may be incorporated into the residual as well as the institutional model. I agree, but in terms of societal connotations the shared values of the residual and the handmaiden distinguish these from the institutional model.

26. Pinker 1971, pp. 88–89.

about the dichotomous nature of welfare associated with the models. For example, the tradition of 'social conscience' theory represents a view of social policy in which the models have come to serve as ideal types.[27] While the residual model reflects the harshness of the Poor Law, the institutional model is tied to the modern welfare state in its most developed form. This highly atheoretical approach, particularly popular in Britain in the 1950s, started from the assumption that 'social policy manifests, through the state, the love that men have for each other.'[28] Welfare development, from this perspective, results from a widening of such sentiments, together with greater knowledge and understanding of social need.

There is a clear methodological and ideological linkage between the social conscience thesis and that of 'convergence theories'. While rejecting the British bias and insularity of the social conscience theorists, the convergence thesis maintains that the welfare state is an integral part of modern capitalist society and that nations of similar levels of development will feature similar welfare arrangements. As countries converge in development, so will their social policies.[29] The welfare state, therefore, is seen by the two theories as the civilised replacement of the minimalist and oppressive ideologies and measures of the Poor Law. Expressed in Titmuss's terminology, the developed welfare state thus represents the replacement of residual with institutional welfare.

Linked to the theories above is the controversy about the relationship between the Poor Law and modern social services. While the view that the schemes developed as a reaction to the Poor Law is linked to the ideas of social conscience and convergence, the critics of this approach maintain that the two sets of services are different systems serving different purposes. Therborn, for example, argues that the much-used expression 'from the poor house to the welfare state is fundamentally misleading from a perspective of social history.'[30] While I question the normative assumptions of the social conscience thesis and the simplistic comparative assessment underlying the convergence thesis, it can be argued that the

27. Baker 1979.

28. Ibid., p. 178.

29. See Higgins 1981 for a discussion of these approaches to welfare. But be aware of new 'convergence in outcome' (Øverbye 1994).

30. Therborn 1983. For an example of the opposite view, see Nestor 1976. A discussion of the two approaches is provided in Fraser 1981.

complexity of the interrelationship between Poor Law services and those of modern welfare reveals close linkages, both in the forms of contrasting policies and in the continuation of the values embedded in the Poor Law.[31] The modern welfare state thus reflects the greater societal differentiation in which it has developed and exists.

The distinction between institutional and residual welfare should not be seen as a dichotomy. Applied to the practical world of welfare, it is best understood as a continuum, with elements of both in the different services provided (with the handmaiden model as a third case, incorporating aspects of the other two). While the Poor Law is a clear example of the residual model, its heirs, social assistance and personal social services, may embody elements of the institutional model in their still-residual character. Likewise, social insurance may retain traits of the residual model.

Possible explanations of change and divergence

The dynamics of income maintenance programmes

There are both internal and external factors that should be addressed in any attempt to explain the changing characteristics of social assistance resulting from the interplay between different forms of welfare. Internally, the size of the clientele and its composition will have bearing on the changing nature of the scheme. A scheme that includes only a small residuum of socially maladjusted people will be viewed differently than a large scheme incorporating, among others, the majority of those suffering from civilian disability. This difference in perception influences political attention and the kind of solutions favoured in meeting the need of the assistance clientele.

In my search for external explanatory factors, I will therefore focus on those most likely to affect the size and composition of the assistance clientele, the legacies of poor relief, and the development of social insurance. Among other factors worthy of examination for future studies are cultural differences between nations.[32] The potential contribution of different explanatory factors will be discussed in Chapter 10.

---

31. See, for example, Abel-Smith 1964.

32. The strong element of subsidiarity in (for example) the German scheme (Sozialhilfe) is probably best explained by a culture which puts great emphasis on the responsibility of the individual and of the family, and on mutual responsibilities between the state and the individual. These elements predate the development of the welfare state.

The Poor Law precedent

If we start from the assumption that policy inheritance influences the path of decisions in the field of welfare, we must turn to the nature of the preceding Poor Law in our search for explanations of the nature of social assistance schemes. Almost all OECD countries have a history of statutory poor-relief arrangements.[33] The similarities between the Poor Laws outlined above were, however, complemented by substantial differences between the national arrangements. These differences become important both in evaluating the extent of policy inheritance versus change and with regard to how the structure and functioning of the antecedent Poor Law influenced the path taken during the transition to modern social assistance schemes. I will focus on the latter here.

The 19th century featured both convergence and divergence in European Poor Law practices. Convergence was (probably) mainly due to the diffusion of liberal(istic) ideas concerning the proper role of poor relief. The English New Poor Law of 1834 serves as an example of a drastic reaction to prevailing mercantilist ideas about extensive public responsibilities for the well-being of the poor. Divergence took two forms. First, throughout Europe the all-purpose workhouse tradition was succeeded by a differentiation into specialised institutions such as orphanages, old age asylums, hospitals, insanity wards, maternity houses, and prisons.[34] This differentiation of care was followed by the creation of separate needs-based cash-transfer programmes for different groups. While this took place within the ambit of the Poor Law in some countries, others established these categorical programmes outside the Poor Law, for example as municipal schemes serving as forerunners of state pensions. As the countries followed different paths, the differentiation therefore brought about further divergence in the characteristics of the programmes for the poor.

The second divergence concerns the extent to which the liberal principles were upheld in national legislation and practice. To implement liberal principles, a strong presence by the state through legislation and finance, as well as an extensive bureaucracy, was necessary. Both could form the foundation for an earlier and more extensive modernisation of poor relief, compared with countries where such instruments were absent. It is therefore not self-evident that a Poor Law incorporating

33. Eardley et al. 1996.
34. De Swaan 1988, p. 47.

principles such as 'less eligibility' and 'the workhouse test' laid the foundation for a harsh assistance scheme to follow.

In this study, the preceding Poor Laws in the two nations will not be analysed in great detail. Instead, I will focus on differences in the degree of centralisation and the role of professionals versus laypeople in implementing poor relief.

The development of social insurance

The differentiation of income maintenance through the extension of social insurance programmes is the factor which will be given the greatest attention in this study. Three main questions will be addressed:

1. How does the development of social insurance influence the path of social assistance?
2. Which factors determine the unequal influence exerted by social insurance programmes?
3. How did the two nations arrive at different systems of social insurance?

The answer to the first question is determined by which aspects of social assistance the researcher addresses. Above I have identified the size and the composition of the assistance clientele at the time of legislation as the focal factors in the study of the institutional characteristics of social assistance. National programmes for an accelerated introduction of social insurance schemes during and immediately after the Second World War often included expressed ambitions concerning the relationship between poor relief and insurance, that is, that insurance was to be developed to minimize the need for poor relief or social assistance. The reduction was discriminatory rather than across the board: new insurance programmes lifted some social categories out of assistance and left others behind.

Albeit with similar aims, the social insurance programmes of the various nations differed substantially in nature, and so did their success in reducing the size and altering the composition of the social assistance clientele.[35] In my search for the causes of divergent influences of social

35. The differences between the social insurance programmes of developed welfare states have been documented in numerous studies.

insurance on the social assistance clientele, I focus on the way social insurance is financed. The method of financing distinguishes systems based on individual contributions from those that also include individuals who are unable to contribute. Further, the system of financing influences the level of benefits paid and thus the degree to which a person can subsist on social insurance alone. Both factors influence whether and to what extent social assistance continues to play a substantial role in public income maintenance.

The main distinction, therefore, is between the contributory principle on the one hand and the taxation principle on the other.[36] A contributory system will, by definition, fall short of including all members of a defined category, for example the elderly. In the case of a strict adherence to the actuarial principle, there will be a long period during which even those covered will receive insufficient benefits due to the length of the contributory period. Contributory systems also vary with regard to the level of benefits. All else being equal, a flat-rate system will provide lower benefits than an earnings-related system. The obvious advantage of a tax-financed system, given an ideal of broad coverage, is that deciding which groups to include becomes a political process. In its pure form, a contributory system includes only those able to pay contributions, thereby limiting the coverage to the economically active. A contributory system offers, however, greater scope for higher benefits for high earners. In the practical world we often find these principles combined, for example, with a tax-financed basic pension, topped up by an earnings-related addition.

The wider historical context

In the analytical framework outlined above, both the dependent variable (assistance) and the main independent variable (social insurance) are income maintenance programmes. Such an approach easily lends itself to a functionalistic analysis. To understand the changes taking place, it is necessary to define and analyse the forces at play leading up to the important departures in social policy.

I will focus on four factors: the interplay between private and public welfare, the role of political actors, the timing of legislation, and the forces governing change versus continuity.

36. Zacher 1980.

The interplay between private and public welfare schemes

This factor is particularly relevant for the analysis of how different countries arrive at different social insurance programmes. To understand the significance of this factor, the question of timing is important. European countries experienced differences in the timing and pace of industrialisation (a commonly accepted background to the rise of pensions); still, most European nations converge in the timing of the establishment of the first social insurance schemes, around the turn of the century. This meant that some countries experienced a longer period of industrialisation before the first enactments. With no public alternatives to the Poor Law, private, self-help, and occupational schemes filled some of the vacuum created by the new needs in an industrial society. Such a development favoured the contributory solution by creating divisions in the working class and thus vested interests (among those covered) in favour of the contributory solution; by showing the feasibility of that solution, where successful; and by influencing the interests of organised labour in this direction. Conversely, a late industrialisation (and simultaneous first enactment of social insurance) facilitates a more united (working-class) interest for the tax-financed solution.

The role of key political actors

My definition of political actors goes beyond political parties to include individual politicians, trade unions, and professional organisations. While the influence of experts and their organisations can be described as pressure from above, the influence exerted by (potential) recipients of welfare, and their organisations, will be seen as pressure from below.[37] In explaining the success of the Scandinavian social insurance programmes, the labourist approach has long dominated the debate.[38] Peter Baldwin's influential work *The Politics of Social Solidarity* has challenged the assumption that the role of the labour movement is the single most important factor in explaining the Scandinavian system.[39] He highlights the particu-

37. Jens Alber (1982, pp. 76–77) argues that all non-functionalist theories, Marxist as well as pluralist, can be labelled as stressing either pressure from below or pressure from above in their interpretations of determinants of welfare.

38. For example, Korpi 1983; Esping-Andersen 1990.

39. Baldwin 1990.

lar nature of risk categories which have been mobilised across the socialist/non-socialist divide. While accepting Baldwin's premise, I will emphasise the difference between the roles of organised labour in my analysis of the divergence in early post-war social insurance policies in Britain and Norway. In the case of assistance and personal social services, by contrast, the development is in both countries largely influenced by pressure from above. In this area the role of professional groups will be given particular attention.

In looking at the role of individual policy-makers, I do not focus exclusively on the role of 'great men',[40] but also discuss the role of politicians who, while in office, proved unable to introduce legislation. This latter group's failed attempts altered the timing, subjecting legislative proposals to a later and different social climate.

The timing of enactment

The majority of the Western welfare states enacted social assistance programmes during the first two decades after the Second World War. Because this was the major period of welfare expansion and differentiation in most welfare states, a transition from the Poor Law to social assistance during the early part of this period took place in an environment which was very different from that of the later part of the period. The timing influences the character of assistance in two ways. First, an early transition will most likely have to cater for larger categories of beneficiaries and greater numbers of 'insurance types', such as elderly and disabled people. Second, the nature of legislation is influenced by the prevailing spirit of the time. While the early post-war period was dominated by a structural understanding of poverty, and thus of the clientele, the 1950s and 1960s saw a resurgence of pathological interpretations of this problem.[41]

Timing matters also in the development of social insurance. I will focus both on the time when the two countries decided how to finance social insurance and, later, on the timing of important policy changes in the post-war period. The strength of the labour movement and the relationship between the Labour parties and organised labour were very different at the beginning of the century compared with the period around the

40. Pinker 1979.
41. Jackson and Valencia 1979.

Second World War. Similarly, in a period of differentiation, the forces guiding the interplay between public and private forms of welfare changed. Linked to this is the changing relationship between and within social classes, which express themselves as different 'risk communities'.[42]

Change versus continuity

In arriving at different models for social insurance, a country's policy inheritance has strong bearing on the choices made at that time.[43] A particular solution chosen at one point will influence the choices to be made at the next crossroads. Thus, for example, the choice of a contributory approach to social insurance establishes individual entitlements to benefits which may complicate the transition to a tax-financed solution. Furthermore, if successful, the chosen approach will have proved its feasibility, and experts, perhaps with vested interests as administrators, will be reluctant to change direction. Similarly, a highly centralised Poor Law system is more likely to be succeeded by a centralised assistance scheme than a situation whereby the state devolves more responsibility to the local authorities for the provision of poor relief.

The case studies

The social insurance schemes and the assistance programmes of Britain and Norway will be compared according to two indexes based on the conceptual model outlined above.

At the end of the Second World War, both nations aimed to develop insurance to reduce assistance to a last-resort scheme. I will analyse in detail the unequal success in the achievement of this shared aim. The extent to which each nation managed to move away from the practices of the Poor Law cannot, however, be measured solely in terms of the numbers remaining in the services which descended from it. I will therefore go behind the numbers and study the *nature* of the assistance schemes and the *composition* of the clientele of these services. The comparison will be made according to the dimensions outlined above

42. Baldwin 1990.
43. See Rose and Davies 1994 for a thorough discussion of the importance of policy inheritance in public policy.

and within the framework of the typologies developed by Richard Titmuss.

Social assistance

Although social assistance is often referred to as embodying the tenets of the residual model, I will start from the assumption that assistance also varies along the institutional–residual continuum.

Table 1.1. Index of social assistance and personal social service characteristics

Indicator	*Institutional*	*Residual*
Responsible authority	State	Local authority
Legal basis	Codified	Framework
Decision-makers	Officers	Laypeople
Provision	Cash only	Cash–care
Target group	Poor plus others	Poor only

Social insurance

As the independent variable of this study, social insurance schemes in the two countries will be compared according to their ability to reduce the number of people relying on social assistance. The main criteria are therefore coverage and the level of benefits. A social insurance scheme failing to include large numbers of elderly and disabled people will be seen to have retained stronger residual traits than one with universal coverage. With a low level of benefits, formal inclusion is not a sufficient criterion for universality or institutional welfare through pensions. Low benefits therefore undermine the coverage through continued dependency on assistance in the form of supplementary benefits. For these reasons I have chosen to focus on old age pensions and the introduction of disability schemes in the two countries.

Table 1.2. Index of social insurance characteristics

Indicator	*Institutional*	*Residual*
Coverage	Universal	Selective
Level of benefits	Standard security	Anti-poverty

The comparative hypothesis of this study can be expressed according to these two indexes. I hypothesise that the cash–care multifunctional social services of Norway will fall on the far right end of the continuum. British social assistance and its social services are hypothesised to feature less residual traits than their Norwegian equivalents. By contrast, the Norwegian model of social insurance will (be expected to) feature stronger institutional traits than its British counterpart.

If this is true, it follows that the social division of welfare in Britain is increasingly between a relatively undivided public income maintenance and a substantial private and occupational welfare arena through which standard security is provided. In Norway, by contrast, equally strong divisions exist, but mainly within public welfare – between a developed social insurance on the one hand and a residual assistance on the other.

Herein lies a possible contradiction: While the Norwegian public income maintenance system in total features stronger institutional traits than its British counterpart, the tenets of the residual model have been maintained to a greater degree in Norway through an assistance scheme which has more similarity to the previous Poor Law than does its British counterpart. This study aims to test the existence of such a contradiction and discusses how and why the contrast between the two nations developed.

Method and data

The choice of data and the method of the study were determined by the kind of issues I wanted to address and the time period chosen for analysis. First, my main interest is the institutional arrangements for the provision of welfare and how these differ with regard to the perception of the target groups for these policies. This approach calls for studies and interpretations of the main departures in policy development. Second, I have chosen to study the first twenty years after the Second World War. The time limitation was necessary to make the study feasible. The particular time period was chosen because these were the formative years for both the expansion of social insurance and the transfer from the Poor Law to social assistance in the two countries. It follows from my emphasis on policy inheritance that the choices made in this particular time period offer the best source of information for understanding the differences between the two countries today.

The choice of the historical period limited the nature of data available for research. While, for example, the level of benefits in social assistance is an important indicator of the quality of the scheme, such data were available only for the United Kingdom, and therefore no comparison could be made.[44] Instead, because my main concern is not the extent of poverty alleviation but the relationship between alternative forms of maintenance, the analysis here focuses on the insurance–assistance benefit ratio, measured by the number of pensioners receiving supplementary social assistance.

I compiled the book by using a number of different sources. First, the most widely used and most frequently cited were secondary sources, in the form of monographs, articles in journals, and post-graduate dissertations. There are two reasons for the reliance on secondary sources. The first is one of economy. The time period, which was one of great legislative activity, and the number of welfare programmes covered forced me to rely on other people's work for much of the study. Important departures and areas insufficiently covered by previous research were subject to comprehensive use of primary sources. Second, while this area of research is new to comparative inquiry, both countries offer a wealth of research concerning social insurance, the personal social services, and social assistance. Often, my contributions are new interpretations resulting from subjecting national evidence and interpretations to the comparative test.

I also referred to professional social work and social service journals for the period studied. In studying the major acts of relevance to the study, I used public documents in the form of departmental white (and green) papers and transcripts of parliamentary debates in both countries.

In addition, I studied the political background and motives behind important policy decisions. Although most of these events are 30–50 years back in time, I have been fortunate enough to meet the key policy-makers in Norway and two distinguished academics in Britain who had an impact on Labour Party social policy in the 1950s and 1960s.[45] In

44. Present-day comparisons also meet considerable obstacles in their attempts to compare benefit levels. See, for example, discussions of these problems in Eardley et al. 1996.

45. From Norway: Rakel Seweriin, Gudmund Harlem, Liv Kluge, Haakon Lie, and Bernt H. Lund; from Britain: Brian Abel-Smith and Howard Glennerster.

Britain, the great tradition of writing biographies provides a source to tap, one much less developed in Norway.

The method used was also determined by the questions I have set out to answer. My aim is to understand diversity in policy in the light of shared challenges and shared objectives. The diversity is identified at the outset: different systems of social assistance. The challenge applies to all developing welfare states – what to do with those falling outside both established forms of maintenance while exhibiting welfare needs that are not universally accepted as deserving of aid. These questions call for an interpretative analysis[46] with an ambition to study differences and similarities in the hope of furthering our understanding of how different causal conditions generate different outcomes.[47]

It follows also from this approach that mine is a study primarily concerned with social policies targeted at particular social groups. The welfare programmes chosen for analysis are therefore identified in relation to these groups. Two sets of services are distinguished: 1) services targeted at the group, mainly social assistance and personal social services; and 2) social insurance, the development of which is seen to have bearing on the unequal provision of the first set of services in the two countries. (Since my focus is on groups in need, the comparison mainly concerns the development of policy areas over time.)[48]

The extent to which theoretical advances in the form of generalisations can be made is clearly limited by the choice of only two countries. This choice must be understood in the light of the limitations discussed above, but it is also a result of the pioneering nature of the study. When I started the research for this volume, the terrain was uncharted, and this is still the first comparative study of social assistance involving an in-depth study of the history of national programmes. While the study has a theoretical ambition, that of contributing to the understanding of welfare state variation, the main objective is therefore to make a contribution to the cumulative task of forming hypotheses for future research in this area.

46. Jones 1985, pp. 23–31.
47. Ragin 1994, p. 109.
48. Higgins 1981, pp. 20–25.

Plan of the book

The remainder of the book is organised around two themes, institutional welfare (Part Two) and residual welfare (Part Three). The first two chapters of Part Two trace the development of Norwegian social insurance. Chapter 2 takes us back to the beginnings of Norwegian social security in an attempt to analyse how Norway arrived at the tax-financed approach to social insurance. Chapter 3 traces the developments in Norway from the Second World War until the introduction of National Insurance in 1966. The main theme is the development of the old age pension and extensions of social insurance to cover new groups.

The study then turns to inquire into the history of British social insurance. Labour was in charge of implementing the Beveridge proposals after the party took power in 1945. The party's change from rejection to acceptance of the contributory system of financing is given particular attention in Chapter 4. The following chapter traces the developments in Britain during the first two decades after the war and discusses how the contributory flat-rate approach proved unsuccessful in taking groups out of assistance dependency.

Part Three focuses on the dependent variable: the role of social assistance in the expanding welfare state. Because of the combination of social care and material aid under the Poor Law in both nations, both social assistance and the personal social services will be addressed.

Chapter 6 follows the transition from the Poor Law, through different government proposals, to the introduction of social assistance in Norway in 1964. The following chapter focuses on the social work element in the cash–care multifunctional Norwegian scheme.

Guided by the findings in the material on Norway, Chapter 8 first discusses how and why Britain nationalised assistance in 1948. The second half of the chapter traces the development of British assistance until the introduction of Supplementary Benefits in 1966. Because Britain separated the personal social services from the provision of material aid, Chapter 9 ventures outside the narrow scope of social assistance by tracing the development of a specialised service to replace the welfare element of the Poor Law. In this chapter the reintroduction of material aid in the social services in 1963 is given particular attention through a discussion of the changing attitudes towards the needs of the poor in general and towards material aid among British social workers in particular.

The Conclusion (Chapter 10) first brings the main findings of the study together. The findings are then discussed in relation to the models of welfare outlined above, and to the ongoing debate regarding welfare regimes.

Part Two
The Evolution of Institutional Welfare

Introduction
Social Insurance: The Foundation of the Modern Welfare State

In the area of income maintenance the development of social insurance represents the gradual replacement of the residual welfare of the Poor Law with services financed, administered, and allocated according to an institutional model of welfare. Universal schemes based on a test of need replace selective means-tested programmes. While Poor Law services had great scope for discretion, social insurance is allocated according to clearly defined statutory rules. The responsibility for the services lies with the state rather than with the local authorities.

As we shall see in the next four chapters, the reality is, however, not so neat, and the differences between the insurance programmes of Britain and Norway become more important than the similarities. Therefore, to carry out this comparison I need, first, to outline the variables by which insurance schemes may differ and, second, to highlight the particular features that will be emphasised in my analysis.[1]

There are three main variables by which the social insurance programmes of matured welfare states vary. First, the *method of financing* takes two main forms. At one extreme is the strictly contributory approach whereby future beneficiaries contribute together with their employers. At the other end of the spectrum is a system whereby the entire cost is covered by general taxation. Both sources of income can be

1. An 'official' definition of social insurance and other social security programmes is provided by the International Labor Organization (1984). When the ILO, for example, defines insurance as 'financed by contributions which are normally shared between employers and workers, with, perhaps, state participation in the form of a supplementary contribution or other subsidy from the general revenue' (p. 4), I find this to be too narrow a definition. In my analysis 'social insurance' will therefore include schemes that are mainly financed by general revenue. Furthermore, unlike the ILO, I also include schemes that include an element of means-testing.

operated on a pay-as-you-go basis, or the money can be accumulated in a fund. A tax system may be based on progressive taxation or, alternatively, a set percentage of income can be paid. As we shall see, the Norwegian and the British system both combined these two approaches; the differences were in the divergent balancing of the two forms of financing. Second, the *level of benefits* may vary in real terms, most importantly in the context of this study in relation to benefits offered through social assistance. Third, the *coverage* of a national insurance system varies between a high degree of universality and a selective approach in which entitlements are restricted by a test of means and/or a test of need. Furthermore, a strictly contributory scheme includes only individuals with contributory records.

The term social insurance comprises services targeted at wide varieties of need situations. A general trend has been for pioneering programmes to cover loss of earnings from work. By extension, groups outside the workforce have been included through a change of emphasis away from work-record to an assessment of need alone. Thus, Flora and Alber found that of the 12 European nations in their study, 6 introduced industrial accident insurance as the first scheme. Five started out with sickness insurance, while only Denmark introduced old age pensions at the outset.[2] The authors describe the close association to the labour market as 'a break with liberal ideas concerning the assignment of guilt and responsibility among individuals.' From this perspective, securing against loss caused by occupational contingencies 'could be rationalised by redefining the old idea of liability for individually caused damage.'[3] Furthermore, these schemes would have very limited coverage, including only individuals who were able to contribute towards future benefits and thereby placing an acceptable burden on the state. When old age receives particular attention from policy-makers at a later stage, this must be understood in the light of the situation of the late 19th century. While disability caused by sickness or industrial accidents was a common need situation, old age pensions grew out of the idea of retirement. Before the first programmes, the rule was to work until old age, and frailty made this impossible. With improved medicine to keep people alive long after frailty made work impossible, the need for a support system outside the Poor Law became pressing for this group also.

2. Flora and Alber 1981, p. 51.
3. Ibid.

My focus on old age pensions in this section must therefore be understood in the light of the purpose of this study. Except in the 1930s, when unemployment dominated the Poor Law in both countries, the transfer of the elderly from the Poor Law to insurance had the greatest impact on support systems in the two countries during the period of analysis. Furthermore, old age pensions set the standard for later extensions of social insurance,[4] thereby lifting new groups out of social assistance dependency.

Moreover, the old age pension represents the most important insurance scheme for a study that attempts to highlight the interrelationship between private and public income maintenance. Traditionally, the need for income maintenance in old age has been an important market for private insurance.[5] The extent and nature of this activity will be seen to have strong bearing on the different paths taken by social insurance in both countries. This influence may take two forms. First, a low income replacement ratio in social insurance allows room for the growth of private insurance. Second, in the case of a contributory system of social insurance, a low ceiling for contributions will have the same effect. A final reason for examining old age pensions is to draw out more clearly the role of the labour movement. Regarding this area of social insurance, the study will highlight the difference in the extent to which welfare was extended beyond coverage of the labour force in the two countries. This, in turn, is of vital importance to the extent of the transfer of claimants from assistance to insurance in the period of this analysis.

The old age pensions (and related programmes) will be analysed according to the three variables outlined above. The following issues will be raised in relation to the variables.

Financing

Until the end of the 19th century the Poor Law represented the only form of public income maintenance. Measures were taken only when extreme hardship occurred. The *ad hoc* nature of relief, together with the composition of the target group, ensured that financing from general taxation was the only alternative. Because receiving poor relief was closely tied to

4. Pettersen 1987; Jones 1985.
5. Kaim-Caudle 1973, p. 131.

punishment, it was hardly a situation towards which potential 'beneficiaries' would have contributed, had they been able. With the introduction of income maintenance programmes aimed at a wider section of the population and designed to meet more foreseeable contingencies, new ways of financing the services were rendered possible. The much greater costs involved gave more impetus to the search for ways to relieve the public purse.

It was, furthermore, in line with prevailing (liberal) notions of self-help that the individual should contribute towards his or her own future maintenance. But, with wages at subsistence level, the practicality of contributory pensions had clear limitations. It was unrealistic that the individual worker, finding it hard to make ends meet as it was, should be expected to provide for the full cost. Furthermore, the first debates on the principle of financing coincided with the emergence of socialist parties, for whom tax-financed pensions soon became a major political objective.

Following on from this connection to labour politics, I will argue that while the taxation principle represents a socialist approach to social policy, the contributory principle is based on ideas traditionally associated with non-socialist ideologies. While the contributory approach stresses self-help and actuarial reciprocity, the main ideas underlying the taxation principle are solidarity through collective responsibilities and the desire to achieve redistribution through welfare. That this latter approach is more in line with socialist ideologies has also been emphasised by other writers. Fraser writes about financing 'via the more socialistic general taxation'.[6] A similar understanding underlies Pinker's equation of the contributory principle with 'the ethic of an economic rather than a social market'.[7]

In Chapter 1, I hypothesised that the difference in the forms of financing chosen by Norway and Britain before the post-war insurance expansion largely explains the varying degrees of success in reducing the scope of assistance in the two countries. My analysis of financing therefore covers two areas. First, I will analyse how the two nations arrived at different positions in 1945. This is the main focus of Chapters 2 and 4. Second, in Chapters 3 and 5, I will outline how the different solutions brought about very different developments of insurance in the two countries.

---

6. Fraser 1984, p. 232. See also Abel-Smith 1953, p. 21.
7. Pinker 1971, p. 90.

Coverage

The establishment of insurance schemes gradually lifted groups out of Poor Law dependency. Until the Second World War Norway and Britain both followed this approach of breaking down the Poor Law 'from without' through the creation of alternatives. In 1948, however, Britain broke with this tradition and attempted to launch a frontal attack on the Poor Law itself. Its abolition necessitated, among other schemes, the setting up of compulsory insurance for the elderly. Norway, by contrast, continued the breakdown 'from without' in the period leading up to the reform of the Poor Law in 1964. During this period the coverage of old age pensions was gradually extended through the easing of the means test, which was finally abolished in 1957. The different roads towards universality in the two nations will be seen to have a bearing on the unequal development of assistance.

Furthermore, this heading also comprises an analysis of the extent to which insurance has been extended *beyond old age pensions* to cover other groups that have little possibility of achieving insurance through a contributory system. The extensions may take two forms. First, separate schemes for different need categories can be established along the lines of an existing insurance programme. Second, existing schemes can be opened for other groups of claimants. In general this involves a liberalisation of the test of eligibility. The extension of disability pensions to new categories of handicapped people is one example. As we will see, the extent to which this can take place depends largely on the form of financing.

Levels of benefits

Put bluntly, it is not an impressive achievement for a state to establish a universal pension if the benefits offered are far from sufficient to cover the essentials for subsistence. Universality, therefore, is in itself not a sufficient condition for a nation to deserve being called an institutional welfare state. The level of pensions therefore has a direct impact on the scope of assistance. With insufficient insurance benefits, recipients may have to turn to assistance for supplementation. This will be one of the main focuses of Chapter 5, where we look at British insurance after the war. Moreover, I will argue that the Norwegian policy of a gradual extension towards universality also proved beneficial for the elevation of benefit levels.

Explanatory factors

The search for explanations aims to answer first of all how the two countries arrived at very different models of social insurance in 1945. In both countries Labour governments came to power in this period. We therefore have to ask why and how the two Labour parties could arrive at very different policies. My analysis of the post-war period will highlight the importance of the method of financing in explaining the divergent development of insurance. Therefore, I must first analyse attitudes towards this question in the two Labour parties in the period leading up to 1945.

Regarding this early period, the difference in *policy inheritance* is considered the most important factor in explaining the contrasting policy choices in the labour movements of the two countries. But although I argue that policy development in both countries represents a case of the victory of continuity over change, I also discuss the extent to which ideological factors played a role, first, in establishing the policy to be inherited and, later, in maintaining support for the specific solutions.

Once established, a particular solution in the form of a welfare scheme gets invested with professional and bureaucratic interests which may resist deviation from the established norm. Furthermore, client groups which feel that the existing solution favours their interests could exert political pressure to preserve these vested interests. Finally, unless the existing schemes have been found to represent a dead-end, their existence and proven feasibility will have an impact on the debate.

Policy inheritance embodies, in the context of this analysis, non-public as well as public precursors to state schemes. While the latter include municipal and state programmes, private and occupational pensions will be considered to be the most important non-public schemes.

In Britain the existence of non-public schemes (self-help programmes such as Friendly Societies, together with the private insurance business) will be seen to have strong bearing on decisions regarding financing, level, and scope of social insurance during and after the Second World War. In Norway, by contrast, self-help and private insurance arrangements had not developed to a degree comparable to that in Britain. The important policy inheritance in Norway is found within the public sector.

The existence of municipal pension schemes proved to influence the choice of a tax-financed insurance system and laid the foundations for insurance schemes with aims beyond meeting the needs of the workforce only.

Neither the creation of a policy nor its later influence on future programmes can, however, be explained without reference to the major political groups involved in the process of policy formation. Although other political parties played an active role in both countries, the differences can best be studied by comparing the contrasting policies of the respective labour movements. Here, I will hypothesise that the Norwegian labour movement played a much more active and constructive role than its British counterpart.[8]

8. Heclo (1973, p. 228) makes a similar point in his comparison of the British and the Swedish development.

Chapter 2
Towards the Norwegian Model of Social Insurance

In this chapter I will analyse the political process which facilitated a change from contrasting positions at the time of the first social insurance initiatives, towards the end of the 19th century, to a near-all-party consensus on the major principles of insurance by the mid-1930s. The emphasis will be on the compromises that made the consensus possible. For both sides of the political spectrum, pragmatism rather than dogmatism proved to have been a necessary approach in this process. In particular, the pragmatism of the labour movement will be seen to have been of great importance. The existence of municipal precursors to later state pensions will be seen to have facilitated the particular consensus reached. The chapter will conclude with an outline of the main elements of the Norwegian model of social insurance.

Security in old age

With the exception of Finland, Norway ranked in 1935 as the country with the narrowest social insurance coverage in Europe.[1] During the following five years Norway experienced the greatest expansion in social insurance coverage of any European country since the introduction of Bismarck's first legislation in 1883.[2] Thus, according to Alber's index of insurance coverage, Norway ranked fourth in Europe by 1940.[3]

1. Kuhnle 1983, p. 147.
2. Ibid.
3. The ranking is based on an index developed by Jens Alber, cited in Kuhnle 1983, p. 148. We should, however, be aware of an important weakness in this index: it includes only state schemes. The levels of benefits and spending were actually higher in Norway due to the widespread existence of municipal pensions in the pre-1936 period.

The development of the Old Age Pension (OAP) both largely explains the country's position as a welfare laggard and, since its enactment in 1936, has accounted for much of the ensuing expansion. Among the countries in Flora's comparison, Norway preceded only Finland (1937) and Switzerland (1946) in introducing a state pension.

In other areas of social insurance Norway figured differently. With the 1894 enactment of the Act on Accident Insurance for Factory Workers, Norway ranked among the first in Europe to introduce such a scheme.[4] Norway's first subsidised voluntary unemployment insurance was introduced in 1906, five years before Britain got its first compulsory scheme for the unemployed. In health insurance the Norwegian scheme preceded the programme enacted in 1911 during the British period of liberal reforms.

These facts highlight two important points: First, they show that one nation may be a laggard in some areas of welfare while at the same time being a forerunner in others. (This furthermore shows the limitations of total spending indexes.) Second, they emphasise the importance of OAPs to the total scope of social insurance.

Why, then, did Norway perform relatively poorly in this important section of social policy? The country was one of the last European nations to be industrialised. General underdevelopment is therefore one tempting explanation. The examples above concerning the development in related areas, however, contradict such a conclusion; in spite of its late industrialisation Norway did carry out pioneering work in some areas of public welfare. Similarly, in the 1830s the liberal ideology underlying the new Poor Law was discussed simultaneously with, and under direct influence of, the events taking place in Britain.

After Norway was freed from Danish colonial rule in 1814, it entered a union with Sweden which was to last until 1905. During this period the country had its own constitution and elected parliament. While Sweden controlled the foreign policy, matters such as social legislation were largely left to the national parliament. As in Britain, the question of pensions had been a political issue in Norway since the middle of the 19th century. This places Norway alongside other European nations in that respect. Simultaneously with its counterpart in Britain, the first Norwegian Royal Commission on OAPs was appointed in 1885.

4. Flora 1983.

However, the political backgrounds to the Norwegian and the British commission were quite different. The Commons committee 'to inquire into the best system of National Provident Insurance against poverty' was to a great extent the outcome of a process instigated by the clergyman Canon William L. Blackley, 'an obscure, but reform-minded curate who had learned about the pension technique both abroad and in his own profession.'[5]

In Norway, by contrast, it was not primarily social engineers who instigated reform. Dating back to the 1850s various labour assemblies were propagandising for OAPs. Still, the labour advocates were mainly reform-minded intellectuals and not workers.[6]

Before 1885 proposed pension schemes were rejected on liberal grounds. Compulsory pensions were seen to clash with the free contractual relationship between labour and capital.[7] However, from 1885 onwards the will to establish a public alternative outside the Poor Law was generally shared.

The two nations reached consensus on establishing equivalent schemes at the same time. But while Britain took just 28 years to enact its scheme, the same process stretched over half a century in Norway. The position as a welfare laggard may paradoxically be explained by the highly ambitious nature of Norwegian social policy at the time.[8] We shall later see that this attitude has sustained and contributed in the long run to a much more benevolent development in the Norwegian pension sector compared with equivalent areas in Britain. The ambitions were directed towards two key areas of welfare: coverage and financing. As early as 1894 the second commission on pensions established a new socio-political norm: the principle of equal treatment. This embodies the idea of a general OAP including all Norwegian citizens. A Conservative (Høyre) member of the Storting, Morell, explained in 1918 the many delays by pointing out that

5. Heclo 1973, p. 159. Blackley was strongly influenced by the development taking place on the Continent. He started his own pressure group for advocating state pensions.

6. Ormestad 1948, p. 29. Pettersen (1982) explains the appointment of the committee in 1885 as a result of labour pressure. Seip (1984, pp. 90–91) argues, though, that the committee was established after prompting from the Swedish king, Oscar II. The government was influenced by the development in Bismarck's Germany. Also, the Norwegian plans were expected to pacify the growing working class.

7. Pettersen 1982.

8. Ibid.

'the spokesmen of the reform have, from the very beginning, aimed to cover a wider segment of the population than would be the case if the aim was restricted to a workers insurance.'[9] This principle was at the time rare in European social policy.[10] The target groups were otherwise still those without means of their own. The Norwegian state was, however, not yet ready to meet the cost that the implementation of such a principle would involve.

The struggle for a compromise on the questions of financing and coverage resulted in a series of committees in the period between 1885 and 1917. The 1885 committee never produced an actual proposal. Due to the enormity of the task, the committee was first asked not to consider old age or disability insurance. The proposal for a sickness insurance was also completed by later committees.[11] In 1894, therefore, a new committee was established. Its work resulted in 1899 in a proposal for an old age and invalidity insurance covering the entire nation. Because of the unacceptable costs involved, a new 'critique commission' was established. The government was still not satisfied after considering its recommendations, and in 1907 a new Folkeforsikringskomite (People's Insurance Committee) was established. Unable to reach agreement on major issues, the committee presented a minority and a majority report. This further delayed the achievement of consensus on the matter until 1914. By that time changes in the value of the krone and the levels of income necessitated new statistics to be worked out before the rates could be set.[12]

A royal commission on OAPs presented its proposals in 1918, one year after the presentation of the new income statistics. This report introduced a change of terminology which reflects the changes in Norwegian social insurance and the increasing divergence between it and British policies. Most important, the term *forsikring* (insurance) was replaced by *trygd* (security).[13] During the following five years the proposed pension was repeatedly debated and reviewed in parliamentary and extra-parliamentary hearings. In 1923 a pension scheme was finally enacted. The majority in the Storting, made up by the Conservatives together with socialists from three parties, pushed through legislation to create a system based on

9. Ibid., p. 30.
10. Kuhnle 1983.
11. Seip 1984, p. 91.
12. Pettersen 1982.
13. Hatland 1987, p. 12.

the principle of financing from general taxation. Eligibility for the scheme was to be subject to a test of means. However, the country was in an economic crisis, and even before the final decision on the matter, it became evident that implementing the scheme would be impossible for the time being. It was postponed indefinitely. Despite a Labour (Arbeiderpartiet) attempt to introduce it in 1926, it was not before the mid-1930s that the scheme could be implemented. However, it proved to be important as a policy decision.

The scheme introduced in 1936 was more or less a duplicate of the 1923 law. This, together with the urgency felt at the time for an alternative to the Poor Law, made the process of enactment swift. I will therefore begin the analysis by focusing on the debate that took place between the presentation of the 1918 proposal and the 1923 legislation. It was in this period that the main questions regarding the nature of the scheme were to be emphasised, both in practical terms and, increasingly, concerning the nature of the key political principles.

The following analysis will thus follow the development according to the key variables of financing, coverage, and level of benefits.

Financing: From the contributory principle to a modified taxation solution

The question how to finance a future pension for the elderly was a key issue in the pension debate from its outset in the mid-19th century. In the 1840s the *amtmann* (county mayor) of Bergen proposed a compulsory insurance scheme for 'those with limited means'.[14] A few years later the radical Thrane movement supported another contributory system, only this time the employers were to cover the full cost.[15] Both proposals were rejected by the Storting on liberal grounds.[16]

During the last two decades of the 19th century, the desirability of a non-Poor Law alternative for the elderly was more vigorously promoted in the political arena. The two proposals mentioned above set the parameters for the division over the question how to finance such a scheme. On the one hand the socialists supported a solution whereby employers, and

14. Seip 1984, p. 258.

15. The Thrane movement was a revolutionary labour group which was active in the years 1848–52.

16. Seip 1984, p. 258.

later the state, were to meet the expenses, while on the other hand Conservatives and Liberals (Venstre) favoured a solution based on the principle of insurance. The debates towards the end of the century strengthened this division, which remained unchanged until 1918.

Although the socialists voiced their views on pensions in various fora, they were, during the important years of the last two decades of the 19th century, not yet represented in the Storting. This partly explains why the committees on pensions were free to focus exclusively on the insurance solution. However, in 1907, when Labour had gained representation in the Storting, the committee still focused exclusively on the insurance solution.[17] The fact that this approach was chosen by the Conservatives and the Liberals can be explained partly by the strong influence of Bismarck's Germany on Norwegian policy at the time.[18] The German scheme was financed mainly by individual contributions.

Having rejected the taxation approach, the committees turned to debating the different solutions and alternatives within the contributory system. This involved the choice between a compulsory and a voluntary system, the role of the state in subsidising the scheme, and the question which groups to include.

The increasing influence exerted by the labour movement forced the planners of reform, however, to produce more fundamental arguments for the desirability of a solution along the lines of the insurance principle. The arguments were in part economic and in part moral.[19] Economically, both the lower cost involved for the taxpayer and the resistance to the introduction of a redistributional scheme favoured a system whereby those who benefited also paid the bill. More important, however, were the moral arguments: 'Insurance was self-help. It fostered self-respect and a correct impression of receiving a return service according to your previous contribution.'[20]

In the 1907 review the non-socialists shared the strong conviction in support of the insurance principle. Seip quotes the Conservative representative Klingenberg: 'I was like many others, on the basis of my purely non-socialist instincts, in favour of the insurance principle.'[21]

17. Seip 1981, p. 41.
18. Ibid.
19. Ibid., pp. 40, 41.
20. Ibid.
21. Quoted in Seip 1981, p. 41.

New alliances, 1918–1923

The five years between the 1918 proposal and the 1923 enactment represent the turning point in the development of Norwegian pensions. In contrast with the strong and contrastive positions before this, pragmatism opened the way for new solutions and compromises. The three most important parties in this context were the Labour Party, the Liberals, and the Conservatives.

The Labour Party launched an attack on the proposal put forward in 1918. The extensive (governmental) review carried out before the 1918 proposal concluded with a proposal for a contributory scheme whereby contributors would pay 2% of their income and in return receive stamps which they had to save until pension age in order to prove eligibility. In addition to rejecting the insurance solution on principle, the Labour Party criticised the proposal on two major points. First, the scheme did not cover the already old.[22] Second, the party envisaged enormous administrative costs.

By this time the Labour Party had gained enough political strength to influence the majority in the Storting to conduct a review based on the taxation principle. The resulting report from the People's Insurance Committee highlighted the illusory nature of the division between tax and insurance. It argued that in effect both systems rely on beneficiaries themselves paying for their pensions 'with their taxes and productive labour in past and present'.[23] The majority support for this argument was a significant step towards political consensus on the question of financing. Hatland argues that the existence of municipal pensions contributed significantly to the change of attitude among the non-socialists.[24] (We shall return to the role played by these schemes later.) Also contributing to this change was support for the taxation principle from unexpected quarters. In 1919 the Norwegian Association of Actuaries decided to support a review of a solution following the taxation principle. Before this the insurance principle had been widely regarded by these professionals as the technically superior solution. Again, the feasibility of the taxation approach, as documented through the municipal schemes, proved important.[25]

22. The proposed scheme excluded persons over the age of 56 at the time of enactment. Seip 1981, p. 44.

23. Debates in the Storting, 1923, cited in Seip 1981, p. 45. Previously, only the Labour representatives had used this argument.

24. Hatland 1987, p. 42.

25. Ibid., pp. 34–35.

The Liberals, who formed a new government in 1921 under the leadership of Otto Albert Blehr, continued to be the strongest advocates of the insurance principle. This government made a new proposal based on insurance in 1921. In hearings this gained little support.[26] The ongoing struggle between the two principles forced Blehr to look for compromises.

By this time the Conservatives, who had reconsidered their position on the question of financing after the latest review, were willing to support a tax-financed system. The majority in the Storting, including the Conservatives, supported this solution because it would involve lower administrative costs and because the already old would benefit. Most important, however, the Liberal proposal was rejected because the contributions were designed to be based on the flat-rate principle. Seip refers to the view expressed by the majority of the review committee in the Storting: 'It would be unreasonable and at variance with fundamental principles of taxation, that poor and rich, single persons and persons with family responsibilities, should be charged equally.'[27]

During the second decade of the century Norway experienced strong economic growth. The increased wealth enabled the government to levy the additional taxes necessary to finance the scheme. While the economic situation thus contributed to the feasibility of the scheme, it was also changes in the economy that finally stalled the implementation of the programme. By 1920 the recession was already starting to be felt. The first measure was to delete the invalidity pension from the plan. When the Storting finally voted on the pension scheme in 1923, it was clear that this was a vote on a principle and not on a scheme to be implemented in the near future.

The first OAP

The implementation of an OAP was given high priority in the 1935 coalition government headed by Johan Nygaardsvold of the Labour Party. In the previous battle over pensions, between 1918 and 1923, it was the non-socialists who were forced to make concessions on the question of financing. The Labour Party was at that time able to pursue and maintain its position of principle. The 1936 pension proposal may, by contrast, be interpreted as a movement to the right by the Labour Party.

While the Labour Party had originally advocated a scheme financed

26. Seip 1981, p. 46.
27. Ibid.

totally by local and state taxes, it now proposed a system whereby the insured person would also contribute to the scheme through the payment of a premium. Furthermore, contrary to the flat-rate approach of the proposal by Blehr's Liberal government in 1921, the individual contributions varied according to the insured person's income. Also, the lowest paid were exempt from paying the premium, which amounted to 1% of net income. A proposed means test and the exemption of the lowest paid from paying contributions added to the redistributional nature of the scheme.

Seip interprets the acceptance of an element of individual contributions as a clear turn to the right by the Labour Party. She quotes the minister of social affairs: 'It is only of limited interest to discuss whether it [the pension scheme] should be built on one or the other theoretical system. The main issue is to find a practicable solution.'[28]

Hatland finds it hard to follow Seip's interpretation of the Labour Party's policy in this period. Referring to the above-mentioned redistributional aspects of the scheme, he argues that it was a far cry from a solution based on the insurance principle. Adding to this, he argues, is the fact that there was no actuarial relationship between contributions and benefits, and that the scheme was to begin immediately and thereby include the already old.[29]

While Seip is partly right in pointing out the turn to the right in the Labour Party, Hatland's interpretation of this as a change of policy that did little to alter the principles held by the party is equally valid. This policy was an expression of compromises necessitated by the political situation at the time.

With this change the Labour Party had also become more pragmatic on the question of welfare. Both Seip and Pettersen consider the mid-1930s to represent the convergence of the socialist and the non-socialist on the question of financing.[30] This pragmatic compromise was later instrumental in the post-war consensus on welfare.

Funding versus a modified pay-as-you-go system

On this question also, contrasting viewpoints from the earlier debates softened up during the time of the 1935 coalition government. From

28. Seip 1981, p. 47.
29. Hatland 1987, p. 55.
30. Seip 1981; Pettersen 1982.

totally rejecting both individual contributions and funding in 1923, the Labour Party in 1935 proposed a fund built up from money paid by contributors.[31]

This fund was, however, given a rather minimal role in the financing of the scheme. The state was to cover 62%, the municipalities 25%, and the fund 12% of the total cost. Most of the fund was reserved to meet the rising costs envisaged due to demographic changes. Also, Keynesian economic theory was starting to make its influence felt in the Norwegian political milieu, and in particular the Labour Party wanted to use the fund to finance housing, agriculture, and other means to enhance productivity. Seip quotes from a pamphlet published by the Labour Party in 1918. The statement highlights the pragmatism in the party on this question as well: 'It would be a different case if society, irrespective of the question of financing, should be interested in creating a big fund as a means to ensure social control over industry.'[32]

With a redistributional element ensured through a combination of, on the one hand, no upper ceiling to contributions (1% of income) and, on the other hand, means-tested benefits, the Labour Party was ready to change its view on the question of funding. For many of the same reasons that made the Labour Party support funding, the Conservatives now opposed it. Pettersen points to the paradoxical situation whereby the Conservatives in 1936 were the only defenders of a principle that before 1918 was supported only by the socialists.[33] The Liberals and the Agrarian Party (Bondepartiet) had earlier (1920) supported the fund for reasons similar to those expressed by the socialists in 1935. With the socialists in power, they still supported the fund, but this time as an instrument to avoid higher taxes in the expected event of growing demand for pensions due to demographic changes. The strongest opponents, the Conservatives, again paradoxically, became the strongest supporters of the fund after the war when the Labour government wanted to use the money in the daily running of the pension.

In this section we have seen that the political parties converged from opposing positions. In particular, the Conservatives entered a more prag-

31. Pettersen 1982, p. 145.
32. Seip 1981, p. 48.
33. Pettersen 1982, p. 144.

matic phase around 1920, abandoning their dogmatic rejection of the taxation solution. Only the Liberals maintained a more prolonged adherence to the insurance principle. In 1935 the Labour Party, in power and thus responsible for carrying the scheme through, showed a greater willingness to abandon some of its ideological positions and accept an element of individual contributions. The combined system of financing worked out through a series of compromises in this period has remained more or less unchanged until the present day.

Coverage: Towards pragmatic selectivity and gradual universality

In a way similar to that affecting the debates on financing outlined above, pragmatism replaced dogma in this question also and gradually brought about a situation whereby compromises and even alliances between socialists and non-socialists could be made.

Early development

In the 1885 Workers' Commission the incompatible preferences of the labour movement in relation to pension coverage were already highlighted. The Labour representatives supported universality in some areas of social policy, while preferring a more selective approach in others. Their priorities depended both on the kind of schemes that were debated and on the proposed means of financing the pension. First, in the choice between various schemes, the socialists preferred universality where 'it was only limited economic resources in question, or where stigma caused by differential treatment would be particularly strongly felt, and where it was seen to be tactically important that the workers were treated similarly to others; for example in education.'[34] These priorities exemplify the struggle between the virtues of *economic* versus those of *social* equality. At the time the former tended to be given priority over the latter. This must, of course, be understood in the light of the poverty that the services were designed to alleviate.

In the case of the OAP, the position taken by the labour movement furthermore depended on the solution to the question of financing. In the

34. Seip 1981, p. 43.

case of a contributory system, the socialists rejected a selective scheme. Such a system would, they argued, become a 'poor tax', with workers paying for their own old age.[35]

The pragmatism of the labour movement in relation to this question appeared when an OAP based on the taxation principle was debated. While supporting universality in principle, the social democrats were willing to sacrifice social for economic equality and support a pension paid for by all wage-earners and allocated according to a test of need. This position, we shall see, was sustained until 1957.

After 1918

In 1918 the Labour Party defended for the first time its dissent from the principle of universality: 'Now it is most important to give help where it is most needed. Later the pension can be gradually extended to cover new groups.'[36]

The Conservatives also supported the principle of universality. The political opponents concurred, however, from contrastive political priorities. The virtues of universality to the socialists must be understood in the light of their hatred of the means-tested Poor Law. By contrast, the main reason for the Conservatives to support universality was based on an 'equality before the law' principle.[37] The Norwegian Conservatives deviated here from mainstream European conservatism at the time.[38] In the Bismarckian tradition, conservative parties tended to support schemes aimed at only the poorer sections of society.

Both the Conservatives and the socialists deviated from their positions of principle in the process leading up to the enactment of the means-tested OAP in 1923, but again they did so for different reasons. By 1923 both groups had acknowledged the limitations imposed by the economic crisis. The Conservatives therefore sacrificed 'equality before the law' in order to make the scheme less costly. By contrast, to the socialists, the

35. Ibid., p. 42.

36. Ibid., p. 43. Seip quotes the proposal for a pension as presented by the Labour Party in 1918.

37. Pettersen 1982, p. 53.

38. Ibid.

redistributional effect achieved by means-testing weighed more than the fear of prolonged stigma.[39]

The first OAP

In 1936 the desire to establish an OAP as soon as possible, together with the still relatively weak economy, ensured continued provisional Labour support for a selective scheme.[40] The Conservatives and the Liberals also continued their pragmatic support for a means-tested scheme.

With universality postponed, the political struggle shifted to centre on how to implement selectivity. Depending on the rules for testing eligibility, a selective scheme may vary from being targeted at only a small minority to covering all but a small section of the group found to meet the basic requirements of need (i.e. those over the age of 70).[41]

In this situation the socialists wanted to include more categories of means into the test than did the non-socialists. This question brought about more debates in the Storting and in the committees than any other question related to the enactment of the first Norwegian OAP.[42] While the socialists proposed to include even very small occupational pensions in the means test, this was strongly challenged by all non-socialist parties. They feared that this proposal would make employers lower the pension benefits below the set limit and thereby bring an end to occupational pensions in Norway.

With occupational pension schemes already restricted to only a small minority of companies, the government saw no reason to contribute to the unequal treatment of workers in different industries by supporting these schemes.

Conservative and Liberal support for giving preferential treatment to occupational pensions must be understood from pragmatic as well as ideological perspectives. Pragmatically, the groups covered were seen to be potential voters for non-socialist parties. Ideologically, support for occupational pensions was in line with the stress on the virtues of self-help in social policy.

---

39. Pettersen 1982, p. 52. For both parties this line of argument is based on the premise that the scheme was financed by general taxation rather than by individual contributions.

40. Seip 1981, p. 47.

41. Reddin 1968.

42. Pettersen 1982, p. 147.

The Agrarian Party, however, supported the socialists in the move to include even the smallest occupational pensions in the means test.[43] Since self-help was stressed as a virtue among the farmers' representatives also, we must look for pragmatic explanations for this move. With very few voters in industry, the saving obtained by restrictive means-testing was more important than supporting the self-help schemes in the cities.

Given the stringent means test imposed, it is perhaps surprising to find that as early as 1940 as many as 76% of the over-70s received benefits.[44] To Hatland this goes to show that the means test was not very strict after all. It could also be seen as a sign of the relatively equal standard of living among the majority of the elderly, and it also indicates the relative absence of occupational pensions in Norway at this point.

In the late 1930s the legislators were too occupied discussing the methods of means-testing to resume discussion of the principle of universal versus selective pensions. This debate re-emerged, however, after the Second World War.

Level of benefits

In his discussion of the road towards compromise between the political parties around 1920, Hatland argues that the level of pensions never became a major controversy.[45] If the Labour Party was to follow its earlier prioritising of economic over social equality, it would have been natural to pursue higher benefits from the tax-financed and means-tested pensions in order to maximise the living standards of retired workers through redistribution. Since this did not happen, Hatland argues that the achievement of social equality through extended *rights* to benefits, which had a symbolic value as a way of distancing the scheme from the existing Poor Law, was given priority over concerns regarding the economic circumstances of the elderly population.

In spite of this, in 1936 the coalition government established two central targets for the development of the new OAP. First, the benefits

43. The Agrarian Party had its support base among people working in the primary industries in rural Norway. In 1959 it changed its name to the Centre Party (Senterpartiet).

44. Hatland 1984, p. 50.

45. Hatland 1987.

offered were to be set at a level sufficient to give a reasonable coverage of what is needed for a person's subsistence.

This implied the adoption of a new approach to public responsibility in welfare. To Hatland this was the introduction of a strategy to alleviate poverty rather than prevent socialist unrest among the working class.[46] In the terminology of Jones, this can be interpreted as the introduction of a 'standard security approach' at the expense of a 'poverty alleviation approach' to welfare. The significance lies in the recognition that the public support scheme should fulfil this aim and that eventually it should not be necessary to add savings or alternative pensions in order to maintain income in old age.

In addition to this, the majority in the Storting gave their support in principle for a universal pension as the ultimate aim.[47] However, with limited resources available, the government was forced to give priority to one goal at the expense of the other. The choice was between a universal pension at a very low level and a selective pension at a higher level. Ultimately, the government gave priority to economic equality over the immediate achievement of social equality. Social equality was a less important problem because the majority of elderly people actually received pensions.

Alternative schemes

In the Introduction to Part Two, I argued that the role played by alternative pension schemes offers an important key to the understanding of the divergent development of British and Norwegian social insurance. There, I also hypothesised that a precursive public alternative would exert an influence very different from that of private or voluntary schemes. We shall return to a comparison along these lines in the Summary of Part Two. The following describes how alternative programmes contributed to the Norwegian model of public insurance before the enactment of the OAP in 1936.

Non-public programmes

Before 1936 in Norway self-help and private insurance did not develop to an extent comparable to that in Britain.[48] This has both directly and indi-

46. Hatland 1984, p. 47.
47. Seip 1981, p. 49.
48. For Britain, see Hannah 1986; for Norway, Hippe and West Pedersen 1988.

rectly influenced the divergence of the courses taken by Norwegian and British pensions – directly, in Norway, because there was no scheme of any significance to stall or influence the course of the emerging state alternatives;[49] and indirectly because the participants in the struggle for pensions had no vested interests to take into consideration.

This is not to say, though, that private and voluntary schemes were non-existent in Norway. The history of Norwegian social insurance features examples of the influence of such schemes being felt and debated. In the negotiations preceding the enactment of the first OAP in 1936, existing occupational pensions were brought into the debate. Due to the postponement of the implementation of the 1923 OAP, the following years saw a growth in occupational pensions. These were, however, limited to large companies. The small-scale nature of Norwegian industry therefore precluded stronger growth.[50]

The proposed means test led to lobbying for certain kinds of earnings disregards. Both the Liberals and the Conservatives wanted to give preferential treatment to income from occupational pensions. This would, they argued, encourage thrift and saving. If, on the other hand, the pensions were counted in full, companies would lower the benefits to just below the limit for earnings disregard.[51]

The Agrarian Party, which was the third major non-socialist party at the time, supported the government in its non-preferential treatment of occupational pensions. This party even contributed to a lowering of the exemption originally proposed by the government. Pettersen explains this as a combination of the party's general desire to save on public spending and the nature of its supporters; farmers and fishermen did not receive occupational pensions.[52] In the enacted pension, occupational pensions received the same treatment as did income from earnings, interest, and private insurance.

In 1936 the government had no clear picture of the prevalence of these schemes, but it was believed that they were so few that there was no

49. The first major occupational pension scheme was established for civil servants in 1917. Later, new schemes grew to cover most public employees and eventually the private sector (Hippe and West Pedersen 1988, pp. 62–70).

50. Pettersen 1982, p. 150.

51. Ibid. See also Seip 1987, p. 229.

52. Pettersen 1982, p. 150.

reason to give them preferential treatment. Furthermore, the fact that only workers who were already better-off would benefit from the scheme contributed to this decision.

Public alternatives to state pensions[53]

Although the role of non-public schemes was not strongly felt in Norway, alternative schemes did play an important role in the establishment and nature of the state-run OAP. The effects on the latter are, however, different when the alternatives are public and not privately run. Starting in 1916 Norwegian municipalities established their own OAPs in order to provide an alternative to the Poor Law for some members of their ageing populations. With the expectation that a state scheme would be carried through shortly, the growth of municipal OAPs accelerated between 1918 and 1923.

Old age and disability pensions

The first scheme was set up in the rural municipality of Storelvdal in 1915. Although the main purpose of the pension was to free the elderly from the stigma of the Poor Law, it still retained many of the principles of the latter. First, a stringent means test was introduced to exclude those who could be supported by their own families. Second, a distinction between deserving and undeserving applicants found its expression in the ineligibility of persons who had a history of absenteeism, drunkenness, or other forms of socially unacceptable behaviour. As an example of the latter, previous receipt of poor relief for reasons other than sickness was grounds for refusal.[54] The programme, which was modelled on the Danish law regulating the 'support of deserving elderly', was soon adopted by many other local authorities, mainly in the south-eastern parts of Norway. By 1922 municipalities constituting 40% of the population had established such schemes.[55]

---

53. I distinguish these from the occupational schemes for state and municipal employees.

54. My description of the Storelvdal and Oslo OAPs is largely based on Hatland 1987.

55. Ibid., p. 18.

The significance of these pensions lies, first, in the fact that, however similar they were to the Poor Law, they were created to offer an *alternative* for groups found deserving of escaping it. Second, and perhaps more important, being wholly tax-financed, they represented a successful pilot project in a period when this approach was struggling to gain acceptance. Adding to these factors, two schemes set up in the capital had a more direct influence on the path taken by Norwegian social insurance.

In 1917 the Labour Party gained power in the Kristiania (Oslo) city council.[56] Along with other radical measures the socialist mayor proposed the setting up of a municipal pension scheme to replace poor relief for the elderly *and* the disabled. Hatland argues that the composition of the committee appointed to outline the scheme was an early indication of its national significance. The members included the chair of the national Labour 'Shadow Committee' on pensions and the later minister of finance in the first Labour government in 1936.[57]

The committee criticised the insurance-based scheme proposed by the Liberal government in 1918. This criticism took two forms. First, the committee argued that the majority of people were unable to make contributions sufficient to avoid poverty in old age and disability. Second, because the proposed pension was not financed solely out of contributions, they argued that it would be more sensible to extend the state subsidy to make it mainly tax-financed. Furthermore, it was pointed out that a contributory system offered no benefits to the already old or disabled. Finally, the high expenses needed to administer a system of individual contributions were considered a waste of resources. The validity of this argument should not be underestimated in relation to a time when 'the main administrative tools were pen and ink.'[58]

The taxation solution, by contrast, was seen to signify that maintenance in old age and infirmity was a public, rather than merely an individual and familial, responsibility. This was expressed in the term 'socialisation' of maintenance. This argument clearly showed that the sympathy was with those impoverished by caring for dependants rather than with the people in need of care.[59]

The Kristiania Committee also discussed the distinction between the

56. The name of the capital was changed back to Oslo in 1924.
57. Hatland 1987, pp. 21–22.
58. Ibid., p. 23.
59. Ibid.

'deserving' and 'undeserving' needy. They rejected the principles of the Storelvdal model on the grounds that it practised a moralising form of selectivity. The Conservative minority of the committee argued that clauses similar to those in Storelvdal should be included in the Kristiania pension. In a sarcastic address to these members, Emil Stang, the chairman, referred to the existence of 'idle persons in all classes'.[60]

We saw above that the report of the Labour Party's People's Insurance Committee formed the basis for a compromise on the question of financing in 1923. The arguments expressed then drew heavily on the experiences of the creation of the Kristiania pension in 1917. The capital had provided a 'test area' for the feasibility of the taxation principle. In this way Stang's committee laid the groundwork for the achievement of a compromise between the advocates of the competing principles of financing on the national level also. Furthermore, Hatland documents that there was direct pressure from the municipalities on the state to finance a future pension out of taxation. When Kristiania enacted its pension in 1918, a request was made to the Storting for a tax-financed state pension. Similarly, a survey of local authorities showed that while only 70 supported the insurance principle, a majority of 145 favoured a tax-financed state scheme.

Mothers' pensions

Although the main influence exerted by the Kristiania experience was through the Old Age and Disability Pension, the less recognised Mothers' Pension scheme, introduced simultaneously, complemented it. Seip and Ibsen highlight how the scheme added a new dimension to insurance by expanding its target groups.[61] Let us first consider how this scheme complemented the local OAP.

Norway played a pioneering role in establishing services targeted at families in general and children in particular. With the Castberg Child Welfare Law of 1915, an important barrier was broken by the introduction of equal rights for legitimate and illegitimate children alike. This legislation also had an economic element in the provision of maternity benefits to unmarried and poor married mothers. Although these benefits

60. Ibid., p. 25.
61. Seip and Ibsen 1989.

failed to be realised due to a lack of state funding, the idea of public responsibility for children and mothers had been introduced.[62] Again, Kristiania preceded the state in creating a viable scheme. When the Kristiania Mothers' Pension was introduced in 1919, the link to a future state scheme was arguably even more explicit than was the case for the simultaneous OAP.

The pension was seen by the Labour representatives as a pile-driver. The municipality had only started what the state ought to take over: the communities 'ought to be at the forefront and show the way to the state, which has the first responsibility.... the communities must ... force the state.'[63] Seip and Ibsen argue that 'local initiatives were here seen as a strategy in what we can call "welfare state building".'[64]

The scheme also proved to influence the discussion of the principle of financing. In the case of the municipal pension, the choice was between financing out of general taxation on the one hand and tying the funding to the wage agreement on the other hand. The latter solution was modelled on the French *caisses familiales*. Labour preferred the taxation solution, arguing that benefits ought to be paid regardless of the father's position in the labour market. Again, therefore, tax financing was favoured as a means to achieve universality.

When the state family allowance was enacted as a universal tax-financed scheme in 1946, the vote was unanimous. The experience with the Oslo predecessor contributed largely to this outcome. In the rejection of the insurance principle in 1946, another argument was introduced. Tax financing proved to be a good method to include the self-employed. This, together with the realisation that an all-inclusive flat-rate scheme involved no redistribution other than that in favour of families with children, made the non-socialist parties accept financing out of general taxation.

Even though some municipalities were forced to close down their programmes during the recession, by 1936 some 43% of the population lived in towns featuring local pensions.[65] By this time the municipal schemes had proved the practicality of a scheme that the government wished to

62. Ibid.

63. Ibid., p. 417. The quote is from city council documents in the capital, 1919–20.

64. Ibid.

65. Hatland 1984, p. 47.

implement nationally. Furthermore, the municipalities had no interest in counteracting the implementation of the state scheme in order to save their own. There were no economic interests vested in the scheme which would be jeopardized by the introduction of a state alternative. On the contrary, the implementation of a state scheme would involve great savings for the municipalities. In fact, as we have seen, many of the schemes were created with the expectation of an early state take-over. This way, their existence added strength to the political arguments expressed by the local authorities.

After 1936, the growth in municipal schemes continued, but then as *additions* to the state pension. We shall later return to how alternative schemes and their influence in Norway contrasted with those in Britain.

Towards an early consensus

Far from being an isolated case, the compromises that facilitated the implementation of the 1936 OAP were part of a wide-ranging political change taking place in Norway in the mid-1930s. After a period of Liberal government, the Labour Party took office in 1935. This happened after Labour's proposed measures to counteract the economic crisis had contributed to growing support for the party. The non-socialist parties had failed to achieve a joint policy to stem the crisis. In particular, the Agrarian Party felt that the policies of the Liberal government did little to help their supporters – the farmers and other workers in the primary industries. This situation facilitated a 'crisis compromise' between the government and the Agrarian Party. The latter gave support for socialist austerity measures, while the government in turn backed policies designed to alleviate the problems of the primary industries.[66]

In addition to the Agrarian support for the minority Labour government, other factors coincided to facilitate the expansive policies embarked on by Labour. Most important, from 1935 onwards there was an upswing in the Norwegian economy. In the period 1934–39, industrial output increased by 40%. Some 140,000 new jobs were created and the GNP increased by 25%.[67] Furthermore, the government accepted the new

---

66. This short account is based on Lorentz 1974, pp. 39–44. Sweden, Finland, and Denmark also experienced similar compromises between socialists and non-socialists in this period.

67. Nestor 1986, p. 51.

Keynesian doctrine of more, rather than less, public spending as a measure to create economic growth.[68] From this perspective, expenditure on social policy programmes was also seen to be productive.[69] The new emphasis on family policies, as advocated in the work of Alva and Gunnar Myrdal in Sweden, was also important in changing the focus and scope of social policy in this period.[70]

The new Labour government established a Social Legislation Committee (Sociallovkomite) as early as 1935. Partly building on existing plans, as in the case of the OAP, the committee soon began to propose new social security programmes. First, the existing health insurance was extended in 1935 to include fishermen and, in 1937, sailors in the merchant marine. In 1937 new programmes for the unemployed, the disabled, and the protection of workers were enacted. It is of particular interest to note that the new state unemployment insurance was financed according to the contributory principle. In contrast to OAPs, this area had a history of voluntary schemes financed through individual contributions. Although it can be argued that unemployment is a more 'insurable' contingency than old age, the choice of the contributory solution can, from the perspective of my analysis, also be interpreted as a sign of the importance of policy inheritance in deciding the form of new schemes.[71] The disability scheme was, however, financed out of general taxation. While the plans of the Labour government outlined a universal scheme, the Act of 1937 (Lov om vanføre) was limited in scope in that it covered only the blind and the severely physically handicapped.[72]

The programmes enacted in the 1930s can be interpreted as representing a change of emphasis in Norwegian social policy. Hatland argues that

68. Yet, Nestor (1986) argues that the extent of this reorientation was limited. In particular, the poorest recipients failed to benefit; the number of people receiving poor relief remained unchanged between 1934 and 1939. During this period social policy expenditure did not increase faster than GNP.

69. Seip 1987, p. 209. Nestor (1986, p. 52) argues, however, that 'the fear of the destructive influence of social policy upon production and the creation of wealth was still present among the majority of the elected representatives.' In particular, this was expressed in the discussion of more extensive unemployment insurance.

70. The Myrdals published their book *Krisen i befolkningsspørsmålet* in 1934.

71. Unemployment benefits are better suited to the contributory solution because the need situation will be preceded by a period of employment. By contrast, not all old people have a work record; a compulsory/universal OAP is therefore more difficult to finance through individual contributions.

72. Kluge 1973, p. 70.

> up to this point the social security acts could be regarded as a kind of labour legislation, one of their objectives being to reduce the political discontent of the working class, but the new old age pension and the aid to the blind and crippled was aimed far more distinctly at alleviating the poverty in the country. Rights were held by virtue of one's being a citizen, not by virtue of being an employee.[73]

Although the changes are also recognised by other writers, some question the extent to which this represented a new direction of policy. Nestor points to the fact that the numbers receiving poor relief hardly decreased at all in the period 1935–39. He also stresses the needs of other poor groups when he argues that the change of emphasis was only limited: 'survivors, disabled, single parents and many of the unemployed were not favoured in this period of welfare expansion.'[74] Seip argues that although the new schemes heralded a new approach to welfare, the extent of expansion was not significant enough to represent a break with the past.[75] Although I agree with Seip in her stress on continuity over change, I find also that the extensions to cover groups outside the (past and present) labour force constituted an important new orientation in Norwegian social policy. Although such extensions were only limited in scope, the importance lies in the recognition of such extensions as a desirable development. Even more important, perhaps, the 1930s legislation established the taxation principle as the main form of financing for Norwegian social insurance. As we shall see later, this facilitated extensions along the lines embarked on in this period.

The change of focus away from the labour force towards the needs of the population at large coincided with a transfer of power within the Labour Party. Lorentz argues that 'while in the 1920s it was the trade unions that decided the policies of the Party, it was now the parliamentary section that decided the policies of the trade union movement.'[76] Although the trade union movement lost some of its autonomy and influence on party policies in this period, the Labour government also strengthened the unions' power base. In particular, through their participation in various boards and committees, the trade unions gained access

73. Hatland 1984, p. 47.
74. Nestor 1986, p. 52.
75. Seip 1987, p. 206.
76. Lorentz 1974, p. 42.

to the state apparatus. The period 1935–39 saw an increase in the number of bodies that comprised representatives from the state on the one hand and employers and employees on the other.[77] Moreover, the 1935 cabinet included two ministers from the trade union movement.[78] If there was an overall loss of power in the union movement, this was certainly not reflected in the level of unionisation: from 1934 to 1938 the membership of the LO (Landsorganisasjonen) increased from 172,000 to 344,000.[79] The new role of the trade union movement may be interpreted as a move in the direction of a more corporate state. A further step in this process was the 1935 'general treaty' (Hovedavtalen) between employers and LO regarding wages and labour relations.[80] This was a further step towards the replacement of class conflicts by co-operation.

In Chapter 4 we will see that in Britain contrasting positions were established between the Labour Party and the unions before the party accepted social policies based on principles very different from those prevailing in the Norwegian labour movement at the same time. The increased influence of the Trade Union Congress on Labour politics will be seen in the 1942 endorsement of Beveridge's liberal social policy. As we shall see later, there is, however, nothing to suggest Labour support for a contributory principle in the case of the more influential Norwegian trade union movement. In Norway a stronger trade union element in the Labour Party *may*, however, have counteracted the 1930s tendency towards greater emphasis on groups outside the labour force. As we shall see in the next chapter, the change of emphasis towards a wider 'catchment area' for social insurance is crucial to the understanding of the development towards welfare based on the institutional model in Norway in the post-war period.

We can therefore conclude that the political situation favoured reforms in this period. Furthermore, the *need* for reform was particularly great in the mid-1930s. Since the onset of the Depression, prevailing economic doctrines had prevented the state from meeting the growing needs with expanded programmes. The situation between 1920 and 1935 has been described as one of 'Sunday silence' in the Department of Social Affairs.[81]

77. Ibid., p. 43.
78. Bull [1968] 1976, p. 135.
79. Lorentz 1974, p. 44.
80. Ibid.
81. Nestor 1986, p. 41.

In combination, these factors facilitated a period of expansion in the area of social policy.

Summary and conclusions

In this chapter we have seen how the socialist and the non-socialist parties converged from contrastive positions in the two key areas of financing and coverage of a future OAP. The compromise reached regarding financing followed the original Labour idea of a system paid for by general taxation. The agreement was due partly to changing attitudes in the non-socialist camp, in particular among the Conservatives, while on the other hand the Labour acceptance of a contributory element made it easier for the non-socialists to reach a consensus.

In the area of coverage the political opponents found common ground regarding the issue of means, while the objectives behind their positions remained different. Thus, in particular the unity between Labour and the Conservatives facilitated a scheme which was selective in coverage but was designed to evolve into universality through the gradual relaxing of the means test.

While the level of the pension was set low in 1936, the existence of the means test was used politically as an instrument to elevate this level before extensions could be made. The fact that the system was tax-financed made the setting of the level a question of political will rather than of the individual's ability to contribute.

The municipal predecessors to the state pension played a constructive role in the creation of state schemes. Being wholly tax-financed, they gave evidence of the feasibility of this solution. Furthermore, they were designed to be replaced by state schemes; thus, they not only had no interest in stalling the state alternatives, but were actually used to put pressure on the state to establish new programmes. Lastly, they led the way in creating schemes for groups previously outside the realm of social insurance.

The consensus of 1935 facilitated a model of social insurance that was designed for expansion. A tax-based system has greater scope for the extension of coverage compared with a system whereby only groups whose members are able to contribute individually can be included. The level of benefits was set low, but there was not, as in Britain, a flat-rate contributory system to curtail its future development.

Furthermore, the programmes enacted in the mid- and late 1930s pointed in the direction of offering welfare to the population at large, rather than restricting the non-Poor Law services to participants in the labour market. According to the model laid out in Chapter 1, this can be viewed as an important foundation for later moves towards institutional welfare. In this model services are allocated according to need rather than previous records (e.g. moral behaviour or individual social insurance contributions).

While this chapter has focused on the achievement of *compromises*, we will see in the next chapter that it was in this period that the foundation for the post-war *consensus* was established. Seip sums up the relationship between the two. She concludes that, in spite of prolonged conflicts over social policy in the 1930s, 'the climate for compromises was better than in earlier days. And at the next crossroad the decisions were binding. Compromise led to consensus.'[82]

82. Seip 1987, p. 209.

Chapter 3

Norwegian Social Insurance, 1940–1967: From Pragmatic Selectivity towards Institutional Universality

The first two decades after the Second World War can be described as a period of uninterrupted Labour Party hegemony in Norway. This provided the party with a unique opportunity to introduce social legislation of its own making. As we will see in this chapter, however, the policies of this period were largely built on the compromises entered into in the mid-1930s and further compromises with the non-socialist parties in the years following the war. While the emphasis of the analysis will be on the post-war years, the years of occupation also deserve attention.

Social policy and the war

Until recently, the Norwegian literature has treated the five years of German occupation as a parenthesis in the development of Norwegian social policy. New evidence suggests, however, that this period deserves closer examination.[1] Three aspects of this history will be addressed briefly. First, new programmes introduced by the Nazi regime may have influenced the path taken after the war. Second, during the years in exile, the Norwegian government continued to plan for the future. Given that this took place in Britain, a third aspect to be touched on is the question of diffusion between Norwegian and British policy-makers in the field of welfare.

During the years of German occupation there was a large degree of continuity as the administration of the individual ministries remained mostly intact. While the political leadership of the ministries was changed, only to a limited degree did the new regime install its own civil

1. The important work here is Sørensen 1991 and 1993.

servants. Rather than making a radical break with the past, the new programmes introduced by the regime represented a high degree of continuity with the past. The question whether this is an example of the victory of continuity over change in social policy or an expression of shared objectives between the Nazi regime and Labour policies falls outside the scope of this study.[2] Labour market policies in the form of unemployment insurance and labour exchanges built largely on existing programmes. In fact, the new regime went further than the pre-war government by extending the 1938 Unemployment Insurance Act to include also those with the lowest wages. When the new Labour government abolished the Nazi scheme and replaced it with its own in 1945, the 1938 Act was extended to include those earning the lowest wages. Sørensen sees this as an example of continuity and influence leading into both the Nazi period and the new democratic regime.[3]

In other instances, the influence of the Nazi government on post-war policy was even stronger. The 1946 Family Allowance Act was close to a blueprint of the scheme introduced by the Nazis in 1944.[4]

The exiled Norwegian government stayed in London during the war. The extent of contact between Norwegian groups attached to the government and British policy-makers has not yet been fully researched. Still, much of the Norwegian literature emphasises the possibility for significant diffusion.[5] In particular the Beveridge Report has been cited as a source of inspiration. While there can be no doubt about the spread of inspiration and optimism crated by the report and its reception, both the extent of diffusion and the relevance of possible contacts need further qualification.

In the British literature, emphasis has been given to the impact of war on social policy. Titmuss in particular has contributed to the discussion of the experience of the Second World War as a determinant of the post-war consensus in British social policy.[6] In Norway this relationship has been given less attention, but both Seip and Kuhnle argue that a similar influ-

2. Sørensen 1991 stresses the latter point.

3. Sørensen 1991, pp. 94–124.

4. Sørensen (1991, p. 140) found a copy of the Nazi Act in the archives of the ministry. In preparing the 1946 Act, the ministry had simply replaced a few words in the wartime text.

5. Kuhnle 1983; Seip 1987, 1994. I will return to the question of diffusion in the Summary of Part Two.

6. Titmuss 1950, 1987.

ence can be traced in the country.[7] The pamphlet *Framtidens Norge* ('The Future Norway') was published by the Norwegian LO in Stockholm in 1945.[8] The main drafting of the report, however, was carried out in London by members of the exiled LO. Haakon Lie, later the political secretary of the Labour Party, was in charge of the editing of the report.[9]

Lie gave a background to the writing of the report that echoed the factors emphasised by Titmuss in his analysis of the war experience: The hardship endured by the Norwegian population during the war called for plans for a better future. Lie drew attention to the terrible winter of 1941–42, which resulted in great losses both in Norway and abroad. In particular, the situation was hard for the Norwegian seamen, who endured great hardship and enormous losses after shipwrecks caused by German attacks on convoys. Indeed, it was the trade union for seamen that first took the initiative to work out a plan for Norway's post-war future, thereby instilling hope and faith in a society worth fighting for.

The pamphlet *Framtidens Norge* outlines, among other things, the plans for a future social policy in Norway. Its recommendations had a clear impact on the post-war plans outlined below.[10] The pamphlet was distributed among Norwegian trade unionists in exile and was also smuggled into occupied Norway.[11]

The persons involved in the writing of *Framtidens Norge* were part of a larger community of trade unionists and Labour Party politicians spending their years in exile in London. We know that during the war there were contacts between these groups and the British labour movement on many levels. Starting in 1942, members of the secretariat in London participated in a number of congresses and annual meetings within both the Labour Party and the Trade Union Congress.[12] As a key political document the Beveridge Report was discussed in many of these arenas of

7. Kuhnle 1983, p. 154; Seip 1987, p. 210. Also, Kjønstad (1987, p. 56) states, 'After World War II the Beveridge Plan played an important part in the development of Norwegian social security legislation.'

8. LO and Norsk Sjømannsforbund 1945.

9. Haakon Lie is widely considered to have been one of the most influential people in the Norwegian labour movement during most of the post-war period. I interviewed him in his home in Oslo on 6 October 1995.

10. 'It is clear that "Framtidens Norge" influenced the shaping of the 1945 "Joint Programme".' Stenersen 1973, p. 93.

11. Ibid., p. 81.

12. Ibid., p. 75.

contact. Knut Getz Wold, a central person in the preparation of the later Norwegian report on social insurance,[13] informed occupied Norway about the report in a radio broadcast.[14]

While I recognise the influence of war in facilitating a feeling of integration and solidarity, and thereby adding to the support for collective measures, my main emphasis is on *the continuity of the consensus achieved in Norway in the mid-1930s.*[15] In this chapter I will outline how the compromises chiselled out in this period resulted in a policy that ensured the combined effect of, on the one hand, universality followed by extensions to include groups other than the elderly and, on the other, a gradual elevation of benefits for the elderly as well as for the newly included need categories. Both are of crucial importance for reducing the number of people depending on social assistance.

In 1945 a coalition government consisting of all the political parties was established. It soon produced a joint programme outlining the policies for reconstruction. The document included a key statement for the development of the welfare state: 'Social insurance will be developed to make the services of the Poor Law superfluous. The social insurance schemes shall be coordinated to form a joint system covering sickness, invalidity, unemployment and old age.'[16]

In 1948 the Labour government presented its first White Paper for a national insurance scheme. The tripartite method of financing laid down in 1936 was unchanged in principle. With the proposed extensions to cover groups other than the elderly, the contribution would be changed to a general 'social insurance duty'.[17] The continued balancing between the virtues of high benefits, universality in the Old Age Pension (OAP), and the extensions to cover new groups was outlined in a stage-by-stage plan in which *economic growth would determine the speed of implementation.* In the first stage the aim was to establish a disability pension. This would be followed by an elevation of benefits. In the third stage priority would be

13. Stortingsmelding nr. 58, 1948.

14. Sørensen 1991, p. 144. These broadcasts, received illegally in Norway, were a major source of information and inspiration during the war.

15. The importance of this period is also supported by Kuhnle 1983 and Seip 1994.

16. Fellesprogrammet 1945.

17. Stortingsmelding nr. 58, 1948, p. 11. I refer to the reports to the Storting as White Papers.

given to the revision of the Health Insurance, the Unemployment Insurance, and the Occupational Injury Insurance. Lastly, the benefits would be further increased, and maintenance schemes would be established for children and widows.[18]

It was not only in the area of financing that the 1948 plan represented a continuation of the principles established through the compromises of the mid-1930s. As we have seen, the gradual extension, first to ensure a universal OAP and later to include other groups, continued. The same was true for the gradual elevation of benefits. We now turn to look at the balancing of these different objectives in the period eventually leading to the introduction of the National Insurance scheme in 1967.

Priority conflict and compromises, 1948–1957

The road towards universality

In the late 1930s the legislators were too occupied discussing the methods of means-testing to embark again on the principal discussion of universal versus selective pensions. This debate re-emerged, however, after the Second World War. In the 1948 National Insurance White Paper, the Labour government stated clearly that the principal aim was a universal OAP. Three arguments were central to the government's determination to abolish the means test.[19] The abolition would

1. stress the character of the pension as a right for all;
2. result in big administrative savings; and
3. encourage saving and work.

However, while recognising the virtues of abolishing the means test, the government in 1948 was not yet ready to introduce a universal scheme. With consensus reached on the principles of this important question, the subsequent ten years saw a struggle over priorities. The Labour government wanted to extend the pension to include benefits for the disabled and widows before including the remaining quarter of elderly people not yet receiving pensions. Another area given priority by the government was the elevation of existing pensions. In 1948 this was also given priority over universality in the OAP.

---

18. Ibid., pp. 84, 85.
19. Hatland 1984, p. 49.

The non-socialists were divided over the issue. The Christian Party followed the socialists in giving priority to the disabled. The three other non-socialist parties all wanted to abolish the means test before pensions were extended to cover new groups.

In 1951 the Storting appointed a standing committee and instructed it to present a report 'with the least possible delay'. It was, among other tasks, asked to consider the means test and give recommendations on whether to raise the earnings disregard or abolish it altogether. In this committee the Labour representatives for the first time gave priority to its abolition.[20] In spite of a united Standing Committee on Social Affairs, the debate in the Storting saw support for an immediate abolition of the means test in 1952 only from the Liberals and the Agrarian Party. The Conservatives now prioritised the establishment of a disability pension. The government also stressed the elevation of the existing pension.[21]

The combination of higher pensions and elevated earnings disregards would gradually bring about a decrease in the number of people being excluded from eligibility after being means-tested.[22] Thus, the role of the means test would diminish. This outcome enabled the majority in the Storting to tie the government to a promise of abolition once the two aims above were achieved. Subsequently the Standing Committee on Social Affairs in the Storting established a twofold goal: by 1957 the basic pension was to be elevated to one-third of average earnings in industry, and the means test abolished.

The Standing Committee on Social Affairs supported a plan for elevated pensions, and thus higher earnings disregards, to reduce the numbers excluded to a point that made it natural to take the small step of fulfilling the ultimate aim of universality.[23] In this way the Conservatives, the Liberals, and the Agrarian Party sacrificed the immediate lifting of the means test while the government gained time for the elevation of rates.

In 1955, however, the Conservatives broke with the established consensus and proposed the immediate abolition of the means test. While they cited the argument for administrative savings, the Conservatives' main worry was the negative impact the means test had on the develop-

20. Pettersen 1987, p. 62.
21. Ibid.
22. In 1952, 82% of those above the age of 70 received pensions.
23. Referred to in Pettersen 1987, p. 39.

ment of occupational pensions.[24] However, this 'solo performance' by the Conservatives made the other non-socialists group together in support of the agreement reached by the Standing Committee on Social Affairs in 1954.

In 1957 the universal pension was enacted, and it was implemented from January 1959. This decision represents a change of principles without conflict. Previously, all public schemes had a redistributive effect resulting from the combining of tax financing and selectivity.[25] Such a redistributional effect in the large and important OAP was therefore sacrificed by the Labour Party in 1957. A change of financing in 1957 also contributed to the diminishing of redistribution through social security in Norway.[26]

With a substantial elevation of the basic pension, the government saw its main objective fulfilled. The OAP now set the standard from which social security could be extended to cover new groups.

Levels of benefits

As we have seen, the central conflict over the question of pensions during this period was between, on the one hand, those who wanted to give priority to universality and, on the other, those who wanted first to elevate pensions to a more decent level. The Labour Party gave priority to the elevation of pensions, while all the non-socialist parties gave preference to the inclusion of the remaining minority of elderly people still excluded from receiving pensions. The extent to which the non-socialist parties shared the Labour desire for elevated pensions, and thereby disagreed only on priorities and timing, is open to interpretation. What we do know is that Labour was the only party explicitly mentioning the standard of benefits in the party political programmes of the first post-war decade.[27]

The Labour government planned and carried out a long-term strategy in this period by tying the gradual extension of the earnings disregard in the means test to the gradual elevation of benefits. Furthermore, the

---

24. Seip (1987, p. 212) shows that only the Conservatives stressed the need for making room for private pensions in their programmes of the late 1950s.

25. The 1946 Family Allowance was universal and non-means-tested. It was, however, redistributional between families with children and other taxpayers.

26. I will return to this issue below.

27. Seip 1987, p. 214.

Labour Party was aware of the significance of the development of old age pensions to the future development of other areas of social insurance. Both because such great numbers were involved and because pensions for the elderly got priority at a relatively early stage, they would set the standard for schemes to be established later.

In the 1948 White Paper the government made some international comparisons between alternative approaches towards pension levels. Here the British 1946 National Insurance Act, together with New Zealand's 1938 Social Security Act, was used to exemplify the 'minimum standard' approach to social insurance. While the equivalent system in the Soviet Union was referred to as an example of the opposite approach, the government chose an intermediate position: 'The Ministry [of Social Affairs] feels that the achievement of *socially acceptable* income maintenance for all members of society is a central responsibility of the public social insurance program.'[28]

To achieve this ultimate aim the government was still not willing to let go of the savings and redistribution resulting from the means test, given the way means-testing was practised in Norway. However, with growing pressure from the non-socialists, and with no resistance in *principle* towards universality in the government, the time was ripe for compromises on the question of pensions. The significant breakthrough came with the 1954 consensus in the Standing Committee on Social Affairs. Here it was agreed that by 1957 the level of pensions was to be raised to one-third of average earnings in industry, while at the same time the means test would be abolished.

Figure 3.1 shows that the level of pensions increased in the period 1945–57. When the means test was abolished in 1957, the strategy of the Labour government had thus proved successful.

Rising benefit rates, 1957–1966

While the compromise in the period leading up to 1957 brought about higher rates, it had been argued earlier that universality would counteract the *further* elevation of rates. It is therefore of particular interest to see what happened to the rates in the period following the 1957 OAP Act. The results appear in Figure 3.1.

28. Stortingsmelding nr. 58, 1948, p. 7; emphasis added.

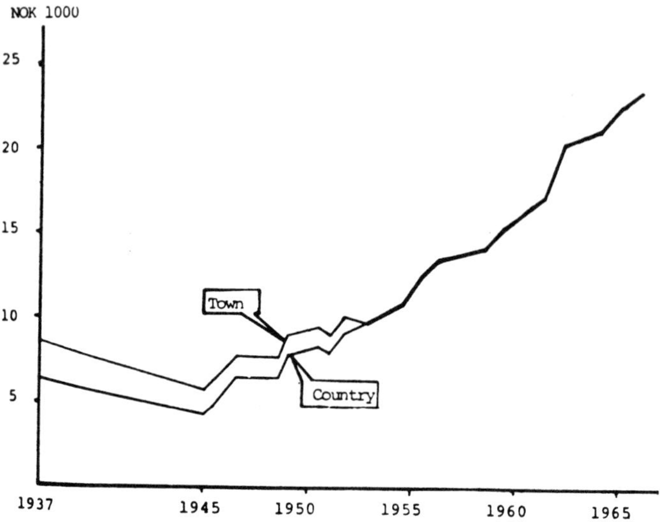

Figure 3.1. Development of old age pensions for married couples. 1982 NOK. (Source: Hatland 1984, p. 51.)

Contrary to what one might expect, the rates rose even more steeply in this period than in previous years. Although there exists no cast-iron explanation for this, some possible reasons can be suggested. In contrast to the situation in 1936 (or 1948 for that matter), the economy allowed for growth in welfare spending. The immediate reconstruction that followed the war was brought to an end. Furthermore, the new groups to be included with the introduction of the universal OAP now had objective interests in exerting political pressure regarding the elevation of benefits. Before 1957 such pressure would have brought about higher taxes and no gain to either the groups excluded from benefits by the means test or their political representatives.

Changes in the methods of financing

The sources of income have remained largely unchanged to the present day.[29] What has changed is the distribution of responsibility among the different sources.

29. That is, in 1976 the contribution from local authorities was abolished.

With the abolition of the means test in 1957, the system of financing was reformed. First, the contribution paid by individuals changed from being paid through general taxation to become a specific membership premium. Second, the employers were to pay a contribution varying according to the contribution paid by the individual employee. Third, the system changed from one of conventional funding to pay-as-you-go.[30]

The main argument for the change from general taxation to premiums lay in the fact that this would make the relationship between contribution and benefit more visible to those involved. This, it was believed, would enhance the popularity of the scheme and make increases in the level of pensions more practicable.[31] The reform thus involved a change towards incorporating a key element of the insurance approach to social security.

The introduction of employers' contributions turned out to be instrumental in the increase in the level of benefits paid. With the change to pay-as-you-go, all increases had to be financed through higher contributions. The Labour government made employers pay for the majority of the increases in the years following 1957. Although reluctant at first, the non-socialists were to follow the same pattern when the first post-war non-socialist government increased pensions in 1965.

The National Insurance Act

Finally, nearly two decades after the publication of the first White Paper, the scheme was approved by the Storting in 1966 and took effect in 1967. This is not to say, however, that no new schemes had been created in this period. While the 1966 Act also established new programmes, its main function was to bring existing schemes together under one umbrella.[32]

The introduction of an earnings-related supplement (ERS)

Before 1967 there was no state-run ERS scheme in Norway, though the question had been raised in the discussion following the 1952

30. The existing fund would be used to regulate the economy of the pension, but no further funds would be accumulated after this date. Pettersen 1987, p. 83.

31. Ibid.

32. I will return to the other social security schemes in the section 'Extensions to cover new groups', below.

Government Report on Pensions. At that time, however, the Standing Committee on Social Affairs in the Storting felt that 'it was not a natural part of social insurance for the time being.'[33] Still, by this statement the government left the way open for a future attempt to create a public earnings-related pension.

In 1960 the LO and the employers' organisation (NAF) made an agreement to establish an additional, but flat-rate, pension (FTP) for their members.[34] This scheme was, however, not designed to be extended to others besides organised workers. Its implementation therefore highlighted the existing differences between those who had the possibility of obtaining a supplementary pension and those who did not. Growing attention to this question was furthermore due to debates in Sweden. In 1957 a referendum there decided in favour of a state-run scheme. This was a big victory for the Labour Party in Sweden, and the non-socialists came out weakened and divided.[35]

That the Norwegian debate a few years later took a somewhat different path must be understood in the light of the Swedish experience.[36] This time the Liberals (the Norwegian counterpart to the losing party in Sweden) supported a state-run scheme. Only the Conservatives opposed this scheme and gave their support to a non-state solution. The existence of the FTP also contributed to the different path taken in Norway. With the only existing scheme limited to organised labour, the non-socialists were less willing to support a future pension based on this scheme than would they have been if it had been freed from organisational ties.

Nor was the Labour Party unanimously in favour of a state scheme. Among some circles in the party there was a desire to replace the old notion of equality (i.e. similar pensions for everybody) with a new equality which sought to diminish the difference between industrial workers on the one hand and salaried staff and civil servants on the other. As the latter groups already had established occupational schemes, this

33. Cited in Hatland 1984, p. 57.

34. The FTP was an ERS-scheme organised by the LO and the NAF. The Labour Party was later willing to sacrifice this pension in order to gain political support from groups outside the LO (fishermen, farmers, and civil servants mainly).

35. In addition to the influence from Sweden, the nature of the FTP and the strong economic growth at the time contributed to the renewed interest in and desire for an ERS around 1960 (West Pedersen 1990, p. 91).

36. Hatland 1984, pp. 57–58.

approach was compatible with a solution along the lines of the existing FTP instead of a universal state-run ERS.[37] In an interview, Prime Minister Gerhardsen expressed support for such a solution.[38]

That a state-run scheme was eventually chosen in 1963 can at least partly be explained by the specific political situation in Norway at the time. In 1963 the Labour government was forced to resign after a mining accident on Spitsbergen. To regain power, Labour proposed an insurance scheme covering the entire working population. This, it was hoped, would win the support of voters outside the Labour Party.[39] Also, a state scheme would ensure public (state) control of 'the savings of the people'.[40] When, in 1965, the non-socialists formed a coalition government, they agreed to abandon their individual party preferences and rally around one solution.[41] By this time the state scheme was widely recognised, and thus compromise by the non-socialists was more feasible.[42]

The scheme, which was implemented by the non-socialist coalition government headed by Per Borten in 1967, involved a strengthening of the standard security approach to welfare. It furthermore had a built-in redistributive element due to graduated contributions, exemptions for the lowest paid, and a higher degree of income replacement for the lower paid than for those with high incomes.

The basic pension after 1967

In Chapter 1, I discussed the importance of incorporating strong, deserving, and well-organised groups into a scheme in order to facilitate its growth and strengthening. I will later compare the British and the Norwegian experience along these lines. For now let us accept that the incorporation of the last 20% or so into the OAP in 1957, and the subsequent growth in rates, may be viewed from this perspective.

37. Seip 1987, p. 218.

38. Cited in Hatland 1984, p. 58.

39. The Norwegian Labour Party has always relied on support from farmers and fishermen.

40. Seip 1987, p. 220.

41. While the Conservatives and the Agrarian Party supported a solution which included private earnings-related pensions, the Liberals and the Christian Party wanted graded pensions within a state scheme. While the Labour Party originally supported a corporative solution, it was the Liberals and the Christian Party that first advocated the eventually enacted state-run solution. Ibid., p. 219.

42. Hatland 1984, p. 60.

If this line of argument is correct, then the creation of a two-tier system in 1967 could have had the opposite effect. In this way, wage-earners could have targeted their political pressure towards the ERS at the expense of the basic pension. This, in turn, could have undergone a decrease in relative value. A possible explanation of why this did not happen in Norway lies in the way the 1966 Act was shaped. It was decided that the basic pension was to be indexed according to the growth in average earnings. More vaguely, it was also settled that pensioners should be awarded their share in the nation's general growth in prosperity.[43]

Hatland shows that in the period 1967–82 the basic pension experienced a growth greater than that of prices in the same time span. Consequently the purchasing power of the pension increased by 14%. Compared with average earnings, however, the pension experienced a slightly smaller growth.

The Special Addition

To ensure higher pensions for those unable to establish entitlement to the ERS, it had, as early as 1964, been suggested that a compensational addition should be made to the basic pension for these groups. The majority in the Storting decided at that point against the proposal and suggested instead an elevation of the basic pension. This would, it was believed, in combination with the subsequent indexing, ensure the same result.

The pressure for a specific addition continued, however, and in 1969 the Storting enacted the Special Addition (*Særtillegg*). Going beyond its original target group – the already-old wage-earners – the scheme also included homemakers and others without income from earnings. It therefore 'attained the character of a guaranteed minimum supplementary pension.'[44]

Representing a 7.5% addition to the basic pension at the time of its introduction, the value of the Special Addition rose to half the value of the basic scheme in 1983. It is therefore within this scheme that the greater part of the growth in pension value for those without ERS has taken place.

43. Hatland 1984, p. 101.
44. Ibid., p. 73.

The prolonged period of dependence on the basic scheme for large groups was furthermore rendered possible by the nature of the rules for establishing entitlement for the ERS. Only after paying contributions over 20 years were pensioners entitled to draw full benefits. In this way support for the basic pension also from large and strong groups of wage-earners was secured.

Extensions to cover new groups

In turning to look at other social insurance programmes, I do so with the understanding that there is a close relationship between the OAP outlined above and the timing, nature, and standard of these schemes. This relationship is expressed in the use of the term 'extension'. Although it follows from the preceding section that the OAP was the scheme from which extensions to cover new groups were made, this is, of course, not to say that groups other than the elderly were included in the OAP. The new schemes covered different contingencies with different needs. Furthermore, the preceding OAP not only showed the way for the new schemes but also laid the foundations on which parallel avenues could be constructed.

The OAP was not, however, the first scheme pointing in the direction of non-Poor Law welfare in Norway. As early as 1894, a workers' accident insurance was enacted. This was later extended to include seamen and fishermen. A compulsory sickness insurance for wage-earners was enacted in 1909.

By 1957 the OAP had attained a combination of universality and relatively high standards of benefits paid. It was awarded on the basis of need irrespective of the claimant's means. This, together with its built-in potential to be expanded to cover other groups, is the reason that I regard it as the foundation on and around which institutional welfare has been built in Norway.[45] Through its development between 1936 and 1957, the OAP showed constructive progress in the field of coverage as well as level of benefits.

The following is an overview of the schemes enacted after 1957 along the lines of the OAP. The pension for the disabled deserves particular

45. The 'built-in potential' results from the adherence to the taxation principle as the main form of financing. The 1957 change towards a membership premium did not alter this picture because it did not exclude non-workers from entitlement.

attention, both because of its large size and because of the role it played in the struggle over priorities in the pre-1960 period.

The Disability Pension (DP)

Simultaneously and in combination with the first proposals for an OAP, a pension for the disabled was first proposed in 1899.[46] In the period from that year to 1919, all the committees working towards the establishment of an OAP included a scheme for the disabled in their proposals. In 1919 this part was left out as a first attempt to make the implementation of the OAP practicable in a period of mounting economic difficulties. In 1936, however, a pension scheme for the blind and severely disabled was enacted together with the first OAP. In addition to an extremely hard test of need (only the completely helpless were included), the scheme had a much harder test of means than that of the OAP. This comprised a test of not only the claimant's income and means but also that of his or her relatives. As a result of these measures to ensure selectivity, only 1,000 blind people and the same number of disabled people received benefits in the first year of the scheme's operation.[47]

With benefits initially lower than those of the OAP, the level of the pension was tied to the OAP in 1947. At the same time the means test was relaxed somewhat. The claimant no longer had to be completely helpless – inability to gain income from earnings became the central criterion. Thus, homemakers, for example, were still excluded from the scheme. Before 1948 the DP was considered a 'downward extension' of the OAP. Therefore, people were allowed to retire as a result of disability before having reached pensionable age. In 1937 it was proposed that only disabled people between the age of 65 and pensionable age (70) should be eligible for the new pension. In 1948 this changed, with age becoming less central as long as the claimant was at least 19 years old. Also, the level of disability required to achieve entitlement was changed that year from 90% to 80%.

The nature of the pension as a highly selective scheme continued, however, throughout the 1950s. In 1955 the minister of social affairs, Rakel Seweriin, was asked what the department would do about the

46. This section is largely based on Pettersen 1987, Part 3.
47. Ibid., p. 69.

means test in the DP when this was abolished in the OAP. She replied by referring to the solutions to this problem adopted by other nations: 'The disability pensions I know of are all means-tested, and I believe it is necessary to stick to that. If a person is able to gain income otherwise, then the disability is not of a nature that calls for state support.'[48] The time was, in other words, not yet ripe for applying the same test of eligibility to the DP and the OAP. Still, in 1957 the means test was somewhat eased.

In the discussion of the OAP we saw how the enactment of a general DP was delayed because the extension and elevation of the OAP were given priority. Thus, the disabled gained little from the early post-war welfare expansion.[49] After the enactment of the 1957 OAP, however, the time was ripe for new initiatives to secure the income maintenance of the disabled. The decade following 1957 can be described as the greatest period of Norwegian welfare expansion. The 1960 DP and its subsequent development accounted for a great deal of that growth. This becomes apparent in Figure 3.2.

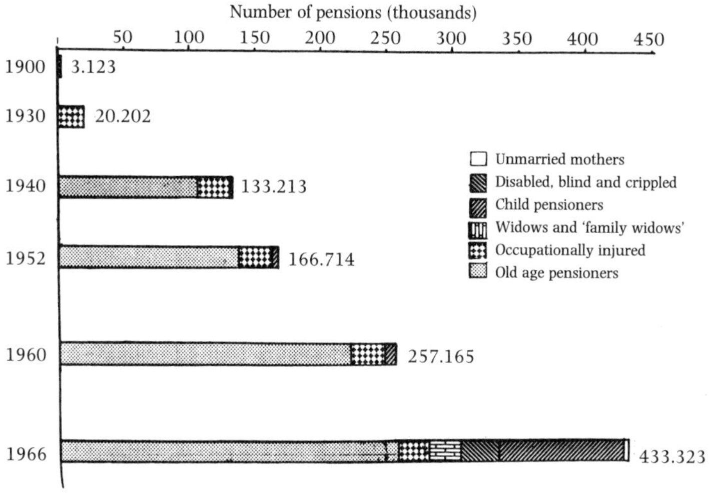

Figure 3.2. Development in the number of pensions under national insurance schemes during the period 1900–1966. (Source: Hatland 1984, p. 54.)

48. Seweriin in the Storting, quoted in Pettersen 1987, p. 77. In Seweriin's statement we see an example of the widespread misuse of the term 'means-testing'. By using the phrase 'able to gain income', Seweriin was really referring to a test of *need*.

49. Seip (1994, p. 195) offers an additional explanation of the slow process of enactment. The inclusion of rehabilitation measures required greater planning and involved greater costs than a pure income maintenance scheme.

At the time of its implementation the new DP was strongly influenced by the OAP. This is true with regard to level of benefits, to methods of establishing eligibility, and to the way in which the funds for the scheme were raised.

From 1947 onwards the level was directly tied to that of the OAP. Due to the strong selective element, only a small minority profited from this before 1960. From that date on, however, the disabled were able to share in the harvest of the struggle for higher pensions in the 1950s. They also benefited, together with the elderly, from the elevation of rates in the years to come.

The 1960 Act restricted the target group to those who could document a work-record. However, with general taxation as the main source of financing, the way was opened for inclusions of groups outside the workforce. It is when such extensions are found desirable that the advantage of the taxation principle over the insurance principle stands out most clearly. Furthermore, it is in accordance with my definition of institutional welfare that services should be allocated more on the basis of need and less on the basis of previous records – be they of work or of contributions.

Having said this, it should be noted that the DP had a contributory element stronger than that of the OAP. Two factors in combination may help explain this outcome. First, the rather vague need requirements of the DP compared with those of the OAP created a fear of 'scrounging', which was less prevalent in the general attitude towards the OAP claimants. Second, most of the needs covered at first were those for which it would otherwise be natural for the individual to seek some kind of insurance.[50] In this way the contributory element would foster a stronger perception of 'rights'. Generally, this is important for the advocates of what are often perceived to be 'unpopular' reforms, as well as for the claimants, with regard to both how they are judged by others and how they themselves see that this concept of rights may ease any potential stigma. With 'old age' as the central criterion, it is somewhat easier to prove 'deservingness'.

---

50. Later, when need categories such as alcoholics were included, this would of course be different.

Changes in the coverage of the DP

The enactment of the 1960 DP involved the inclusion of a great number of new claimants who had not been eligible for benefits from the preceding disability and blindness scheme. After its introduction in 1936 that scheme had showed only a small growth, and even by 1955 only 4,500 people were receiving benefits.

The OAP had set the standard whereby need became the central element in the test of eligibility. It was, however, both more difficult and more challenging to general notions of 'deservingness' to implement an equivalent standard in the DP. Therefore, the years after the enactment of the first general DP represent a *gradual shift in the view of what constitutes need.* It was not until 1969 that the first deliberate attempt was launched to break with the tradition of bringing the cause of the problem into consideration. Labour's Odvar Nordli, who was later to become prime minister, argued that year in the Storting that 'to a great extent we have built up a system where the level of the benefit, as well as the form in which it is given, varies according to the situation of the insured. It seems right in the future to consider the situation of the insured, and not the reason why this situation has emerged.'[51]

In the years between the 1960 enactment and the above statement, however, there was a gradual extension of the coverage of the DP. Indirectly, the extensions were conditional on greater acknowledgement of need regardless of cause. The liberalisation of the test of eligibility took three forms. First, the degree of disability required was lowered from two-thirds in the 1960 Act to 50% with the introduction of National Insurance (NI) in 1967. Second, there was a liberalisation of the nature of the symptoms that could create entitlement. In particular this extended the pension beyond physical disability towards an increasing acceptance of mental and social disabilities. Third, the requirement to establish 'objectively registerable symptoms' was abandoned.

The liberalisations cannot be fully understood with reference to a more generous social policy alone. In many areas of health and welfare, the 1960s represent the zenith of the belief in the value and results of *treatment.* Simultaneously with the enactment of the DP, the law introducing Rehabilitation Benefits came into being. This offered income maintenance

51. Quoted in Pettersen 1987, p. 92.

for people undergoing medical treatment or occupational rehabilitation. The belief was that with successful rehabilitation the majority of those awarded Rehabilitation Benefits would soon be back in the workforce. Instead of being immediately awarded DP, the sick or disabled person received a provisional benefit while in rehabilitation. This would, it was believed, counteract the passiveness and terminal dependence often associated with the DP.[52]

The government expected the rehabilitation programme to restrain gradually the trickle of new clients into the DP. When this optimism eventually proved wrong, it was difficult, even if desirable, to reverse the trend and introduce stricter tests of entitlement. Furthermore, the forecasts of the number of clients were unrealistically low. On the basis of a combination of the Swedish experience and the municipal DP in Oslo,[53] it was expected that after three years of operation the number of clients would stabilise at around 70,000.[54] The great number of people who satisfied the criteria, together with unrealistic expectations about the possibilities of rehabilitation, proved the prognosis dramatically wrong. By 1966, the year the National Insurance Act was passed, the number of clients had reached 100,000. Subsequently the growth exploded, and by 1972 the DP was providing benefits for a record 154,000 people. It was in this latter period that the majority of the 'symptom-liberalisations' and the lowered disability requirements were introduced.

Other schemes

The establishment of a wide-ranging, non-means-tested DP was by far the most important extension of social insurance after the introduction of the 1957 OAP. Still, this development alone did not bring about what turned out to be the greatest period of welfare expansion in Norway.[55] Simultaneously with the incorporation of the DP into NI, Norway witnessed a

52. In Chapter 6 we will return to a discussion of the notion of 'rehabilitation' as a key issue in the relationship between the DP and the Social Care Act.

53. Oslo had a long history of municipal DPs. This was also true for many other local authorities. By the time of the 1960 enactment, 20,000 people were covered by municipal DPs. This compares with 4,500 in the state-run disability and blindness scheme.

54. Pettersen 1987, p. 85.

55. Hatland 1984, p. 51.

development whereby a wide range of need categories found their way into the great bosom of National Insurance.

In part these were groups already demarcated and covered by specific schemes, and in part newly established need categories defined and lifted out of social assistance and/or family dependency. While the widows and unwed mothers may serve to exemplify the former, unmarried persons forced to live at home ('family nurses') may represent the latter.[56] Common to all these groups is that incorporation into NI involved an enhancement of their welfare, not only in terms of entitlement, but also in terms of their relative position in the welfare hierarchy.

In 1964 a scheme was introduced to provide benefits for widows and mothers. From an international perspective this scheme represents a piece of welfare pioneering because unwed mothers were also included. Moreover, the new scheme for 'family nurses' represented unique legislation at the time. The NI scheme came into effect on 1 January 1967. It replaced the previous schemes relating to OAP, DP, Widow and Mother Benefits, Survivors' Benefits for children, and Rehabilitation Benefits. In 1971, Health Insurance, Unemployment Insurance, and Occupational Injury Insurance were also incorporated into NI.[57]

Tentative explanations of the extensions

The gradual incorporation of groups into social insurance in Norway after 1957 offers more than an account of an expanding welfare state. Studied in more detail it also reveals a picture of internal differences between the various incorporated groups. This applies both to the nature of the groups *per se* and to the way in which they are perceived by policy-makers and the public at large.

I have earlier hypothesised that individuals and groups experiencing contingencies deemed more 'deserving' stand a better chance of being incorporated at an early stage, compared with those suffering from less

56. 'Family nurses' are unmarried persons who have been forced to stay at home to give necessary care and attention to parents or near relatives. This reform, which was unique to Norway, gave these people a right to a pension when their parents died.

57. The latest group to be incorporated into NI were separated and divorced parents in 1981.

socially accepted problems.[58] This distinction furthermore relates not only to the nature of the contingency itself but also to the degree to which the person is seen as responsible by having inflicted the problem on him- or herself. The latter is particularly important to the public attitude regarding deservingness. In the DP this found its expression in the earlier incorporation of physical disabilities as against mental problems. In this hierarchy social disabilities, for example those resulting from alcohol and drug abuse, were incorporated at a later stage than the two above. This latter extension was part of the 'symptom-liberalisation' I have described.

Another factor that will be seen to have influenced the timing of incorporation is the relationship between the need category and the labour market. As we have seen, disabled workers were incorporated earlier than, for example, disabled homemakers. In the chapter on Norwegian social assistance (Chapter 6), I will pursue this discussion further and study the welfare offered to the groups excluded wholly or partly from NI.

Political and ideological aspects of the extensions

So far my discussion of the relationship between the OAP and the subsequently established schemes has focused on the practicalities of the extensions through the inclusion of parallel schemes. I have showed how the solution to the question of financing rendered possible the inclusion of groups with little or no possibility of establishing a contributory record (for an insurance-based scheme). Furthermore, the OAP created a non-means-tested scheme offering universal benefits at a relatively high level. Given the possibility of inclusion, this constituted a form of social security attractive to groups still not incorporated into social insurance.

The dynamics of the extensions that took place can thus be summed up as follows: The technical solution in the form of a mainly tax-financed social insurance constituted a *prerequisite* for inclusions. Furthermore, the relatively high level of welfare made inclusion desirable for 'outsiders'. But neither the technical solution nor the desirability of the scheme constitutes a *sufficient* explanation of the inclusions that took place. To gain a better understanding of the developments described in this section, I must therefore include further explanatory factors. The two central pro-

58. I will return to a discussion of the notion of 'deserving' and 'undeserving' clients in the concluding part of the study.

grammes for post-war social insurance, as outlined above, also offer a key to understanding the gradual extensions of insurance in the two decades following 1945.

First, in 1945 the Joint Programme of the coalition government established the goal of 'developing social policy in order to make the Poor Law superfluous'. Later, in 1948, the important National Insurance White Paper was presented by the Labour government. This document includes explicit discussions of the questions analysed above. Two important sections stand out: 1) level of benefits and 2) coverage. First, in the discussion of the level of the future pensions, a distinction was made between a *minimum standard* on the one hand and *income replacement* on the other. We saw that the Norwegian government argued for an intermediate solution. The basic level of social insurance aimed eventually to offer 'socially acceptable income maintenance for all members of society'.[59] In comparing Britain and Norway, we see that the two countries shared ambitions with regard to coverage but that Norway had higher ambitions concerning level. A cautious note was included in the acceptance of economic growth as the main determinant of the speed with which the reforms would be implemented. Thus, although ambitious goals had been established, it was generally agreed that all the aims concerning level and coverage could not be achieved immediately. Therefore, the 1945 aim of *replacing rather than abolishing the Poor Law* was still valid in 1948. But rather than being satisfied with general aims only, the government established in the 1948 White Paper the need categories that should eventually be covered by the proposed NI, and stated the order of the reforms to be implemented. The aim was to establish a system as close as possible to universal coverage against loss of earnings. This would require insurance in the cases of old age, disability, unemployment, and loss of supporter.

With the general aims established and the first step towards extensions through inclusions taken with the 1960 DP, a new explanatory factor may have come into play. The acceptance of the needs of one group in the form of incorporation into NI may create pressure from non-included groups sharing similar problems. If this is true, groups that could create channels through which their interests could be expressed and pressure exerted might be expected to enjoy an advantage. However, it falls outside the scope of this study to analyse the nature and extent of such

59. Stortingsmelding nr. 58, 1948, p. 7.

influences in the period. I will, though, return to the question when looking at the non-inclusion of the assistance clientele into NI.

Summary and conclusions

In this chapter we have seen that Norwegian post-war social insurance represents a continuation of the policies forged through the compromises of the mid-1930s. Crucially, the tripartite method of financing, whereby the state, the employers, and the individual all contributed towards the cost of the scheme, continued. The strong dominance of public funds made this a programme based on the principle of tax-financing, incorporating elements of the insurance principle through individuals' and employers' contributions. The significance of the emphasis on tax-financing became clear when extensions to include groups that had no contributory record were deemed desirable. Also, the gradual extension towards universality through the easing of the means test was continued after the war. Finally, while the benefits were set low at first, the expressed aim was to move towards a high degree of income replacement when the economy allowed for this. I therefore find that although the war may have had an influence on the level of ambition in social insurance, the course of the envisaged development remained unchanged. In the Summary of Part Two, I will return to the other aspect of the question of the impact of the war, when I consider the extent of diffusion between British and Norwegian policy-makers in this period.

We have seen that the conflict over priorities in the first post-war decade facilitated the achievement of two major objectives. The gradual extension towards universality in the OAP was accompanied by a gradual elevation of benefits in that scheme. However, the third objective set out in 1948, extensions to incorporate other groups into social insurance, was delayed in this process. Thus, the disabled, for example, gained little in this period. In general the Labour government in this period continued its long-established pragmatic approach to priorities, whereby *economic equality*, through a levelling out of the differences in living standards, was favoured over the long-term goal of *social equality* through equal treatment of rich and poor in periods when income maintenance was needed.

When universality was achieved in 1957, however, the time was ripe for extensions to be made. As extensions were made according to the principles and standards established in the OAP, the newly incorporated groups finally benefited from the post-war developments. Moreover, from the late 1950s onwards the economic and political climate favoured extensions as well as further elevations of benefits. Finally, when the ERS was introduced as part of the 1967 National Insurance scheme, the particular solution favoured a further elevation of the basic pension also.

At this point it is tempting to speculate about what the outcome might have been if, first, universality in the OAP had been achieved earlier, in accordance with the wishes of the non-socialist parties, and, second, the extensions to include other groups had been given priority over universality in the OAP and/or the elevation of benefits in that scheme. Judging from the dynamic that existed between the elevation of benefits and coverage in the 1950s, I find it not unlikely that such an alternative development might have stalled the development of benefits for all groups covered by social insurance in Norway. There would have been a 'thinner spread' when limited resources were allocated (remember the prominence given to economic factors in setting the pace). Also, with a mainly tax-financed scheme, it could be that the political desire to elevate pensions would have been less widely shared if large groups of, for example, people suffering from mental disorders had entered the scheme. From this perspective, old people are seen to be generally accepted as a highly deserving group. It is therefore possible that in the long run groups such as the disabled benefited from the long wait until they were incorporated into a scheme with benefits already elevated to a relatively high level of welfare. This offers, however, little comfort to the large groups of disabled people and their families who had to rely on poor relief throughout this period.

Again, therefore, as in the early part of the century, the particular ambitiousness of Norwegian social insurance was characterised by 'cautious haste'. In the Summary of Part Two, we will see that this contrasts sharply with the British approach of 'as much as possible as early as possible'. Most important, the two approaches had very different consequences for the relationship between social insurance and assistance and their respective client groups in the two countries. This will be discussed further when we turn to social assistance in Part Three.

Chapter 4

British Labour and Contributory Pensions: From Rejection to Acceptance and Implementation

With the 1946 National Insurance Act, the Attlee government started implementing the recommendations of the Beveridge Report. Although this and later social insurance legislation did more than merely duplicate the Beveridge blueprints, it did not deviate from Beveridge's central principles of social insurance. We shall return to the Beveridge Plan and its implementation in the next chapter. For now the significant aspect of this plan is that social insurance was based on a system of finance in which people would be awarded benefits by viritue their previous individual contributions. The contributions were equal for all participants in the scheme, and so were the benefits. Labour's support for these principles contrasted sharply with the party's position before the first Old Age Pension (OAP) in 1908.

In this chapter I focus on the contributory principle, for two reasons. First, in Chapter 2 we found that the Norwegian choice of a mainly tax-financed social insurance proved to be the cornerstone of what I called the 'Norwegian model of social insurance'. To understand the roots of the British model, in itself as well as in relation to its Norwegian counterpart, we therefore have to analyse how and why Britain arrived at the opposite solution regarding this key aspect of social insurance. While both the Norwegian and the British Labour Party from the outset were committed to the taxation principle, employing many of the same arguments, the British party left this position before taking office in 1945. Second, in Chapter 3 we saw that the tax-financed solution proved instrumental in the achievement of a gradual elevation of insurance benefits and the extension towards a more universal scheme in the post-war period in Norway. In the next chapter I will hypothesise that the British choice of a contributory approach was equally important in determining the development of British insurance in this respect. The unequal success of the two approaches to insurance will, in turn, be seen to be the main factor explaining the divergent scope and nature of social assistance in the two countries in the same period.

When we focus on the Labour Party in this period, the reason is that without its support the implementation of the contributory principle would not have been possible in 1946. This follows from the fact that the Attlee government ruled with majority support in Parliament, unlike the two earlier Labour governments.[1] It cannot be ruled out that the inability of those minority governments to break the policy inheritance of contributory social insurance was a result of 'ruling without power'.

In the Introduction to Part Two, I argued that while the taxation principle has traditionally been advocated by socialist parties, the contributory principle is equally associated with conservative and, in particular, liberal social policy. In Chapter 2 we saw that the Norwegian Labour Party adhered to the taxation principle while gradually accepting some contributory elements. However, this compromise contrasts sharply with the programme enacted in Britain after the war. The 1946 legislation will therefore be seen as a departure from socialist social policy.

This, then, was when the British Labour Party departed from the line taken by its Norwegian counterpart. With both parties in power in the immediate post-war period, the ensuing divergence between the two welfare states resulted from the contrasting policies of the first Labour majority governments in the two nations.

The objective of this chapter, therefore, is to analyse the standpoint of the British Labour Party with regard to the contributory principle of financing in the years leading up to the party's definitive acceptance of the principle through its implementation in 1946.

I will argue that, rather than representing a sudden break with earlier policy, the position taken by the Labour Party in the 1940s was the end product of a process of gradual acceptance of the contributory principle. This process will be seen to have begun as early as 1910. The factors that made this change possible will, however, be traced still further back. The final turn towards full acceptance will furthermore be seen as a non-decision: it was never discussed in principle within the party nor brought into the parliamentary arena by Labour MPs.

1. Ramsay MacDonald formed two minority Labour governments, in 1924 and 1929. In 1931 he formed a government with the Liberals and the Conservatives.

The analysis first focuses on the Labour Party's policies in the pre-Second World War period. We will then go on to study Labour and Trade Union Congress (TUC) publications in the period leading up to the parliamentary debate on social insurance in 1943. The next section highlights the contribution of Labour representatives during this debate. Finally, the findings will be discussed in relation to existing literature which, directly or indirectly, addresses the subject of this chapter.

The Labour Party and contributory OAPs before the Second World War

The purpose of this section is to find out when, how, and why the Labour Party came to accept the contributory principle. But before we do so, a short overview of the actual development of the OAP in relation to the variable of financing is necessary, not only as a backcloth against which to see Labour policies, but also to present an explanatory factor, inasmuch as policy inheritance will be seen to play a role in determining later policy decisions.

In 1908 Lloyd George's Liberal government instituted the first British OAP. The scheme, which was based on the taxation principle, remained more or less intact until 1925, when it was changed to be financed mainly from individual contributions. Pensioners entitled to benefits under the previous scheme continued, however, to receive a non-contributory benefit. After the introduction of the 1925 scheme, therefore, three types of pensions for the aged coexisted:

1. a non-contributory pension paid between the ages of 65 and 70 for those eligible for National Health Insurance (NHI);
2. a partially contributory pension for NHI-eligible pensioners after they reached the age of 70; and
3. a non-contributory pension for those aged 70 or older without an NHI record.

While the last two remained means-tested, the first became exempt.[2] Apart from minor technical changes, the 1925 scheme remained largely unchanged until the Second World War.[3]

2. Thane 1982, p. 199.
3. Heclo 1973, p. 209.

Labour's attitude towards the contributory principle in the first half century of the party's existence appears to be distinguished by three stages. The first period, partly predating the establishment of the party, saw a united labour movement behind a firm rejection of contributory pensions. This period culminated with the 1908 enactment. The second stage saw the party on the move over this question. This started with the debate leading up to the 1911 contributory National Insurance. The end of this stage is harder to date; there was a gradual transition to the third stage in the 1940s, when the question of financing became a non-issue.

Struggle for non-contributory pensions and party consolidation, 1899–1908

A natural starting point for this analysis is the 1899 establishment of the 'National Committee of Organised Labour on Old Age Pensions' (NCP). The committee consisted of representatives of trade unions, trade councils, Friendly Societies, and co-operative societies. It was established 'with the avowed aim of gaining a free state pension of 5 shillings a week for every citizen at age 65.'[4]

Heclo argues that 'the force of labor behind pensions was scarcely organized as such; indeed pensions helped advance the organization of the British labor movement as much as the reverse.'[5] In the years leading up to the 1908 enactment, the fight for a non-contributory pension became an issue around which the young labour movement could unite. Before this period conflicting interests counteracted the unification of the movement and the ultimate aim of establishing a parliamentary party.

The NCP rejected a contributory scheme on the grounds that it 'would interfere with the activities of the Friendly Societies and that it would offer no help to women, the poorest and those in need of immediate aid.'[6] At the outset the Friendly Societies rejected the idea of a state pension altogether. Towards the end of the century, however, they realised that a pension could be to their advantage. By this time the societies were facing economic problems because their members continued to draw 'sickness benefits' for much longer periods of time than previously. According to

4. Ibid., p. 166.
5. Ibid., p. 165.
6. Ibid., p. 167.

the societies' policy, a member was entitled to benefits when he was too frail or ill to work. However, improved health and medicine extended the period from this point to the time of death. For this reason the societies were unwillingly taking part in the 'invention of retirement'.

When they changed their attitude and welcomed a state pension to relieve them of some of this burden, they could not, however, accept a contributory scheme. As they faced economic problems due to high expenditures, it became increasingly important to safeguard their only source of income. A state contributory scheme would have introduced a competitor vying for the limited savings of working people; therefore, the extension of the practice of self-help became subordinate to the protection of vested interests. The role of the Friendly Societies at this point thus represents a variant of what Kaim-Caudle describes as the situation in which 'insurance companies have an interest in impeding the expansion of public welfare.'[7] The interrelationship between public and non-public welfare will, as we shall see, continue to dominate the development of British social insurance.

In 1904 the Labour Representation Committee made non-contributory, universal OAPs 'the first plank' in the social reform programme of the new Labour Party.[8] Thane argues that the Treasury played an instrumental role when contributory pensions were rejected in 1908, its main concern at that point being the cost involved in administering the individual contributions.[9] To answer whether it was the rejection by the Friendly Societies of a contributory pension, the Treasury's objections, or the Labour campaigns for a non-contributory scheme that most determined the 1908 outcome falls outside the scope of this analysis. We will, however, return to the question in the Summary of Part Two, where I compare the routes towards the first non-contributory OAP in the two countries.

The success of the struggle, in terms of social policy as well as in terms of the wider political objective of consolidating the labour movement, undoubtedly gave the non-contributory approach a *symbolic value* that later made openly departing from it difficult.

---

7. Kaim-Caudle 1973, p. 132. See also the Introduction to Part Two for an outline of this argument.

8. Heclo 1973, p. 171. The Labour Party was established under its new name in 1906.

9. Thane 1982, p. 82.

Practical acceptance and rhetorical dissociation, 1910–1930

In practical terms, however, the united stance was short-lived.[10] This brings us to the second period, which started with the support for the 1911 contributory National Insurance by a majority of Labour Party MPs. To understand this 'apparent volte-face', we must consider a third argument that had been used by the labour movement in its rejection of contributions a few years earlier.[11] The TUC feared that payment of contributions could undermine the wage-earners' ability to pay union dues, and thereby have a negative impact on union membership.[12] In a necessary attempt to seek co-operation and support from voluntary organisations in the insurance field, the Liberal government sent a TUC delegation to Germany to study the records of contributory insurance there. The delegation came back with a most favourable report. The most important of their conclusions was that the contributory scheme appeared to have stimulated the growth of trade unions. By electing representatives to the bodies administering the scheme, the trade unions had gained strength and importance.[13] Mountford concludes that the impact of the German experience, together with actuarial problems in the trade unions' own insurance schemes, 'was enough to overcome any practical or theoretical objections they might have.'[14] Furthermore, she attributes Labour's parliamentary support to the influence of the unions, particularly those for skilled, well-paid workers, on the party as a whole. A further point which strengthens this line of argument is the way in which the 1911 scheme came to be administered. Friendly Societies, trade unions, and insurance companies were given responsibility for the day-to-day running of the scheme.[15] With skilled workers dominating both the trade union movement and the Friendly Societies, it is not surprising that this decision eased union opposition to the new schemes.[16]

10. My analysis of this time period relies heavily on Mountford 1984.

11. Ibid., p. 40.

12. Ibid., p. 43.

13. Ibid., p. 48. See also Hennock 1987 for an in-depth study of the German influence on British social policy in this period.

14. Ibid., p. 53.

15. Thane 1982, p. 85.

16. The interests of these groups may have coincided with those of the better-off. Baldwin argues: 'In a sense, it was Asquith and Lloyd George's success in financing

There were still groups within the party which objected to the policy shift, notably the Fabians, the Independent Labour Party, and unions with nothing to gain from contributory pensions.[17]

Although the 1911 National Insurance Act did not include OAPs, both the introduction of contributory social security and the Labour support for the scheme as a whole set important precedents for the later development of social insurance.[18] Before Labour was forced to decide on the method of financing once again, there was a period in the 1920s during which pre-1911 attitudes enjoyed a renaissance. The means test attached to the 1908 OAP, as well as the diminishing values of benefits in the period 1908–20, made the Labour movement intensify its struggle for a universal non-contributory pension offering benefits sufficient for subsistence. This was expressed through resolutions moved by Labour MPs.[19]

The first real test of the changing attitudes within the Labour Party after 1911 came with the short-lived Labour minority government in 1924. Mountford has studied in detail the socio-political activities of both MacDonald Labour governments. She challenges interpretations positing the main cause of government inactivity to have been 'ruling without power'.[20] She argues convincingly that 'parameters imposed by the Treasury, not by the Palace of Westminster, were what constantly pressed on the policy making process.'[21] In other words, the greatest failure of the two governments was their inability to challenge economic orthodoxy.

An increase in the deteriorating OAP benefits and, perhaps more important, a shift in the financial arrangement of sickness and unemployment benefits to the non-contributory approach would indeed have implied considerable increases in public expenditure. The 'failure' of the

---

non-contributory pensions through progressive taxation that made necessary British social policy's volteface in a contributory direction. Because they had already been able to enlist middle and upper-class efforts on behalf of the poor, the political rationing of any further golden eggs was painfully apparent. Recipients would themselves have to help finance benefits directly were there to be any further expansion of social insurance.' Baldwin 1990, p. 101.

17. Mountford 1984, p. 60.

18. 'The importance of the 1911 (health and unemployment) insurance act for old age pensions lay in establishing a working system of contributory insurance that could serve later as a precedent for pensions.' Heclo 1973, p. 196.

19. Ibid., p. 205.

20. This was Philip Snowden's own phrase. Mountford 1984, p. 65.

21. Ibid.

two minority governments under Prime Minister Ramsay MacDonald must therefore be judged in the light of the political economy of the time.

Of more specific interest are the attempts made by Philip Snowden, the chancellor of the 1924 Labour government, to ease the means test in the OAP. He announced in that year that a scheme could be found to achieve that important Labour aim. Mountford states, however, that 'it seems almost certain that the scheme he had in mind was the product of the deliberations of the Anderson Committee.'[22] It was on the recommendations of this committee that the Conservative government in 1925 introduced the first contributory OAP in Britain. If Mountford is correct, this represents further evidence that the Labour Party was willing to sacrifice the non-contributory principle in social insurance.

Heclo similarly concludes that the desire for a universal pension at subsistence level, combined with Labour's inability to challenge economic orthodoxy, forced the party to accept contributory pensions in the mid-1920s. He quotes Snowden's observation that 'the case for universal pensions is not really logical. I can imagine circumstances where [they] might be justified if the country had means to squander and it knew of no other purpose to which they could be devoted.'[23] Heclo obviously sees this as a turning point in the struggle over the future source of finance when he states that, 'with defection of the major defenders of the 1908 Pension Act, it was now only a matter of time until British social policy finally turned to contributory old age pensions.'[24]

Again, the Treasury played a key role in the policy-making process. I have mentioned that the 1908 OAP offered very low benefits. The weekly rate of 5 shillings was 2 shillings below the lowest amount which, according to Rowntree, could support one person.[25] The stringent means test detracted further from the ability of the pension to alleviate poverty in old age. At the time it was described as a pension for 'the very poor, the very respectable and the very old.'[26] By 1925 the value of the pension had decreased further. While the pension at that point was 10 shillings per week, the corresponding rate for poor relief was often 15 shillings.[27] The

22. Mountford 1984, p. 133.
23. Hansard, 25 June 1924, quoted in Heclo 1973, p. 205.
24. Heclo 1973, p. 205.
25. Thane 1982, p. 83.
26. Ibid.
27. Thane 1982, p. 142.

government was therefore under great pressure to increase the level of the benefits. On this occasion the Treasury's argument was that it could 'only countenance an increase if pensions were shifted onto an insurance basis.'[28]

Once enacted by a non-Labour government, the 1925 scheme met, however, with a frontal attack from Labour MPs. All the arguments from the debates leading up to the 1908 enactment were remobilised.[29] 'The Bill bristles with anomalies inevitable in the case of a contributory scheme', said Arthur Greenwood.[30] The party in general and Greenwood (the later advocate of the Beveridge proposals) in particular showed that the non-contributory principle, because of its symbolic value, had not yet been abandoned by the mid-1920s. In practical politics, however, the party showed at best an inability to find ways to counteract the means test other than by contributory income maintenance. Labour thus appears to have come half-way to accepting the contributory principle.

During the late 1920s there was growing resentment among the Labour Party grass-roots membership towards contributions. According to Mountford this strengthened the position of those in the parliamentary party arguing for non-contributory pensions.[31] Yet, on their return to power in 1929, the Labour ministers again proved unable to break the policy inheritance of contributory income maintenance. The party, determined to prove itself 'responsible', lacked the know-how to counteract the advice of established experts in the field of social insurance and, not least, the realities of the national economy.

In her conclusion Mountford states that by 1926 the party had realised that the contributory route for some inevitably meant the means-tested route for others.[32] While only some of the people in present and future need were able to contribute, the remainder were still forced into the means test of the Poor Law. Furthermore, in 1931 claimants realised that a contributory scheme entailed no greater rights for the beneficiary than did a non-contributory scheme.[33] In combination one would expect that these insights

28. Ibid., p. 143.
29. Mountford 1984, p. 168.
30. Ibid., p. 169.
31. Ibid., p. 209.
32. Ibid., p. 308.
33. Ibid., p. 311. In Chapter 8, I will return to the breakdown of the contributory system in the 1930s.

and experiences would have been sufficient for the party to see through the argument that Beveridge had put forward since 1907 – that only through contributions could the right to non-means-tested benefits be achieved.

To explain why the new insight achieved in 1926 did not have any decisive impact on the views taken by the party, Mountford points to the nature of the party itself: 'Primarily it served the interests of the higher paid, male trade unionists, and it was this section of the working class who, for much of the period under consideration (1908–31), had more to gain from the operation of the contributory principle than to lose from it, given the limited possibility of alternatives.'[34]

The final move towards full acceptance in the 1930s

This period was one of inactivity in the field of OAPs. In fact, even the rates set in 1925 remained unchanged until 1939.[35] For British income maintenance as a whole, however, the period was one of drastic changes, both in the nature of schemes and with regard to the balance between various groups in the struggle over social policy.

The change of focus was provoked by the arrival of mass unemployment. The struggle over unemployment benefits (UB) will be dealt with, however, only to the extent that it had repercussions for the later development of social insurance in general and OAPs in particular.

The analysis will focus on three areas. First, I will examine the development of UB *per se*. Second, this development will be studied in relation to the changing power structure within the Labour Party. Third, particular attention will be given to the role played by William Beveridge.

During the 1920s the number of unemployed rose to more than 1 million. The payment of UB therefore became a mounting responsibility for the governments in charge. The insurance fund proved, not surprisingly, unable to cover the cost, and by 1931 the contribution paid by the Exchequer amounted to nearly one-quarter of all government expenditure.[36] That successive governments continued to increase the length of the period of entitlement must be understood in relation to the political cost involved in subjecting such great numbers to the Poor Law.[37]

34. Ibid., p. 313.
35. Thane 1982, p. 198.
36. Deacon and Bradshaw 1983, p. 15.
37. Ibid.

Eventually, however, the burden proved too great, and in 1931 Transitional Payments were introduced. With this scheme, all unemployed persons who had either paid fewer than 30 contributions over the last two years or drawn benefits for more than 26 weeks in one year were excluded from the insurance-based UB. To cater for the newly established category, numbering 900,000 people, Transitional Payments were set up to be paid at government employment offices. The significance of the reform lies in the fact that these new payments were made subject to a test of means administered by the local Public Assistance Committee. In effect, therefore, this group of unemployed were once again subject to the Poor Law. It was with the introduction of Transitional Payments that the notorious 'household means test' was introduced into British social policy. This refers to the extension by which the means of everybody who shared a dwelling were taken into account. This is the scheme usually referred to when the British post-war welfare state is seen as a reaction to the experience of means-tested income maintenance in the 1930s.

For the unemployed things became worse still with the establishment of the Unemployment Assistance Board in 1935. Its main objective was to counteract the tendency towards generous treatment of the unemployed by some local authorities.

It should come as no surprise that the crisis in general and the experience of UB in particular had political repercussions beyond the realm of social policy. For the Labour Party this was particularly strongly felt in the autumn of 1931. To finance the mounting costs of UB, the second Labour government was forced to seek foreign loans. Under the terms of these loans, 'considerable economies had to be made in public expenditure.'[38] This was the background for the imposition of the means test. The government fell, however, over this issue shortly afterwards. An important minority in the cabinet refused to accept a 10% cut in the insurance-based benefit. The introduction of a means test was, however, endorsed by all ministers. The crisis that this event brought about within the party was further heightened by the 'solo performance' of MacDonald in immediately entering into a coalition government. The TUC in particular felt betrayed by this move. It was not consulted on the matter. The TUC was later instrumental in having MacDonald excluded from the party.[39]

38. Ibid.
39. Pelling 1985, pp. 72, 73.

Pelling argues that in the power vacuum that resulted from MacDonald's fall, the TUC gained much greater influence within the party. He sees this change as part of a more general phenomenon: 'As is usual when the parliamentary party is at the bottom of its fortunes, most of its members were trade unionists, especially miners.'[40] Another vacuum was created by the inactivity of what Pelling describes as 'the long moribund Fabian Society' in this period.[41] He concludes that 'in this period of disorder among the more committed Socialists and intellectuals, the General Council of the TUC under the leadership of Bevin and Citrine abandoned its usual role of being the sheet-anchor of the party and instead moved in to take the helm.'[42]

Following this development the newly appointed National Council of Labour became the central arena for the shaping of Labour policy in the mid- and late 1930s.[43] The TUC held 50% of the seats in the council, the rest being divided between the parliamentary section and the party organisation. It would be wrong to infer that greater influence by the TUC on the party would necessarily have led to a move to the left. Although such an influence might have been exerted with regard to industrial relations, in the area of social policy the TUC has always represented sectional interests more than those of the working class as a whole. This tradition proved important in the crucial years that were to follow.

As a consequence of the division of UB into a means-tested and a contributory non-means-tested scheme, two advisory bodies were set up. William Beveridge was brought in to be the chairman of the Unemployment Insurance Statutory Committee, which gave advice on the running of the insurance-based scheme. With this appointment, Beveridge re-entered the process of social policy-making. While he took part actively in shaping social insurance before the First World War, he spent most of the inter-war years being 'more often the critic than the architect of new insurance schemes.'[44] For Beveridge himself this work was instrumental in strengthening not only his own desire for a contributory pension scheme but also his belief in the popularity of this approach among ordinary people. Working on the committee allowed him to get in close

40. Ibid., p. 74.
41. Ibid., p. 76.
42. Ibid., p. 77.
43. Ibid.
44. Harris 1977, p. 346.

contact with popular attitudes: 'He was greatly impressed by the strength of support for insurance among the organized working class, and by their willingness, even eagerness, to pay larger contributions for broader coverage – in striking contrast to the widespread hostility to insurance that he had found in 1916.'[45]

With the division into two UB schemes – and two corresponding advisory bodies – it was exactly the 'organized working class' with which Beveridge came to work together on the committee in the years to follow. Beveridge himself gives particular emphasis to the co-operation with the head of the Social Insurance Department of the TUC, J.L. Smyth. This relationship was to form 'an admirable foundation for the discussions on social insurance that were to follow in 1942.'[46]

Discussions in the labour movement, 1940–1943

We now turn to look at the internal discussion in the labour movement in the period leading up to the parliamentary debate on the Beveridge Report. As we will see, this debate produced no questioning of the principles of the report by Labour MPs. This does not, however, necessarily mean that the issue was not debated internally in the party. It is conceivable that the early implementation of a much-needed national insurance scheme was considered so important that the party decided no time should be wasted in debates over principles.

It was not until 1943 that the first political polls were published in Britain, showing increasing support for Labour. In 1942, however, nothing pointed towards a post-war Labour election victory. In view of this it is possible that the Labour Party was willing to sacrifice principles in order to realise some of the undoubtedly progressive proposals embedded in the Beveridge Report. If this line of reasoning is correct, then one should expect to find evidence of discussions on principles in the party in the period leading up to the parliamentary debate.

To test this, let us look first at the report from the 1942 Annual Labour Conference and then at the official Labour Party periodical *The Labour Organiser* for the period 1941–43. The 41st Annual Labour Party Con-

45. Ibid., p. 359.
46. Beveridge 1953, p. 226.

ference was held in May 1942, six months before the report was published. The later minister of social insurance in the Attlee government, James Griffith, moved a resolution by which the conference welcomed 'the establishment of the Interdepartmental Committee'.[47] The resolution went on to stress the Labour objectives of comprehensiveness, adequate payments, family allowances, and the establishment of a National Health Service. In his following speech Griffith expanded on the main points of the resolution. Of particular interest are his arguments relating to comprehensiveness. He referred to the anomalies created by the piecemeal development of social security to that point, concluding, 'We believe the time has come when we ought to build into one comprehensive system the whole of these social services. What we propose is that there shall be one scheme administered by one Minister, *one contribution,* and one benefit.'[48]

What Griffith did, in effect, was to make the acceptance of the contributory principle an underlying assumption upon which his proposal was built. It is therefore particularly interesting to study the debate following the resolution. In this debate two amendments were moved. The first concerned family allowances. Not unexpectedly, a delegate from the trade union movement proposed the withdrawal of family allowances from the resolution. The amendment met with heated debate and was finally defeated by a majority of nearly two-thirds.

The second amendment, moved by J.J. Tinker, asked the Congress to add new section (e): 'That contributions from wages and industry be discontinued and the total cost of all Insurance Schemes be met from Exchequer Funds.' Tinker argued his amendment on four points. First, noting the fact that the state was partly involved in the financing of the scheme as proposed by Beveridge, he asked, 'why cannot we ask the state to meet the whole of it?' Second, he referred to the fact that 'the contributory method has grown up with us, and it is difficult to break away from it.' He was, however, overly optimistic about the ability of the party to break an established policy when he went on to say, 'If we are going to set about a new society there is nothing we cannot break away from.' Third, he acknowledged that 'our people who are negotiating have already committed themselves to the contributory system.' Again he

47. Labour Party 1942a, p. 132. This is the committee behind the Beveridge Plan.
48. Ibid. My emphasis.

asked the conference to change that commitment. He concluded by addressing those workers who thought that because they were 'not subscribing directly', it was 'a loss to their dignity because they [were] getting something for nothing.' Referring to the non-contributory pensions for these groups, he asked somewhat sarcastically whether the conference believed that lord chancellors and judges 'blush for shame' when they claim their (state) pensions.

Except for the important question of redistribution, Tinker raised all the earlier Labour objections to the contributory principle. Far from setting off a heated debate, the amendment was totally ignored. Only when the head of the National Executive, B. Ayrton Gould, summed up the debate before voting was the motion addressed, and then only because it had to be voted on. She referred to the contractual obligation of the party to the contributory principle and concluded, 'if you are to try to put it all on the Exchequer, what you are going to do is to tie up our hands in the working out of the details of the scheme.'[49] The amendment was defeated by 1,226,000 to 237,000 votes.

The Labour Organiser

The party periodical ran a series of articles on the Beveridge proposals in 1942 and 1943. The editor attempted to spark a debate with a rather provocative editorial in the December 1942 issue. His main argument was that the Beveridge proposals did nothing to bring socialism nearer and left 'the whole structure of society unchanged'.[50] Apart from these wide-ranging considerations, he also touched on the more immediate deficiencies when he stated that 'with Beveridge in full swing the capitalists need only raise prices and the benefits become negligible.'[51] This shows an awareness of the weakness of the system in times of inflation. The root of the problem – the tying of benefits to flat-rate contributions – was, however, not raised. The article triggered no polemic, and the only response in the following year did little but repeat the arguments of the editorial.[52]

49. Ibid.
50. Labour Party 1942b.
51. Ibid.
52. Labour Party 1943.

Contemporary literature

A different insight into the mood of the time can be gained by studying the literature discussing the Beveridge Report around the time of its publication. Again, I will limit my focus to the labour movement. The first book is a very popular account written by a journalist from the TUC-controlled *Daily Herald.*[53] The second book is included because, in addition to having been the most thorough evaluation of the proposals at the time, it contains the official Fabian Society reactions to the report.

In the first few pages Frederick J. Scheu presents the main thrust of his book *British Labor and the Beveridge Plan:* 'While Liberals and some progressive Conservatives are favorable to the Plan, the main driving force behind it is the British Labor Movement.'[54] In the context of my analysis the desire to prove paternity of the plan is more interesting than its outcome. Now, one should be careful about making Scheu a representative of the views of the labour movement as a whole. He presents, however, a convincing picture of a movement united behind the Beveridge proposals. His claim of Labour paternity is less convincing, though, and his characterisation of Arthur Greenwood as 'grandfather and godfather of the Beveridge Plan' is at best an exaggeration.[55]

Again, the most interesting aspect is the total absence of an evaluation of the contributory principle. Correctly, Scheu notes that 'scepticism within the labor movement was confined to ... children allowances.'[56] His account of what was debated within the movement appears to be correct.

Of greater political significance is the book *Social Security,* published by the Fabian Society.[57] In addition to presenting a Fabian scheme of social security, the book contains articles that, according to the editor, William Robson, offer 'the most thorough critical examination the Beveridge report has so far received.'[58] This promise, together with the historical role played by the Fabian Society as a stronghold of Labour's theoretical considerations, indicates the significance of the book for this study.

In the preface, Robson first stresses the independence of the Fabian

53. Pimlott and Cook 1982, p. 72.
54. Scheu 1943, p. 5.
55. Ibid., p. 110.
56. Ibid., p. 90.
57. Robson 1943.
58. Ibid., p. 1.

group in relation to the Beveridge Committee by stating that, by the time of the appointment of the Beveridge group, the Fabian Sub-Committee 'had already embarked on some hard thinking'.[59] We can therefore expect an independent presentation of Fabian proposals, not only a response to Beveridge's plan. With the history of the Fabian Society in mind, it is thus surprising to read Robson's conclusion about the relationship between the two plans: 'Taking the matter all in all, it is remarkable how large a measure of agreement exists between the Beveridge Report and the Fabian plan.'[60] Although there is no direct connection, striking dissimilarities appear when we juxtapose this response and that of the Fabians to the Liberal reforms early in the century. Although the Webbs' Minority Report to the Poor Law Commission did little more than propose the scheme to which the 1911 National Health Insurance Act became the 'antithesis', at least it produced exactly that.[61] Such critical power was absent forty years later.

This is not to say that the Fabian plan was totally in line with that of Beveridge. The Fabians proposed, for example, a separate rent allowance to compensate for higher rents in the cities.[62] This was in turn rejected by Beveridge, to whom a 'flat rate of benefits' was one of the key principles. Like Beveridge, the Fabians focused on the anomaly of the Approved Societies. Through the administration of the National Health Insurance by the societies, recipients were drawing unequal benefits for equal contributions.[63] In their criticism of the handling of contributory insurance, the Fabians ignored the principle of insurance as such. Similarly, they criticised private insurance and advocated a compulsory state scheme as less wasteful.[64]

The firm rejection of contributory insurance in the 1909 Minority Report stands in stark contrast to the 1943 Fabian plan, in which the same principle was reduced to an implicit assumption and thereby accepted without being debated. The plan portrays a Fabian Society with critical powers that were still enfeebled after being 'long moribund' in the 1930s.[65] Furthermore, it represents a continuation of the process

59. Ibid.
60. Robson 1943, p. 4.
61. Pinker 1971, p. 89.
62. Robson 1943, p. 2.
63. Ibid., p. 238.
64. Ibid.
65. Pelling 1985, p. 76.

Mountford described as starting as early as 1911: the Fabians' increasing acceptance of political realities. It was, as we will see in the next chapter, not until the mid-1950s that the Fabian Society was to restore its critical powers in regard to social policy.

In the absence of a strong Fabian Society, we need to look elsewhere for expert critical examinations of the contributory principle. This is found, not on the left, but in the independent group Political and Economic Planning (PEP).[66] In their memorandum regarding the Beveridge Report, they argue that 'the contributory insurance method will ultimately prove unworkable as the basis of a completed system of income maintenance services. There is a strong case for financing children's benefits, medical services, long term incapacity cash benefits and pensions out of taxation.'[67] In the labour movement the shortcomings of the system were, as we will see in the next chapter, first understood by Griffith in 1946. I raise these two facts because they indicate that with a better 'think tank' at hand, the labour movement might at least have understood what they were silently accepting. This is not to say, however, that the outcome would have been any different.

The analysis so far has established that there were no discussions on the principle of contributory social insurance within the labour movement's most representative bodies in the period leading up to the parliamentary debate on the report.

The parliamentary debate, 16–19 February 1943

Perhaps the most central figure in Labour's involvement in social policy at the time was Arthur Greenwood. As minister without portfolio in charge of post-war planning and reconstruction, he was in 1941 responsible for the appointment of Beveridge as chairman of the Interdepartmental Committee.[68] He opened the Labour contribution to the debate by moving the following resolution on behalf of the party: 'that the House welcomes the Report'.[69] He went on to explain how the report

66. The PEP was an independent, non-party research organisation founded in 1931 and supported by subscriptions from industry, commerce, and private individuals and by grants from trusts and foundations. Crossman 1981, p. 258n.

67. Cmd 6405.

68. Addison 1975, p. 169.

69. Hansard, 1943, 1617.

had been received by the labour movement: 'The Labour Party, the Trade Union Congress General Council, and the Cooperative Movement have given it a warm welcome in its broad outlines.'[70] In particular, he referred to a resolution adopted unanimously by The National Council of Labour, 'the most representative working class organisation in this country', in which it approved 'the principles laid down in the Report'.[71] Greenwood then went on to introduce the issue which was to arouse the most controversy in the days to follow, the timing of the implementation of the proposals: 'Delay will be disastrous. Early action would hearten the people of this country and of other countries and would give Britain the moral leadership in the universal struggle for social security for all peoples in all lands.'[72]

In broad terms the division in the House on this issue came to be between, on the one hand, Labour advocating early legislation and, on the other, Liberals and Conservatives advocating a postponement until after the war had been won. The exception from this polarisation was a group of 40 young Conservatives who also favoured early legislation and the immediate setting up of a Ministry of Social Security, a key issue.[73]

Today, what strikes the reader of the voluminous minutes is that the principles on which Beveridge based his recommendation were never brought into the discussion. It is particularly interesting that the contributory principle received no attention from Labour MPs, as this was an approach to which the party had traditionally objected. In fact, the only reference to the principle was made by a Tory representative, Mr Hudson, who, in agreeing with Labour's Mr Barnes on the 'non-political nature of the proposals', concluded that 'contributory pensions, I would remind my own Honorary Friends, is a good Tory principle.'[74] By not objecting to this claim, Barnes, and in effect Labour, approved a Tory principle under a 'non-political' guise.

Although the contributory principle was never explicitly endorsed by Labour MPs, their acceptance of it can be traced in many contributions to the debate. Mr Clynes first quoted from an editorial in *The Times* (16 February 1943): 'It is significant that although the finance of the schemes

70. Ibid.
71. Ibid.
72. Hansard, 1943, 1628.
73. Scheu 1943, p. 100.
74. Hansard, 1943, 1780.

has not passed unchallenged, no substantial body of opinion, certainly no organisation with claims to represent the manual workers, has seriously objected to the high price in terms of compulsory weekly contributions which wage earners will be called upon to pay for the greatly expanded range of benefits provided under the new scheme.' To explain the validity of the claims in the article, Clynes went on to say, 'The workman has come to understand that the money will flow back to him in several forms when he is in the greatest need. It is good that the report carries a message of encouragement to the masses of the workers to put as much as they can for this sensible purpose.'[75]

Another important Labour representative, Herbert Morrison, implicitly endorsed the principle when he argued for the equity of 'flat-rate benefits for flat-rate contributions'.[76]

Other MPs attacked the unfairness of the existing benefit structure as practised by Approved Societies. A statement by the Conservative Mrs Cazalet Keir had implications similar to that of Morrison: 'I do not pretend in any way to understand its [the benefit structure's] intricacies, [but] one thing seems to be agreed by everybody, that unequal benefits for equal compulsory contributions should no longer be tolerated and that people should get equal benefits for equal contributions.'[77]

In only one case can criticism be traced, and then only indirectly. Tom Brown complained about the means-tested pension for the already old. He argued that pensioners were hesitant to apply because of the stigma attached to means-testing. In his view the chancellor should have wiped out the means test once and for all: 'The fact that they were born on and attain the age of 60 on a certain date should be sufficient to guarantee them a pension.'[78] No reference was made to the impossibility of the achievement of this aim in a contributory system. As we have seen, the Labour Party had realised much earlier that the contributory way for some leads to the means-tested way for others.

This account of nearly unanimous praise of the Beveridge proposals by the Labour Party should certainly not, however, lead us to conclude that the party necessarily considered the plan to be socialist. Consider, for example, this statement by Barnes: 'I say as a convinced socialist that I do

75. Ibid., 2008.
76. Ibid., 2038.
77. Ibid., 1721.
78. Ibid., 1803.

not support the Beveridge Plan because it is a socialist plan. It is not. To me, frankly, it is a common sense method of meeting our peace-time casualties under the prevailing system, the capitalist system.'[79] Similar reasoning underlay Mr Buchanan's statement: 'Often I have thought in the past that he [Beveridge] was reactionary.... But I take the Report as a whole.'[80]

The 1943 non-decision: Possible explanations

The fear of the means test

First, let us consider the extent to which previous experiences with the means test can explain Labour's acceptance of the contributory principle as outlined in the Beveridge Plan. When the means test is referred to as a 'backcloth' against which the emergence of modern British welfare is seen, it is usually the more specific experience of 'the household means test'[81] of the 1930s that is in focus.[82] According to T.H. Marshall, 'Nothing in the history of social policy, except perhaps the old mixed workhouse, has inspired such hatred and detestation as this household means test.'[83]

Beveridge therefore probably conveys an accurate picture of prevailing British attitudes in referring to 'the strength of popular objection of any kind of means test'.[84] His ensuing extrapolation of this as a reason for the 'established popularity of compulsory insurance' and 'the phenomenal growth of voluntary insurance' appears to be a rhetorical extension of the argument. One could argue that any established schemes that avoided means-testing would have enjoyed similar popularity. In Britain this happened to be contributory insurance in the immediate past. As we have seen, there are reservations even to this truth; it was the failure of contributory unemployment benefits which subjected large numbers to the household means test in the 1930s.

79. Ibid., 1770.

80. Ibid., 1783.

81. While the Poor Laws, dating back to 1601, included family responsibility as their first principle, the household means test extended this to include people living in the same household, whether or not they were related. See also Chapter 8.

82. As a foreign observer of British social policy, I am struck by the weight that is given to the experience of means-testing in studies of the history of income maintenance in Britain.

83. Marshall [1965] 1985, p. 69.

84. Cmd 6404, para. 12.

In assessing the impact of the experience of the means test on Second World War social policy planning, Deacon and Bradshaw outline the two aspects on which analysis most frequently focuses: 'First, the public were now less inclined to see poverty as the result of personal failing or irresponsible behaviour. Second, there was a far greater awareness of the misery and hardship it had caused in earlier years.'[85] Although they question the degree to which both the Conservatives and the Labour Party desired its total abolition, they do not challenge the impact its history had on policy-making in the 1940s. In their interpretation, the Beveridge Plan allowed for enough means-testing for the Conservatives to accept it and little enough to ensure Labour support.[86] The 'acceptable' means-testing in this assessment was that of National Assistance as a safety net under National Insurance.

If we are to accept that the experience of the means test had a direct impact on Labour's acceptance of Beveridge's contributory principle, it must be on the assumption that Labour had finally accepted the argument that Beveridge had been hammering at since 1907: that only through contributory social insurance could the means test be avoided. Labour had, however, reason to expect more means-testing than what was expected to follow from the role of National Assistance as envisaged by Beveridge. Experience had proved that the contributory route for some leads to the means-tested route for others.

The popular 'hatred' was directed more towards the specific 'household means test' than towards means-testing in general. The abolition of the household means test in 1941, and its replacement with an *individual* means test, brought about an increase of a quarter of a million recipients from the Assistance Board.[87]

This reform involved a change away from means-testing mainly the unemployed to subjecting old people applying for supplementary pensions to the test. The latter scheme did not encounter great hostility, and there was no failure in take-up. The continued impact of the means test on the policies of the labour movement would therefore seem to be dependent on a fear of a return to the means test of the 1930s – that is, a fear of post-war mass unemployment and a return to the *household* means test.

85. Deacon and Bradshaw 1983, p. 31.
86. Ibid., p. 47.
87. Fraser 1984, p. 213. See also Chapter 8 for a further discussion of this development.

According to Deacon and Bradshaw, Beveridge's estimate of 8.5% post-war unemployment was generally considered to be too optimistic.[88] Judging from the experience of the First World War, when mass unemployment followed, it is not unlikely that this reasoning was behind the labour movement's continued fear of the means test.

This leaves us with two possible interpretations of Labour's standpoint in 1943. Either the Labour movement was suffering from political amnesia in which the experiences of the 1930s, when contributory pensions failed to stave off the means test, were forgotten, or (given that they expected widespread unemployment and a possible return to the household means test) the party was willing to accept even a substantial role for means-testing in the future.

The 'amnesia hypothesis' cannot be properly tested with the material we have available, though focusing on the actual drafts of social policy documents worked out by bodies within the labour movement might go some way towards doing this. As we will see in the next chapter, Attlee was far from well equipped with blueprints when he took office in 1945. The only plan I can find was the Fabian proposal, which bore striking similarity to that of Beveridge. Given this lack of plans of its own, it is perhaps understandable that the Labour Party was inclined to adopt an ostrich posture. Furthermore, by concentrating on advocating early legislation for the proposals, it could hope to draw on the spirit engendered by the war and ensure the enactment of the undoubtedly progressive elements of the Beveridge Plan. Given that a post-war election victory was not yet in sight, this reasoning becomes plausible.

The 'intellectual vacuum' caused by the decline of the Fabian Society hindered an informed debate within the labour movement. Traditionally, Fabians have played an instrumental role in shaping the social policy of the Labour Party. In the gap between the Webbs early in the century and the Titmuss group at the London School of Economics from the mid-1950s onwards, the party was left without this important influence.[89]

Still, even with the necessary expert advice provided, it is unlikely that the party would have rejected the contributory approach in 1943. As we have seen, the 1930s saw a shift of power towards the TUC. For the

88. Deacon and Bradshaw 1983, p. 44.

89. It should be noted that Richard Titmuss was never a member of the Fabian Society. He played a key role, however, in its activities during the 1950s and 1960s.

group in control of the party, Beveridge's contributory insurance proposal represented, therefore, a principle they had advocated since 1910. The means test, in this situation, was a price that the party was willing to accept. A harsher, and perhaps more speculative, extension of this line of reasoning is that the experience of the 1930s might have sharpened the divisions within the working class in relation to welfare. Dating back to the 19th century, the divisions between, on the one hand, the better off and better organised workers who enjoyed exclusive welfare rights through occupational self-help schemes and, on the other, the less organised, less skilled workers excluded from this area of welfare, had rendered joint working-class interests and demands in social policy difficult. The 1930s, we must bear in mind, brought an increase in the standard of living for the three-quarters of the workforce still employed. For these groups, means-testing the others might have been seen to promise lower taxation and, no less important, an antidote to 'scrounging'. According to Derek Fraser, 'This majority of the nation, in asking the unemployed to take the full brunt of the depression, displayed a lingering feeling that somehow the men out of work deserved to be less eligibly placed than the rest.'[90] Similarly, Harris concludes that 'the TUC delegation to the Beveridge committee was in fact in many ways a remarkable embodiment of the traditional sterling virtues of the labour aristocracy. The delegates were strongly in favour of contributory insurance; they were contemptuous of "dodgers", of the "very poor" and of "the type of person who will not join a Friendly Society".'[91]

We can therefore conclude that while the relationship between contributory pensions and means-testing appears not to have been fully understood by the Labour Party, such an understanding would probably have done little to change the attitudes among the dominant groups within the party at the time.

The financing of the National Health Service

The National Health Service Act of 1946 established a tax-financed universal health service in Britain. The Labour Party strongly supported this solution. The popularity of the contributory principle within the Labour

90. Fraser 1984, p. 195.
91. Harris in Winter 1975, p. 48.

Party became evident, however, in the final scheme presented by Aneurin Bevan. He preserved an element of contribution by arranging for part of the National Insurance contribution to be used in the financing of the National Health Service:[92] 'Thus was born the popular myth that the health service is paid for out of insurance contributions, whereas in fact it was never intended that the insurance fund should contribute more than a fraction of the cost.'[93]

There are several possible interpretations of why a different form of financing was chosen for the health service. According to an ILO publication on social security, 'The state may assume all or the greater part of the charge for certain benefits which are considered particularly conducive to social welfare, such as family allowances or a national health service.'[94] Indeed, when enacted in 1945, family allowances in Britain were also financed out of general taxation.[95]

Another possible explanation that would include family allowances relates to the question of deservingness. While many of the contingencies covered by National Insurance could be seen to be at least partly the individual's responsibility (in this way, the tradition of self-help had also ingrained in the population a responsibility to 'save for a rainy day', even if that was one of old age), it is easier (at least in a European context) to find general support for a solidaristic system in the unforeseen event of bad health.

A third interpretation is that, while there was an underpinning safety net in the form of National Assistance in the case of income maintenance, such a system neither existed nor was proposed as a part of the future health services. Health insurance therefore needed to be fully universal. With universal coverage and less fear of 'scrounging', the case for a tax-financed solution was easier to argue than in the case of income maintenance. Tied up with this was the issue of 'work-testing', which is central to income maintenance because such a scheme usually originates from schemes targeted at the workforce and later extended to cover the generation at large.[96] With no underpinning scheme and thus a fully universal health service, there was no need for a work test through the payment of

92. Fraser 1984, p. 233.
93. Ibid.
94. International Labor Organization 1984, p. 117.
95. Thane 1982, p. 243.
96. I will return to this theme in the next chapter.

individual contributions. By contrast, both the work test and the National Assistance scheme were key elements in the contributory National Insurance.

Policy inheritance

Lastly, the significance of established traditions as an explanatory factor deserves particular attention. This influence has two dimensions. First, the insurance principle was established as the accepted norm for social insurance. A return to non-contributory insurance would therefore have required convincing arguments for the public at large and the policy-makers to accept it as a feasible alternative. Second, since its introduction in 1911, the experience with contributory insurance meant that large groups had already acquired rights to present and future benefits. As we will see in the next chapter, Beveridge's proposals largely built on the framework of established schemes. A change to a non-contributory system would have involved much greater and more complicated reforms than those proposed by Beveridge.

Heclo bluntly addresses the first of these considerations when he states that the contributory flat-rate principle was 'imported into the postwar British welfare state because that is the way things had been done since 1911.'[97] Taken out of context, this statement appears to be rather deterministic. However, the evidence presented by Heclo, as well as my research, indicates that the momentum towards contributory pensions after 1911 was increasingly difficult to reverse, even though it may have been desirable to do so.

Conclusions

The British Labour Party's relationship to the financing of pensions represents an example of a struggle between, on the one hand, wider political objectives and, on the other, the pursuit of factional interests within the political group. The wider objectives of redistribution and state responsibility were allowed to dominate until 1910. Although the non-contributory stance was firm and well founded in that period, it is also worth noting that a non-contributory pension was then deemed the least

97. Heclo 1973, p. 256.

harmful solution to the sectional vested interests already present within the labour movement – that is, those of the members of Friendly Societies.

Already two years after the implementation of the 1908 OAP, these interests, as represented by trade union commitment to and benefits from non-public insurance, made themselves felt. The Labour Party's support for the contributory 1911 National Health Insurance thus marked the start of the party's gradual swing towards full acceptance of the contributory principle.

From this time on, *realpolitik* reduced the taxation principle to the status of political rhetoric. The main reason for its postponed execution was the value it had gained as a unifying factor for the organised labour movement in its infancy. Attention was thus drawn to it only when non-socialist governments extended the scope of contributory insurance.

This process was accelerated in the late 1920s by the inability of the two Labour governments to challenge economic orthodoxy and thereby avoid Exchequer transfers in order to save the non-contributory OAP. In the 1930s the shift of power within the party in favour of the trade unions ensured the final move towards full acceptance of the contributory principle.

Meanwhile, the momentum of policy inheritance added to the difficulties of the few who still advocated a non-contributory approach. A change of the method of financing would, at this point, have necessitated a firm and united stand behind this principle. The British Labour Party that was asked to consider the Beveridge Plan in 1942–43 lacked such unity.

From being the central topic of political disputes over social policy in its early days towards the end of the 19th century, the contributory principle of social insurance was established by 1940 as a cornerstone in the British tradition of welfare. It is therefore not surprising that the final move towards full acceptance and implementation of the principle was taken in the form of a non-decision by the Labour Party.

Kevin Jeffery challenges the notion that a welfare consensus was reached during the Second World War.[98] By focusing exclusively on the Conservative Party in testing this hypothesis, Jeffery makes the implicit assumption that a welfare consensus according to the Beveridge principles entailed a move by the Conservatives in a collectivist direction.

98. Jeffery 1987.

Although my study does not attempt to contribute conclusive evidence to that debate, the findings presented above suggest that the consensus reached resulted mainly from the *Labour Party*'s making a final rightward move towards traditionally liberal social policy.

Chapter 5

Residual Universality and Increasing Selectivity: Social Insurance in Britain, 1946–1966

In the previous chapter we saw how the contributory flat-rate system was established as the main source of finance for social insurance in Britain after the Second World War. In this chapter we shall study the effects of the choices made during the war on National Insurance's first 20 years of operation.

Instead of attempting to give a full analysis of British social insurance in this period, I will focus on very specific areas. The themes arise from the findings in Chapter 3, where I analysed the development of Norwegian social insurance in the same period. My analysis in that section pointed to the significance of the question of financing for the development of social insurance. In the previous chapter I treated financing as a dependent variable, focusing on the reasons why the two nations arrived at different solutions. In this chapter 'financing' will first be dealt with as an independent variable. The variables it will be seen to influence are those of 'level of benefits' and 'coverage' (or 'comprehensiveness'). Later, however, we shall see that the question of benefit levels in particular brought about new debates and, eventually, changes in the ways by which British insurance was financed.

The Norwegian experience showed that the choice of a mainly tax-financed OAP in 1936 made a prolonged role for means-testing, and thereby selectivity, acceptable to the Labour Party. Although universality was the ultimate aim, selectivity became the pragmatic means to achieve the combined results of redistribution and the elevation of the basic pension. Furthermore, the choice of the taxation principle in Norway made the question of which groups to include in the process of extending social insurance a political, rather than a practical, issue.

In Britain the choice of a contributory scheme will be seen to have had equally strong implications for the post-war development of pensions. My hypothesis is that the British development differed from that of Norway in two main ways. First, the contributory flat-rate system of financing impeded the development of the level of National Insurance (NI) benefits.[1] In effect, therefore, the greater spillover of the elderly to social assistance dependency through National Assistance (NA) supplementation in Britain compared with Norway resulted largely from the choice of the contributory flat-rate system of financing. Second, the gradual incorporation of groups other than the elderly into social insurance, as seen in Norway, was made more difficult in Britain. A contributory system can incorporate only those who are enabled or compelled to pay the required contributions. As we will see, the choice of the contributory system excluded, for example, large groups of disabled people from social insurance and left them in continued dependency on social assistance.

Referring back to the main hypothesis of this study, the choice of how to finance social insurance is the main cause of the differences in the salience and form of assistance and in the composition of the clientele in the two countries. In Part Three we shall return to the divergent influences this has had on the *nature* of social assistance.

Although the comparison will highlight the less favourable development of British social insurance in the first two post-war decades, this is not to say that the British social reformers were less ambitious than their Norwegian counterparts. On the contrary, Britain took a much greater *initial* step on the road towards universal social insurance in 1946. But as we shall see, British universality was built on insecure foundations, the undermining of which was to create conditions much more conducive to selectivity in the long run.

The chapter consists of four main parts. First, the sections of the Beveridge Report relevant to my analysis will be briefly outlined. Second, the actual development of the level of the OAP will be analysed, starting with the 1946 National Insurance Act. In the third part we will look briefly at the income maintenance offered to groups corresponding to those gradually incorporated into social insurance in Norway. Fourth, we shall return to the question of financing, covering the renewed debate on

1. As we will see, it was the flat-rate principle that impeded increased benefits. In itself contributory insurance is by no means less conducive than tax-financed schemes to a positive development of the levels of pensions.

this issue in the mid-1950s. Following this chapter I sum up Part Two and contrast the development of social insurance in the two countries.

The Beveridge Plan

The importance of the Beveridge Report as the blueprint for British post-war social insurance is well established. I argued in the previous chapter that the Labour Party's acceptance of the main principles of this plan can be at least partly explained by the intellectual 'vacuum' that existed within the British labour movement during this period. The political influence (or lack of it) of intellectuals in the British policy-making process becomes even more clear when we look at the way in which the plan was conceived and hammered out. The writing of the report highlights an important difference between the British and Norwegian polities. When new legislation is planned in Norway, the normal procedure is for the government to set up a commission with a clearly defined mandate. A broadly composed committee, usually comprising representatives of the relevant organisations as well as the government, subsequently drafts the detailed plans within the framework laid down in the mandate.[2] In the British tradition, by contrast, the system works very much the other way around. A committee is given a relatively autonomous role in working out plans and recommendations. Its mandate is usually limited to defining the areas of policy that it is supposed to concentrate on. Through hearings, the affected groups are able to express their views. After its completion the plan is subject to parliamentary readings. With the affected groups entering the policy-making process at this late stage, influence on policy decisions is probably dependent to a larger degree on clearly worked out ideas and reactions to the proposed policy; in Norway the corresponding groups are included at an earlier stage. The greater need for independent, considered opinion as a counterweight to the power embodied in the committees adds to the significance of the 'intellectual vacuum' outlined in the previous chapter.

The Norwegian model, which can be described as featuring stronger corporate traits, thus probably offers more opportunities for affected interest groups to play an active role in the shaping of policies. The different ordering of the process together with the different composition of the

2. Arntzen and Knutsen 1980, p. 63.

committees may account for the greater role played by individual, politically unaccountable policy-makers in the British system. Ashford argues that 'the disjointed character of British policymaking gave enormous powers to civil servants, probably more than in any other political system.'[3] In the history of modern British social policy, few have taken more advantage of this aspect of the policy-making process than William (later Lord) Beveridge. Paul Addison goes as far as describing the Beveridge Plan and its outcome as 'a brilliant coup by one man'.[4] Ironically, Bevin's main motive for appointing Beveridge to head the Interdepartmental Committee on Social Insurance was to escape the irritation of an adviser with whom he had grown increasingly impatient.[5] Neither the then 'bitterly disappointed' Beveridge nor Bevin could envisage the importance of the work that was to follow.[6] Thus, Beveridge not only filled the intellectual 'vacuum' but also used to the fullest the possibilities that the British political system provided for an individual to influence the course of policy development. The Interdepartmental Committee seldom met, and when they did, the purpose was usually for Beveridge to inform them about the progress of his work. The final report was signed by Beveridge alone.

The plan outlined 'six principles of social insurance':[7]

1. Flat rate of subsistence benefit
2. Flat rate of contribution
3. Unification of administrative responsibility
4. Adequacy of benefit
5. Comprehensiveness
6. Classification

The first two principles concern the nature of financing and the level of benefits. As we have seen, the contributory principle was itself made an implicit feature. Because I discussed this in the previous chapter, I will not treat it here.

Both the 'minimum' approach, as expressed in the term 'subsistence

3. Ashford 1986, p. 245.
4. Addison 1975, p. 212.
5. Thane 1982, p. 244.
6. Ibid., p. 245.
7. Cmd 6404, para. 303.

benefits', and the flat-rate approach left room for, and indeed necessitated, a prolonged reliance on voluntary insurance in order to achieve an acceptable level of income replacement in old age and other need situations. It could also be argued that Beveridge in his outline focused more on *delimiting* the role of public insurance than on securing what in Norway was referred to at the time as 'socially acceptable' levels of benefits. Thus, Beveridge's notion of a minimum approach implied not only the importance of the 'floor' below which no one should fall but also the equally important notion of a 'ceiling' above which, according to Beveridge, social insurance had no role to play. In the words of the report, a flat rate of subsistence benefit 'follows from the recognition of the place and importance of voluntary social insurance in social security.'[8] Again, therefore, the existence of a large non-public insurance sector influenced the scope and nature of British social insurance. This contrasted sharply with the influence exerted by 'alternative schemes' in Norway.

The principle of 'subsistence' required benefits higher than those of existing schemes. Referring to the 'floor' aspect, Vic George argues that 'Lord Beveridge considered the subsistence principle the central idea of his report.'[9] Beveridge later wrote that 'without this the report would be little more than a rationalisation of existing powers.'[10] This, together with its comparative significance for my study and its ultimate fate, makes the subsistence principle worthy of closer examination. In relation to poverty, the term arouses associations with early-19th-century American prison experiments carried out to establish how little people could survive on.[11] The analogy is not too unreasonable. Beveridge based his subsistence level on research carried out by Rowntree in York in 1936. Rowntree's notions of subsistence were based on highly scientific work conducted by nutritionists.[12] It would be wrong to evaluate these notions on the basis of later definitions of relative poverty. My point is that the level represented an absolute minimum on which people could survive (that is, if they had the knowledge of professional nutritionists). To compensate for the rise in prices since 1938, Beveridge added 25% to the figures established by Rowntree.[13]

8. Ibid.

9. George 1968, p. 33.

10. Lord Beveridge, 'Social Security under Review', *The Times*, 9 November 1953. Quoted in George 1968, p. 33.

11. Townsend 1979.

12. Shragge 1984, p. 44.

13. George 1968, p. 44.

In his outline of the 'flat rate of contribution' principle, Beveridge gave no reason why the contribution also had to have a flat rate. But a sense of equity surely underlay the statement 'all insured persons, rich or poor, will pay the same contributions for the same security.'[14] It was by *this* choice, not by the contributory principle in itself or even combined with flat-rate benefits, that the Beveridge Plan excluded the possibility of redistribution between groups through social insurance.

The third principle represents perhaps the greatest achievement of the plan. The piecemeal development of British social insurance had created a variety of schemes based on different principles and administered by different public and non-public authorities. The unification of the various schemes to achieve fairness and administrative efficiency was therefore a major task. Under the slogan 'all-in insurance', such a unification had first been advocated by the Conservatives in the mid-1920s.[15] I will not, however, analyse further the extent to which this principle was realised.

The fourth principle expanded on the notion of subsistence. 'Adequacy' implied that benefits should be 'sufficient without further resources to provide the minimum income needed for subsistence in all normal cases.'[16] Thus, although it left room for voluntary insurance, it '[did] not assume that in any case.'[17] Beveridge introduced another aspect of 'adequacy' by stating that benefits would continue indefinitely without a means test, 'so long as the need continues.'[18]

'Comprehensiveness', as Beveridge explained in regard to the fifth principle, implied that social insurance 'should not leave either to national assistance or to voluntary insurance any risk so general or so uniform that social insurance can be justified.'[19] The people covered by social insurance were divided into six 'classes':[20]

I. Employees, that is, persons whose normal occupation is employment under contract of service.

II. Others gainfully occupied, including employers, traders and independent workers of all kinds.

14. Cmd 6404, para. 305.
15. Thane 1982, p. 196.
16. Cmd 6404, para. 307.
17. Ibid.
18. Ibid.
19. Cmd 6404, para. 308.
20. Ibid., para. 19.

III. Housewives, that is married women of working age.
IV. Others of working age not gainfully occupied.
V. Below working age.
VI. Retired above working age.

There was no clear demarcation between social insurance and social assistance. Under the joint heading 'Social Security', Beveridge listed all the need categories covered. The combined scheme provided income maintenance in the cases of 'interruption or destruction of earnings power and for special expenditure arising at birth, marriage or death.'[21]

The sixth principle, 'Classification', was used 'to denote adjustment of insurance to the different circumstances of each of these classes and to many varieties of need and circumstance within each insurance class.'[22]

In what follows the focus will be on the extent to which the realisation of the two first principles has influenced the fate of the fourth and fifth principles – that is, *the extent to which the contributory flat-rate benefit successfully provided the defined need categories with adequate benefits.* Adequacy will be measured as the extent to which these categories *actually* stay out of social assistance dependency. 'Comprehensiveness' will in this context be seen to involve 'adequacy', as well as the extent to which individuals belonging to the defined groups are administratively incorporated into social insurance. In other words, if a group of claimants is still dependent on NA for supplementation in order to achieve subsistence benefits, I do not consider the group to be comprehensively covered by social insurance. I start the analysis by looking at the implementation of the central Beveridge principles in the 1946 National Insurance Act under the Attlee government.

Subsistence through supplementation

Except in one important respect, the Labour government adopted Beveridge's subsistence principle. While Beveridge had proposed a 20-year build-up period to reach subsistence levels in the case of retirement pensions, the 1946 National Insurance Act established near-uniform benefits for all categories.[23] The Act gave entitlement to full pensions with immediate effect to all those covered by the 1925 Act, and the build-up

21. Ibid., para. 17.
22. Ibid., para. 309.
23. Fraser 1984, p. 229.

period for future beneficiaries was reduced to 10 years. Beveridge's scheme would, by contrast, have depended to a larger degree on supplementation from NA in the first 20 years of operation. 'Adequacy', in Beveridge's terminology, would not be achieved for the comprehensive NI until 1966.[24]

The degree to which subsistence was attained in 1946 is, however, open to discussion. Although the Labour government raised benefits to meet the rise in living costs since 1938, the benefits introduced were still in real terms below those calculated by Rowntree. When the government established benefit rates in 1946, it was believed that these were at subsistence level. By 1948 when the scheme came into operation, inflation had, however, already undermined these rates. By this time rates were definitely below subsistence level.[25]

Thane argues that the Labour government made no commitment to bring benefits up to subsistence level in the future.[26] Furthermore, section 40 of the new Act provided for quinquennial reviews of rates. With the cost of living rising in the years to follow, this proved detrimental to the real value of the benefits. But more frequent reviews proved difficult to carry through because of the way the scheme was financed. Because Labour followed Beveridge's flat-rate contributory system, any increase in benefits had to be met by increased contributions. Under the flat-rate system, this would place the greatest burden on the poorest contributors. Thus, the British universal insurance scheme took the form of a convoy, where, of course, 'the speed is that of the slowest ship.'[27, 28]

---

24. The higher initial costs involved in the 1946 Act brought about a change from the proposed system of funding to a 'pay-as-you-go' system. Because this necessitated state subsidies to meet deficits, it can be argued that the change involved an undermining of Beveridge's insurance principle.

25. Fraser 1984, p. 230.

26. Thane 1982, p. 254.

27. Griffith, Minister of Social Insurance, speaking in 1948, quoted in Fraser 1984, p. 229.

28. During the second reading of the National Insurance Bill in 1946, an alternative method of pegging benefits to a cost-of-living index was discussed. The Labour Party rejected the idea, however, on the basis of past experience. The method had been tried during the First World War, but broke down soon after. Also, it was argued that this would leave pensioners with smaller increases than they would otherwise achieve. This, of course, proved to be a false prediction. George (1968) also rejects as 'equally unconvincing' the contemporary argument that this method would involve a decrease of pension value in the case of a reduction in the cost of living. Experience had shown that this was very unlikely to happen. Furthermore,

It was not until 1958 that the benefits reached the level proposed by Beveridge.[29] I therefore turn now to look at the actual development of a scheme which not only was established with benefit levels that were generally accepted as being inadequate but also had built-in curtailments to growth. In studying NI benefits, the main focus will be on how they compared with benefits offered through NA.

NA benefits were established two years later than NI rates. The increased cost of living was taken into account, and the rates were consequently set at a higher level. This, together with the availability of discretionary allowances as well as allowances for rent, accounts for higher benefits from NA from the launch of the scheme.[30]

Figure 5.1 shows developments in the relationship between social assistance, social insurance, and average earnings in the period covered by this analysis.[31] From the table we can see that NA allowances continued to stay above the rates set for NI benefits. Because of more frequent rises in NA (14 times compared with 7 for NI), the basic NA benefit was higher than insurance benefits in half of the years between 1948 and 1967. With rent and discretionary allowances taken into account, assistance allowances were substantially higher for the entire period.[32] While NA allowances outpaced the rise in prices each year, those relying solely on insurance benefits for their subsistence also experienced a decrease in the purchasing power of their benefits between 1949 and 1955. If we compare these rates with average weekly earnings, a different picture emerges. Over the period as a whole, both insurance and assistance benefits rose slightly more than earnings. It is worth noting, with the specific time period in mind, that before 1965 NI benefits also dropped behind average earnings.

Not surprisingly, the low level of NI benefits compared with NA brought about growth in the number of social insurance beneficiaries receiving assistance supplementation. Figure 5.2, from the Report of the Phillips Committee, shows the growth in the years 1946 to 1953.[33] This

---

George rejects the fear of inflationary pressures exerted by such indexing when he asks, 'what social justice is there in a society which expects its weakest members to act as a buttress against inflation?' George 1968, p. 35.

29. Shragge 1984, p. 45.
30. George 1968, p. 212.
31. Ibid., p. 211.
32. Ibid., p. 212.
33. Cmd 9333, p. 57.

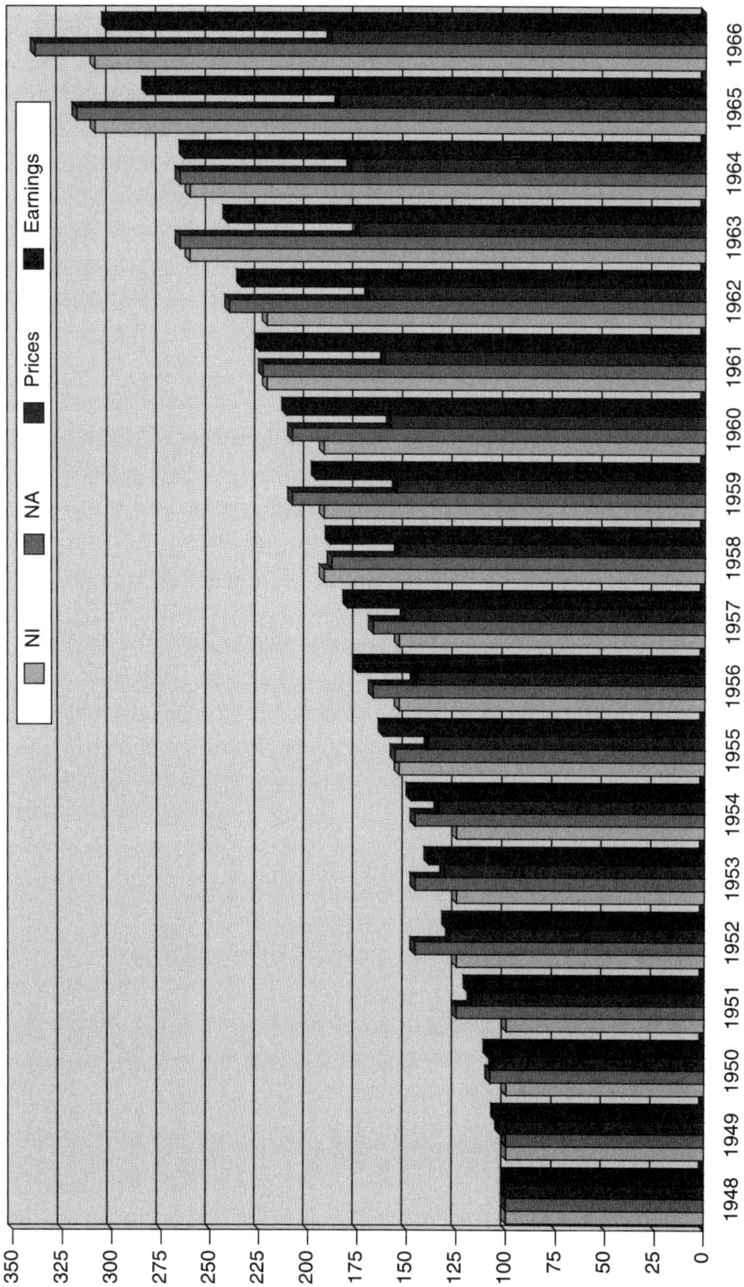

Figure 5.1. Indexes for NI benefits, NA allowances, retail prices, and average earnings, 1948–1966. Single people. (From George 1968, table 57. His sources were annual reports of the MDNI and NAB Ministry of Labour Gazettes.)

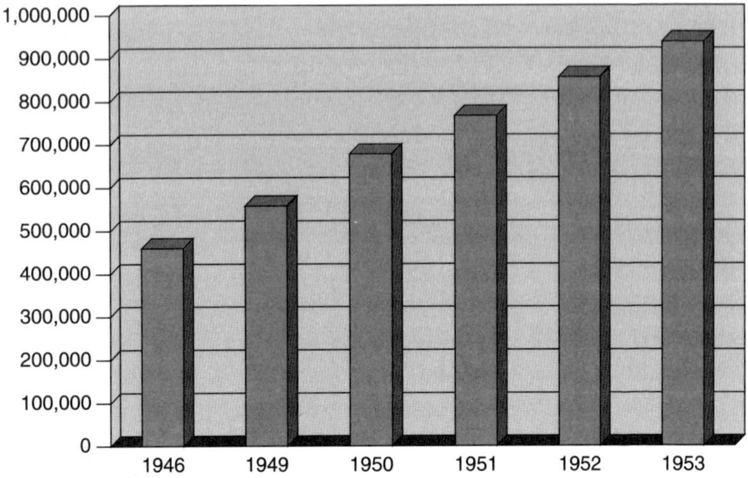

Figure 5.2. Numbers of National Assistance grants in supplementation of retirement pensions.

survey does not cover wives, the inclusion of whom would bring the numbers up by approximately 20%.[34] As we see, the numbers increased every year, although more slowly towards the end of the period. In an early reference to the problem of 'take-up', the Phillips Committee admitted that 'some witnesses have told us, however, that there are still some old people who do not apply for assistance despite the fact that they may be eligible.'[35]

In Table 5.1 the wives are included, and we can also see the percentage of old people relying on NA.[36] Most notable here are the 26% of NI retired pensioners receiving assistance supplementation. The experience of approaching the Assistance Board was no different for those still receiving a non-contributory old age pension – nearly half of the elderly. For the particular period under investigation, however, the group merits less attention in this analysis, as this scheme was gradually being phased out.

The work of the Phillips Committee, from which the above material originates, represents the first major review of social security after Beveridge. The Conservative government which instigated the committee was, as we can see, left with a choice between two possible options, given

34. Ibid.
35. Ibid.
36. Cmd 9333, p. 8.

Table 5.1. National Assistance grants, 1953

	No. of old persons (in thousands)	No. provided with NA (in thousands)	% provided with NA
NI pensioners (incl. wives)	4,310	1,110	26
Non-contributing pensioners (incl. wives)	345	162	47
Other old persons	2,280	128	6
Totals	6,935	1,400	20

that its intent was to enhance social security. It could either 1) launch a major strengthening of NI in order to *float the pensioners off assistance dependency;* or 2) *abandon the ambition to reach subsistence level for the pension,* or, rather, a level which made NA supplementation unnecessary except in exceptional circumstances. In essence, therefore, the choice was between a universal and a selective approach to social security. The recommendations of the Phillips Committee followed the latter course and thereby advocated the abandonment of the major principles of the Beveridge Report.

First, with regard to the level of benefits, the report states:

> A contributory scheme cannot, in our view, be expected to provide a rate of benefit which would enable everybody, whatever their circumstances, to live without other resources either of their own providing or by way of national assistance. Even if a 'subsistence' rate of pension could be related to some average of need or requirement, a large increase in the pension would be required to make any substantial reduction in the number of pensioners at present receiving supplementation. As so much of the cost of national pensions has to be met from general taxation an attempt to provide a subsistence rate for all without regard to need would appear to be an extravagant use of the community's resources. Indeed, where only limited resources are available it is argued by some that the emphasis should be upon the improvement of assistance scales – which would benefit those, by definition, most in need – rather than on improvement in the rates of insurance benefits.[37]

37. Ibid., p. 56.

Although the wording is vague and non-committal, there can be no doubt that the statement represents a departure from Beveridge's central principles of 'subsistence' combined with 'adequacy' and 'comprehensiveness'.

Not surprisingly, the acceptance of a permanent and significant role to be played by assistance presupposed a *rehabilitation* of NA:

> We wish to stress that a changed attitude on the part of the public to the whole problem of national assistance is needed. In the minds of many it appears to be simply the successor of former systems of poor relief. In the welfare state as we know it today 'national assistance' subject to a needs-test is available for many purposes, though under a different name. For instance, the value of a state scholarship is related to the parent's income and, though paid by the Ministry of Education, is really a form of national assistance.[38]

By distancing the scheme from the Poor Law through the comparison with other selective, but non-stigmatised, schemes, the committee attempted to enhance the acceptance of NA without changing the scheme itself. This may be compared with the many changes in the name of assistance introduced in both countries. All exemplify attempts to enhance the status and acceptability of assistance through cosmetic changes without necessarily introducing simultaneous reforms of the schemes themselves. Moreover, the use of the term 'needs-test' instead of 'means test' in the quote above was most likely intended to serve a similar function.

In the context of the previous development of the pension, these recommendations should come as no surprise. Politically, however, they were highly controversial. Informed criticism followed shortly in the Fabian pamphlet *New Pensions for the Old*, co-authored by Brian Abel-Smith and Peter Townsend.[39] Referring to the subsistence principle, they point to the lack of discussion underlying and following the 'abandonment of the central idea of the Beveridge Plan'.[40] The authors furthermore point to the lack of evidence on which the recommendations were based. This critique was also aimed at the Conservative minister who endorsed the suggested reforms. They argue that 'it would seem rather hard to come to reasonable decisions about the level of social security benefits

38. Ibid.
39. Abel-Smith and Townsend 1955.
40. Ibid., p. 4.

without knowing something about the circumstances of those for whom the benefits are intended.'[41]

It is surprising, though, that no mention was made of the problem of 'take-up' in the criticism of a move towards greater reliance on means-tested benefits, particularly since the Phillips Committee itself, as we saw above, pointed to the possibility of people's refraining from applying despite being eligible.[42] In a contemporary pamphlet Abel-Smith discusses the problems of means-testing at length without touching on the problem of non-take-up.[43] It was not until 1962 that evidence was presented showing the degree to which old people avoided claiming assistance. In the conclusion of their book, written in 1962, Cole and Utting estimate that 'over 12% of all old people units, nearly half as many again as are at present receiving Assistance, are entitled to help from the Assistance Board, but are not getting it.'[44] One reason for low take-up in assistance was the problem of 'stigma by association', that is, the association of social assistance with the preceding Poor Law. The fact that memories of the Poor Law were fresher in the early post-war years gives reason to believe that this problem was even greater in that period than later.

In spite of the reluctance to elevate pensions expressed by the Phillips Committee as well as by the minister in charge, it was the Conservative government of the day which first managed to raise pensions to the levels of 1946. Heclo argues, though, that this was 'less because of changes in party or interest power than because of a freer spending climate following the post-Korean decline in defence expenditure.'[45] This was followed by a further increase with the 1959 National Insurance Act. That same year, however, NA benefits were elevated to bring them once again above NI benefits.[46] In the following six years the relationship between NA and NI did not change significantly. After the steady rise in the numbers of NI pensioners receiving NA supplementation in the period 1948–52, the high proportion (around 23%) remained unchanged throughout the period leading up to the 1966 legislation.[47] The growth in the number of

41. Ibid., p. 5.
42. Cmd 9333, p. 57.
43. Abel-Smith 1953.
44. Cole and Utting 1962, p. 98.
45. Heclo 1973, p. 257.
46. George 1968, p. 227.
47. Ibid., p. 228.

Table 5.2. Assistance allowances according to category of recipient (percentages)

	1949	1965
Supplementation of insurance benefits:		
Retirement pensions	48.2	59.9
Sickness/industrial injury	7.9	7.5
Widows' benefits	7.5	4.9
Unemployment benefits	2.6	1.7
Supplementation of non-contributory OAP	8.5	5.6
Assistance to persons not receiving pensions or benefits:		
Persons registered for employment	3.1	3.9
Persons over pension age	5.4	6.4
Persons under pension age	16.7	13.1

pensioners in this period furthermore accounted for a growth in the percentage of old people receiving assistance in relation to other groups.

Table 5.2 summarizes the changes in the composition of NA claimants for the period. From this table we see that in 1965, more than three-quarters of the weekly NA allowances were being paid to persons over pensionable age. The development that was highlighted in Figure 5.2 thus continued after 1953, and NA increasingly became a supplementary scheme for old age pensioners. While the number of old age pensioners receiving supplementary assistance that year was 938,000, this increased to more than 1.4 million in 1965.[48]

The low level of NI benefits, in relation to NA as well as to what was needed for subsistence, thus largely explains the central role that assistance continued to play, far beyond that intended by the Beveridge Plan and the 1946 legislation.

In Table 5.2 we see also that the second largest group receiving assistance was 'Persons under pension age'. Behind this collective term we find a group of particular comparative interest: disabled persons not qualifying for sickness benefits. In the Norwegian data we saw that after the elevation of the old age pension, the main cause of the reduction in the numbers receiving assistance was the gradual inclusion of the disabled into NI. The relatively numerous presence of this group in NA indicates a different development in Britain.

48. Berthaud and Brown 1981, p. 140.

I therefore turn now to give a short outline of what happened to the corresponding groups in Britain.

Further limitations to comprehensiveness

We saw above that the low level of benefits forced growing numbers of NI beneficiaries onto NA for supplementation. Dependency on social assistance is even more extensive and permanent for those disabled from birth or childhood. For these groups assistance represented, more likely than not, their sole source of income.

The case of disability highlights a fundamental contradiction in the Beveridge Plan and its implementation. Under the heading 'Comprehensiveness', Beveridge writes that social insurance 'should not leave either to national assistance or to voluntary insurance any risk so general or so uniform that social insurance can be justified.'[49] The contradiction arises when this is matched with the way by which entitlement is achieved. Being a strictly contributory system, social insurance following the Beveridge recommendations comes into play only after a person, in addition to falling within an eligible need category, has paid a specific number of contributions. However 'general or uniform' the person's specific need category is, this does not in itself entitle him or her to benefits. Because the payment of contributions was organised in relation to paid employment, eligibility was established through the labour market. In relation to disability this excluded from benefits those who had never entered paid employment – homemakers and those disabled from birth or childhood are two obvious examples. It is surprising that George does not make the connection when he expands on his observation that 'social policy in this country, unlike that of many other European countries, does not recognise civilian disability.'[50] Instead, Britain introduced sickness and industrial accident schemes, both directly connected to work. This must be understood in the light of the history of the British disability insurance. The scheme originated in the 1911 National Insurance Act as an arrangement for insured employees organised through Approved Societies. When the scheme was first introduced, the benefits equalled those of the then non-contributory old age pension. Its value decreased

49. Cmd 6404, para. 308.
50. George 1968, p. 104.

dramatically in the years leading up to the Second World War, when it was equivalent to less than 11% of the average earnings of a male manual worker.[51] With the 1946 National Insurance Act the scheme was incorporated and the name changed to 'sickness benefits'. These were, however, payable for an unlimited period of time, as long as the sickness lasted. While the OAP 'blanketed in' the already old, sickness benefits had a much more 'curtailed universality'. First, the claimant needed to have been insured as an employee or as a self-employed person for at least three years before the sickness, and even then would receive benefits only if he or she was incapable of work because of some specific disease or disablement.

The change in the definition of 'disability' towards considering these individuals as either sick or unemployed in the 1946 National Insurance Act is a further example of the proximity of work and welfare in this programme. Moreover, the 1944 Disabled Persons (Unemployment) Act was based on the assumption that adequate employment could be found for all the employable disabled. As this did not prove possible, the failure added to the great numbers of disabled in assistance dependency.[52]

Beveridge's 'classes' appear at first sight to be comprehensive in covering the entire population: non-working people would, according to the plan, be covered under 'Class IV: Others of working age not gainfully occupied'.[53] This particular category was, however, excluded from unemployment as well as disability benefits.[54] This anomaly left large groups of congenitally disabled persons and others with no work-record excluded from receiving NI benefits before they reached pensionable age.

An appendix to the 1959 report from the National Assistance Board presents the first post-war survey of persons under pensionable age in receipt of weekly NA allowances. The group appears on the bottom line of Table 5.2 above. Because of their sickness or disability, these claimants were not required to register for work as a condition of receiving assistance.[55] The report points out that they were not the only group of disabled persons among the NA recipients. Although the blind enjoyed more favourable conditions, they received their entire income maintenance

51. Kaim-Caudle 1973, p. 169.
52. Berthaud and Brown 1981, p. 139.
53. Cmd 6404, para. 19 II.
54. Ibid., para. 19 V.
55. Cmd 1085, p. 51.

from the National Assistance Board.[56] Furthermore, many disabled persons received NA to supplement NI benefits.

Among the 128,000 beneficiaries, the largest single group was the 'mentally defective'.[57] Two-thirds of the sample investigated were said to have been disabled from birth or childhood. The same proportion had received NA benefits for five or more years. Therefore, if we take the congenitally mentally disabled as an example, there can be no doubt that this is a group 'so uniform that social insurance can be justified'. Muriel Brown sums up this anomaly by pointing out that different amounts of money are paid 'according to the source of disability rather than its extent.'[58]

The dependency of large numbers of disabled persons on NA continued throughout the period of my analysis. In 1967 Sally Sainsbury found that nearly half her sample of 211 disabled men and women depended wholly or partly on supplementary benefits.[59]

Another factor which undermined Beveridge's claim of universality was the arrangements made for married working women. Because NI offered unfavourable conditions for this group, they were allowed to opt out of the scheme and remain dependent on the entitlements of their husbands as main bread-winners.[60] With growing numbers of women joining the labour force in the post-war period, the assumption of female dependency has proved wrong, and the lack of compulsion in the inclusion of women into NI proved a further limitation to the level of comprehensiveness achieved.

The composition of NA claimants was thus greatly influenced by two aspects of NI. First, the failure to raise NI benefits, not only to subsistence level but also to the level of NA, left great numbers of NI recipients in NA dependency through supplementation. Second, the failure of social insurance to include large need categories left certain groups totally dependent on NA for their income maintenance – groups that in Norway were gradually lifted out of social assistance dependency. In Table 5.2 we saw the consequences this development had for the composition of NA recipients.

56. Ibid.
57. Ibid., p. 52.
58. Brown 1982, p. 206.
59. Reported in *The Guardian*, 6 May 1967. Quoted in George 1968, p. 185.
60. Abel-Smith 1983, p. 11.

The number of social assistance claimants in Britain increased from 2,750,000 in 1949 to 3,491,000 in 1966.[61]

The exclusion of large parts of the non-working population highlights an important obstacle to the achievement of institutional welfare through the contributory principle of social insurance. As I argued in Chapter 1, a feature that distinguishes institutional from residual welfare is the allocation of services according to need alone, that is, not restricting benefits to those who have been entitled through merit, for example participation in the labour market. In Norway, we saw that the expansion of insurance increasingly included groups outside the workforce. The development of disability pensions therefore offers a good example of the difference between the British and the Norwegian approach. Shragge uses the term 'work-testing' to highlight the close tie between work and welfare in Britain.[62] I focus on this aspect of British social insurance once more because of the implications it has for the degree of success of social insurance in its proclaimed aim of minimising social assistance. Through the relation of insurance to work, large sections of those permanently in need of benefits are excluded from NI. This is also of great importance to the *composition* of social assistance claimants, a question to which I will return later.

Renewed debate on the contributory flat-rate system

Before summing up the development of British social insurance, I will return briefly to the method of financing. In Britain the re-emergence of the debate on how to finance social insurance is closely tied to the question of superannuation. For that reason it will be juxtaposed with the solution of that same question in Norway. The analysis of the Norwegian development of earnings-related supplements (ERS) showed that it was after the combined achievement of universality and the elevation of scale rates to one-third of average earnings that the question of ERS was included on the political agenda.[63] Thus, in Norway the establishment of ERS was a move in the direction of 'standard security', which was

61. George 1968, p. 224.
62. Shragge 1984, p. 29.
63. LO had prepared the establishment of a committee to inquire into the issue as early as 1952. See discussion above.

deemed to be desirable once an acceptable basic pension had been achieved.

Examination of the UK development reveals a contrastive background. Research focusing on the miserable conditions of large numbers of NI pensioners compelled a questioning of the aspects of the pension causing this decline. Inflation was, as we have seen, allowed to undermine the value of the pension in the first decade of its operation. The results of the deterioration of benefits were brought to light by research carried out by the 'Titmuss Group' at the London School of Economics.[64] In addition to Richard Titmuss, the most prominent figures in this new breed of intellectual Fabians were Brian Abel-Smith and Peter Townsend. Abel-Smith wrote in 1953 that 'it is commonly claimed that Britain's social services are "the envy of the world".' Although he left the validity of that claim open, he stated that 'in terms of the level of insurance benefits Britain's position is far from that of a world leader.'[65] In a later study Abel-Smith and Townsend revealed not only that poverty persisted to a much greater extent than was generally believed but also, perhaps to the even greater surprise of many, that old age and not unemployment was the main cause of destitution.[66] The same pamphlet furthermore pointed out the growing divide between 'two nations in old age': 'an underprivileged majority' relying on NI benefits, often supplemented by assistance, for their subsistence; and a 'privileged minority' which, by contrast, consisted of some 6.5 million better-off persons covered by private occupational pensions.[67] The development of private and occupational pensions was, as we have seen, one of the cornerstones upon which the Beveridge Plan was constructed.

These findings led to a questioning of the central principles of British social insurance. In 1953 Abel-Smith scrutinised the contributory flat-rate principle in *The Reform of Social Security*. First, describing it as a system of taxation (which it really is), he highlights its *regressive* nature by claiming that 'the contribution is not just a flat rate levy or poll tax, but a tax adjusted to ability not to pay – a larger sum is taken from the poorer than the richer.'[68] In 1948 the minister of social insurance, James

64. The 'Titmuss Group' consisted of Richard Titmuss, Brian Abel-Smith, Tony Lynes, and Peter Townsend. I will return to the influence of this group in Chapter 8.

65. Abel-Smith 1953, p. 2.

66. Abel-Smith and Townsend 1955.

67. Ibid., p. 6.

68. Abel-Smith 1953, p. 18.

Griffith, had admitted that 'we have reached the limit of what we can do by flat rate of contribution and in future we shall have to give further consideration to see whether some method of financing the insurance scheme other than that of flat-rate contributions can be found.'[69] The system was allowed to work for another five years before Abel-Smith highlighted its shortcomings in 1953. In the same pamphlet he refutes the assumptions on which Beveridge's advocacy of the contributory flat-rate principle was based. Abel-Smith also points out that the growth of private insurance, rather than being an expression of its popularity, only proves 'that people want money available when they need it.'[70] (Reaching the same conclusion, I argued above that any system which could provide this would in turn gain some popularity.) Referring to people's rejection of the rationale for means-testing, Abel-Smith makes it plain that 'the fact that people don't like a means test can only prove that they don't like a means test.' He concludes that 'neither observation tells us anything about the method by which people want money to be collected.'[71]

In the pamphlet *National Superannuation*, published in 1957, the Titmuss Group take their findings and recommendations further into the political world by outlining 'labour's policy for security in old age'. It was here that a turn towards earnings-related benefits in return for earnings-related contributions was first presented as the solution to the problem of raising pensions to subsistence level and beyond. The Conservatives adopted the recommendations and were the first to implement them, with the Boyd Carpenter system, which came into effect in 1961.[72] While the struggle against persistent poverty had been Labour's main reason for advocating ERS, the actuarial situation regarding the NI was the main motive for the Conservatives.[73]

The division between 'two nations in old age' continued, however, with the favourable conditions for 'contracting out' into occupational pensions following the Boyd Carpenter Plan. Under this system, companies that could prove they offered occupational pensions as good as or better than that of the state pension were allowed to opt out of the state

69. Hansard, 16 July 1948.
70. Abel-Smith 1953, p. 19.
71. Ibid.
72. Heclo 1973, p. 273.
73. Ibid., p. 270.

scheme. In the years following the 1946 NI, the development of these schemes had strengthened the role of private insurance to the extent that any withdrawal of their slice of the insurance cake would have been extremely difficult, even if politically desirable. Between 1953 and 1965 the number of persons covered by occupational pensions increased from 5 million to 12 million.[74] Again, therefore, the presence of alternative non-public schemes had a far greater influence on social insurance in Britain than in Norway. The weight of this policy inheritance increased year by year.[75]

While the addition of an earnings-related supplement to a scheme usually indicates a turn in the direction of 'standard security', in Britain its introduction provides a further example of the 'poverty alleviation' approach to social security.

Summary

The findings of this chapter can be summed up in three points. First, under the system of flat-rate contributions, 'actuarial soundness' required pensions to be set at a relatively low level in 1946. Second, the same system later became an impediment to attempts to elevate the benefits to subsistence levels, and large groups of NI pensioners were therefore left in continued reliance on NA for supplementary benefits to bring their income maintenance up to subsistence levels. Third, the strong adherence to the contributory principle as the basis for establishing entitlement excluded large sections of the population even though they met the need conditions. In combination, the 1946–66 developments left large, uniform, and 'deserving' need categories in social assistance dependency either for supplementation or for their entire income maintenance.

74. George 1968, p. 166.

75. The same pattern was repeated when the Labour Party introduced *its* first ERS with the Castle system in 1975; contracting out continued to be a part of the system.

Summary of Part Two

The Unequal Development of Social Insurance

In this part I have emphasised differences between Britain and Norway in their development of social insurance in the first two post-war decades. The four chapters do not aim to give a comprehensive analysis or comparison of social insurance as such. Instead, I have focused on policy areas and issues of particular importance to the success of social insurance in reducing the number of people left in social assistance dependency. The background to the programmes enacted after the war was analysed in Chapters 2 (Norway) and 4 (Britain). The post-war developments were the topic of Chapters 3 (Norway) and 5 (Britain).

Similar ambitions, different methods and means

Documents from the immediate post-war period on social security in the two countries appear to express the shared ambition of developing social insurance in order to replace the income maintenance of the Poor Law. However, the plans outlining how this was to take place signalled the two countries' different approaches to the problem. In Britain the Beveridge Plan expressed as a main ambition the discontinuation of the means test.[1] In Norway, by contrast, the emphasis was on the gradual process of making the Poor Law superfluous through the creation of alternative social insurance programmes. This process of breaking down the Poor Law 'from without' had been pursued by both countries in the half century preceding the Second World War. The implications of Britain's departure from this approach through the 1948 abolition of the Poor Law

1. The emphasis on the means test as the crux of the degradation of the Poor Law must be understood in the light of people's experience of the extended 'household means test' in the 1930s.

will be addressed in Part Three. But the difference was also significant for the development of social insurance in the 1946–66 period. The two approaches brought about very different social insurance systems in the two countries towards the end of the period.

I have given equal weight to the creation of these two models of social insurance and to the subsequent development of services. The main difference between the two models is that while the Norwegian system was financed mainly from general taxation, the British model adhered more to the contributory principle.[2] The differences between the two approaches emerge first when we look at the balancing of the three sources of financing. While the Norwegian system accepted a major state responsibility from the outset, the development of the British pension relied to a greater extent on the ability of the individual to make significant contributions.[3] While the fear of administrative costs favoured the tax-financed solution in 1908, the much more costly insurance of the post-war period necessitated the savings and constraints of the contributory approach.[4]

For both countries, I found that policy inheritance was the most important factor in explaining the nature of the model arrived at before the launch of the post-World War II reforms. In analysing the respective policy inheritances, I distinguished between alternative public precursors to state schemes and private and occupational alternatives. In Norway the existence of municipal pension schemes facilitated the choice of a tax-financed state old age pension in two ways. First, it showed the feasibility of this approach at a time when it was considered inferior to the contributory approach by many social insurance specialists. Second, the municipal schemes did not favour any vested interest by way of acquired rights or professional interests tied to their administration. On the contrary, they were created in the expectation of a future state take-over.

In Britain, by contrast, there were no equivalent municipal schemes. Dating back to the Friendly Societies and private insurance companies of

2. Both the Norwegian and the British system were based on tripartite forms of financing, with employers, employees, and the state all contributing towards the cost of the insurance schemes. In Norway the municipalities also contributed until 1976.

3. Both the choice of a contributory scheme and the later reluctance of the state to contribute the necessary funds have been ascribed to the power of the British Treasury and its unwillingness to contribute towards social programmes. Abel-Smith has argued that decisions in British social policy have been determined first and foremost by the treasury's desire to find the cheapest possible solution.

4. Abel-Smith (1983) makes a similar point about the National Health Service.

the 19th century, non-public income maintenance schemes have played a much larger role in Britain than in Norway. It was not until after the Second World War that considerable development of new private and occupational schemes took place in Norway. Throughout the period, tax concessions favoured this development in Britain. One of the main reasons that the first British OAP (1908) was financed through general taxation was the fear that a contributory solution would threaten the economic interests of the insurance industry. Two years later, the contributory approach was established as the main model for British social insurance. This was made possible through the involvement of the insurance industry in administrating the state schemes. In both cases, therefore, the non-public insurance sector had a decisive impact on the course taken by public insurance in Britain.

When Beveridge proposed a comprehensive social insurance scheme along contributory lines in 1942, two main factors facilitated the necessary Labour support.[5] First, the effect of occupational and private pensions had been to increase the divisions within the working class. Its better-off and better-organised segments – whose experience of these schemes had been positive, and who had a vested interest in their continuation – formed the power base of the party in the late 1930s through their dominance of the Trade Union Congress (TUC). Also, the Labour Party was suffering from an intellectual vacuum during this period. In a party that tended to leave the fundamental questions of social welfare to the expertise of intellectuals (in particular, the Fabians), the lack of informed opinion in the period after the Webbs and before the arrival of the 'Titmuss group' cannot be underestimated. The importance of this failing in the 1940s became clear when Abel-Smith (and others) documented the need to rid social insurance of the 'strait-jacket' of the flat-rate contributory approach. Thus, the Labour Party's ultimate acceptance of Beveridge's argument that only through the contributory approach could rights be insured and the means test avoided must be understood as resulting from a combination of ignorance and vested interests (in addition to the element of political expediency mentioned above).

In Norway an apparently contrastive power configuration may have contributed to the divergence. When Labour gained power in 1935, the

5. It was the Labour government of Clement Attlee that enacted the 1946 National Insurance law.

party became the centre of power within the labour movement. While policies before this time were greatly influenced by Landsorganisasjonen (LO, the Norwegian equivalent of the TUC), the trade unions began to take on a less dominant role in the shaping of Labour policies. Although highly speculative, an argument can be made that this change ruled out the possibility of an insurance solution favouring the sectional interests of organised labour, which might have introduced a stronger element of 'work testing' similar to that established in Britain with the 1946 National Insurance Act. Moreover, the 1930s in Norway was the period when intellectuals favouring collective measures entered the political arena as advisers to the Labour Party. In this way Keynesian policies strongly influenced the path taken by the Labour government from 1935 onwards. Although there were similar wartime measures in Britain, an equivalent influence did not become manifest there until after the war.

Social insurance, 1946–1966

In Norway the tax-financed and means-tested scheme excluding high earners continued after the Second World War along the course established in the 1930s. Gradual elevation of benefits was favoured over the immediate achievement of universality through the abolition of the means test. When it was finally abolished in 1957, the aim of 'socially acceptable benefits', outlined by the Labour government in 1948, was largely achieved. By this time, political pressure and the economic climate facilitated further extension of social insurance, based on the model of the OAP, to include large groups still depending on assistance for their income maintenance. The taxation principle allowed for the incorporation of new groups regardless of their ability to contribute towards the cost of the programmes. The extension of social insurance was therefore a *political*, rather than a practical, question. In 1967 the level of benefits was further raised through the establishment of an earnings-related supplement to the basic pension. Again, the relative absence of occupational and private schemes facilitated a universal, state solution. For the same reason there were comparatively few constraints on the level of the supplement as an instrument designed to further standardise security through public welfare.

Thus, while Britain and Norway shared the ultimate aim of universal social insurance, Britain took a much greater initial leap towards that aim with the 1946 National Insurance Act. From the outset, however, the scheme, which was largely based on Beveridge's proposals, carried built-in restrictions that impeded the achievement of universality. Being a contributory scheme, it could include only those who paid contributions or for whom contributions were being made. This excluded the disabled and other groups outside the workforce. For working women, participation in the scheme was made optional.

The impediments to comprehensiveness proved even greater in the practical implementation of the scheme. Once the contributory solution had been chosen, it was decided that both contributions and benefits were to be set at a flat rate. The shortcomings of this approach were not foreseen at the time of implementation. As early as 1948, however, the minister of national insurance realised that the development of a flat-rate contributory system was analogous to 'the speed of the convoy being that of the slowest ship'. In the relative hardship of the early post-war period, no minister was willing to pay the political cost of raising the necessary contributions and the unreasonable burden this would put on the lowest paid. With unexpected inflation, the pension benefits, already set very low in 1946, failed to reach subsistence level. A more favourable development of National Assistance in terms of benefit levels contributed to a massive spillover from National Insurance of pensioners in need of assistance for supplementation. Furthermore, the contributory principle in itself ensured the continued exclusion of large groups. Even if there had been the political will to incorporate the civilian disabled, for example, their inclusion would have involved violating the principle upon which the entire scheme was constructed.

When an earnings-related supplement (ERS) was introduced in 1961, its main function was to bring more funds into National Insurance, which found itself running in the red, and not, as in Norway, to extend the level of insurance in the direction of greater standard security. Another factor limiting the impact of the ERS was, once again, the influence exerted by the non-public insurance industry. Meeting its demands for 'opting out' laid the groundwork for the gradual residualisation of the public earnings-related programme. For the same reason, the level of the ERS was set very low from the outset in 1961.[6]

To sum up the unequal development with reference to the theoretical

6. Berthaud and Brown 1981, p. 144.

models discussed in the introductory chapter: Compared with Norway, Britain took a much greater first step towards the institutional model of welfare with the early post-war social insurance legislation. National Insurance achieved an initial comprehensiveness much greater than the patchwork of social insurance still in existence in Norway at that time. Furthermore, while British National Insurance offered a non-means-tested service, the Norwegian means test in the case of the old age pension was not abolished until ten years later. If we look at the total extent of means-testing within public income maintenance, the picture is, however, very different. While Norway, through the extension of social insurance after 1957, experienced a decrease in services provided after a test of means, the picture was the opposite in Britain. Both the spillover to National Assistance and the non-inclusion of significant need categories ensured a continued and growing reliance on means-tested benefits in Britain during the period of this study. The universality of the 1940s was thus followed by a growing selectivity by default. At the end of the period, therefore, Britain featured a residual model of social insurance. This resulted from the combination of low levels of benefits and the restricted coverage of social insurance.

The examination of British and Norwegian social insurance highlights two important aspects. First, although the post-war plans featured similar goals, contrastive approaches brought about both very different means to these ends and, consequently, very different degrees of achievement. Furthermore, the differences in approach can be understood only in the light of the contrasting public and non-public policy inheritance in the two countries.[7]

With divergence as the main finding, there is reason to return briefly to the interpretations of other writers who have addressed the relationship between British and Norwegian social security development. The two countries have a long history of cultural ties. With Britain being the dominant one, there is reason to expect to find an element of learning and diffusion, in particular from west to east across the North Sea. The experience of the Second World War, with the Norwegian government in exile in London, strengthens such an expectation. Adding to this is the

7. This conclusion corresponds with Ashford's, who stresses the importance of the inter-war period in shaping the post-war policies of the five countries in his comparison. See Ashford 1986, p. 244.

importance of the Beveridge Report as a planning document which received much attention also outside Britain.

In Chapter 2, I questioned the existence of widespread diffusion between Britain and Norway during and after the Second World War. Norwegian post-war policy represented first and foremost a continuation and extension of the policies laid down in the mid-1930s. Still, this does not exclude the possibility of an element of learning and influence from Britain in the years that followed. Anne Lise Seip's understanding of the relationship between British and Norwegian policy around the period of the Second World War appears to be based on two assumptions.[8] First, she argues that the Beveridge Plan was a result of its author's gradual radicalisation. Discussions of this question found in the British literature all stress, however, Beveridge's lack of radicalism. What *is* apparent is that he changed from a traditional, free market liberal to an advocate of greater collective measures in social policy. Harris describes Beveridge in this way:

> He has often been portrayed as a collectivist liberal with a continuous commitment to social reform dating back to his days as sub-warden of Toynbee Hall in the early 1900s; but in fact his views on politics and society were a great deal more ambivalent than this view would suggest. Ideologically he veered between an almost total commitment to the free market, and a belief that the free market was corrupt and inefficient and should be replaced by a strong, impartial administrative state.[9]

Similarly, Abel-Smith argues that 'Beveridge was a man of the centre, and at varying times he had had both leftist and rightist leanings, but he was never a socialist.'[10] Moreover, when the Labour Party accepted his recommendations in 1942, they did so for pragmatic reasons and not because they had any illusions that his ideas were socialist in nature. A Labour MP, Mr Barnes, summed up the understanding within the party: 'I say as a convinced socialist that I do not support the Beveridge Plan because it is a socialist plan. It is not. To me, frankly, it is a common-sense method of meeting our peacetime casualties under the prevailing system, the capitalist system.'[11] In a party lacking plans of its own, such political expedience becomes all the more important.

8. Seip 1981.
9. Harris in Winter 1975, p. 240.
10. Abel-Smith 1983, p. 11.
11. Hansard, 1942, 1770.

The second assumption underlying Seip's argument was a change in the social policy of the Norwegian Labour Party. Hatland, however, has convincingly challenged the perception that the party's policy in the late 1930s represented a turn to the right.[12] This indicates that there was less common ground between Beveridge and the Norwegian Labour Party than Seip's argument supposes.

Although the differences between the British and Norwegian post-war plans are greater than the similarities, this conclusion does not exclude the possibility that influence was exerted by the undoubtedly trail-blazing Beveridge Report. In particular, the emphasis on comprehensiveness and unification of separate schemes in the report was adopted in the Norwegian post-war plans. Still, the recommendations of the so-called Philadelphia Declaration, proclaimed by the International Labor Organization in 1944, appear to have exerted an equally strong influence on the 1948 White Paper on social insurance.[13]

The pamphlet *Framtidens Norge* ('The Future Norway') called for a unification of the different social insurance programmes then in existence. This proposal was made with reference to the Beveridge Report, in which 'unification of administrative responsibility' was a key principle.[14] While this was not a new idea, in Norway or in Britain, the Beveridge proposals brought it further and showed the way towards its implementation.

The search for more direct diffusion through personal contacts between British and Norwegian policy-makers has revealed little new evidence. In fact, the interviews with politicians, as well as the study of contemporary sources and later (auto)biographies, lead me to conclude that there was surprisingly little contact between the exiled Norwegian politicians and British politicians and civil servants during the war years.[15]

12. Hatland 1987.

13. Stortingsmelding nr. 58, 1948, p. 19–28.

14. LO and Norsk Sjømannsforbund 1945, p. 77.

15. Nordby 1989; Stenersen 1973; Sørensen 1991; interviews with Rakel Seweriin and Haakon Lie.

Part Three
Residual Welfare in the Expanding Welfare State

Introduction
Unequal Beginnings: The Poor Law Heritage

Perhaps to an even greater extent than the association between social insurance and institutional welfare, the Poor Laws of the 19th century epitomise the service delivery and wider societal connotations of residual welfare. Although the history of the Poor Laws of the two countries features differences, I take as my starting point that for the purpose of my analysis the similarities are dominant. In fact, the Norwegian Poor Law of 1845 was to a large extent influenced by the British New Poor Law of 1834.[1] In both nations the Poor Laws were financed and administered by the local authorities. With some exceptions, politically elected laypersons played an active role in assessing paupers for benefits. These benefits were kept low for reasons of economy, but also in order to create incentives for work, charitable activities, and private care from the family. The personal contact between pauper and administrator added to the saving by making benefits conditional on the pauper's willingness to accept individual guidance from the guardians. Economy was moreover achieved by more explicitly punitive measures. While both nations employed the restriction of citizenship, through the loss of franchise and disqualification from taking public office, the British system went further by establishing less eligibility as a rule and the workhouse test as the ultimate deterrent.

Paradoxically, it seems that a main cause of Norway's inability to introduce this latter method of saving was the lack of the resources needed to build the necessary workhouses. The dominance of rural, rather than – as in Britain – urban, pauperism was further justification for the choice of outdoor, rather than indoor, relief in Norway. It made more

1. Seip 1984, pp. 52–64. Still, Seip argues that although the Act was influenced by liberalist ideology, aspects of personal freedom figured more prominently in the Norwegian debate than in the ideas underlying the British system.

sense to give an impoverished peasant family a sack of potatoes or some seed-wheat, thereby enabling them to survive on their meagre patch of land, when moving them to a workhouse would involve taking responsibility for all their material needs. In Britain, by contrast, an urban labourer had fewer self-help possibilities and would therefore be more likely to become totally dependent on the public for the survival of his family. In this situation the workhouse 'made more sense'. In this way, the earlier industrialisation in Britain influenced the divergence in the implementation of schemes based on similar ideologies.

One important early difference that should be mentioned is the much greater central control over Poor Law services in Britain. In Norway the Municipal Acts of 1837 ensured a high degree of municipal autonomy.[2] The tradition of a framework law, enabling the municipalities to have a major influence on the implementation of assistance schemes, continued throughout my period of analysis.[3] This difference between the two countries becomes particularly relevant when we turn to look at the process leading up to the nationalisation of assistance in Britain in 1948. With this enactment Britain also broke with what had been a shared tradition of breaking the Poor Law down 'from without' through the creation of alternative schemes. In Norway, by contrast, this process continued during the first two post-war decades. This will be seen to represent a key factor in explaining the divergence in this period.

When we use social assistance and the personal social services to exemplify the residual model, we do so because these schemes in combination have inherited the main functions of the Poor Law. The extent to which these functions have been maintained by their modern alternatives, however, varies considerably. A key area is therefore the relationship between income maintenance and attempts to make the client more self-reliant. In the personal social services the laypersons' repressive measures were to a large extent replaced by a more therapeutic approach, whereby professional social workers became responsible for most of the direct contact with the clients. While the functions of social work and cash allocation continued to be combined in Norway, these were separated into two services in Britain in 1948.

---

2. Arntzen and Knutsen 1980, p. 79.

3. See Seip 1984, pp. 65–77, for an overview of the formative years of Norwegian Poor Relief legislation.

The fact that mine is a study more of the social services than of the experience of approaching them will influence my discussion of the users of these services. The differences in the size and composition of the clientele will therefore be discussed as some of the factors that determine the nature of assistance and of the personal social services. In particular, the extent to which the services have continued the Poor Law tradition of serving only the poorest section of society will be seen to have had a marked impact on the degree to which the residual traits of the Poor Laws have been maintained in their modern-day versions.

Chapter 6

From Social Assistance to Social Care in Norway: A Study of a Legislative Process

The plans for the future of social assistance were only indirectly commented on in the first Norwegian post-war document, which outlined, among other things, a programme for the income maintenance schemes to be developed. With the proposal to 'develop social insurance in order to make assistance superfluous', the coalition government decided to continue a long-established policy of diminishing the scope of assistance rather than abolishing or reforming the scheme itself.[1]

By 1948, however, the 1900 Poor Law bore too strong a resemblance to a social policy from which the government of the day wished to distance itself. It was felt that the word 'poor' (*fattig*) in the existing legislation was 'incongruous with prevailing opinion'.[2] Thus, throughout the 1948 legislation, the word 'poor' was replaced with 'assistance' (*forsorg*). Similarly, the blueprint for social insurance, also published in 1948, signalled a changing attitude towards the Poor Law: 'The Department [of Social Affairs] will later consider the question of establishing a form of social assistance covering cases which still fall outside the boundaries of social insurance, but where the help ought not to bring about the legal effects of receiving assistance.'[3] In 1950 a committee was appointed to 'review existing assistance legislation and bring forward proposals for a new act.'[4]

Officers from the Poor Law administration played an instrumental role by advocating the need for a committee. They argued that there would be

1. Fellesprogrammet, 1945.
2. Ot.prp. nr. 24, 1945, referred to in Utkast til lov om sosialhjelp, 1953 (1953 proposal).
3. Stortingsmelding nr. 58, 1948.
4. Utkast til lov om sosialhjelp, 1953.

a continued need for social assistance even after social insurance had been allowed to develop.[5]

The proposals of the committee, presented in 1953, mark a major departure from the policies of the existing assistance legislation. It was, however, to be another ten years before the final departmental response to these proposals was put forward. The focal point of this analysis is the divergence between these two plans for social assistance schemes designed to replace the existing Poor Law.

In attempting to explain the divergence, I will focus on the targeted clientele. I believe that changes regarding the social assistance clientele in the 1950s strongly influenced the direction of policy concerning the group. The role played by the target clientele in a process of policy formation is, however, multi-faceted. To convey the complexity of the ways in which the nature of the particular group influences the course taken by policy-makers, I will employ the phrase 'perception of the clientele'. This concept incorporates an objective, a subjective, and an active element. The objective element is the actual size and composition of the group. Myths, arising from ignorance or misinformation, may add a subjective element to the policy-makers' understanding of the size and composition. The active element, that is, considerations regarding the kind of services and methods required to help the clientele, may be guided by a combination of the two aforementioned factors. In addition, prevailing approaches to welfare, in the form of methodology advocated by the dominant professions, will have bearing on the subjective and, consequently, the active element.

Thus, in methodological terms, the clientele will be considered an independent variable influencing the nature of the services to be established – the dependent variable. In this perspective, 'perception of the clientele' becomes an intervening causal variable.

My focus on the relationship between assistance and insurance guides the choice of areas highlighted in the analysis. The correlation between the two areas of income maintenance will be seen to have taken two forms. First, social insurance had a direct impact on assistance in the period because the extension of the scope of insurance was the main reason for the reduced number of people relying on assistance. Sub-

5. Seip 1994, p. 225. The chairman of the committee was Trygve Mohr, one of the most politically active figures in the Poor Law administration.

sequently, this also led to changes in the composition of the assistance clientele. Second, and more indirectly, the new notion of rehabilitation originated in social insurance and was subsequently applied in a modified version to social assistance.

I will first give a brief account of the committee's proposal. Second, this will be juxtaposed with the subsequent departmental response, which was presented ten years later. In this section I will focus partly on the extent to which the two proposals represented diverging socio-political approaches, and partly on the consequences these differences came to have regarding the nature of the schemes proposed. In a third section I will expand the scope of the analysis by examining the changing approaches in the light of developments outside the policy areas in question. The fourth and last section offers a brief presentation of the new scheme as it was finally enacted in 1964.

The sources used are parliamentary papers, secondary sources, and interviews with two cabinet ministers who played key roles in this era.

The 1953 proposal

While the 1948 reform was only cosmetic, the 1950 committee proposed a totally new social assistance scheme. The proposal starts out with a clear-sighted critique of the 1948 reform: 'The change of name has done little to enhance social assistance, so as to distinguish it from poor relief. To be a recipient of assistance carries today the same invidious connotations as did the poor relief board.'[6] In a further comment on the 1948 reform, we find the first mention of those being left behind in the ongoing process of making the Poor Law superfluous: 'By extending the scope of social insurance we enhance the position of those incorporated. This does not, though, improve the position of those still depending on assistance.'[7]

Thus, the committee made an important departure from previous considerations of the Poor Law: social assistance would, even in the event of a successful development of social insurance, continue to exist for the foreseeable future. Responding to this reality, the committee's report represented a genuine attempt to break with the past and establish a new scheme more in line with the existing and planned income maintenance

6. Utkast til lov om sosialhjelp, 1953, p. 13.
7. Ibid.

services of social insurance. In this respect the above quotations are representative of the flavour of the report. It is therefore particularly interesting to see what recommendations the committee came up with.

My outline of the recommendations is informed by two objectives. First, I will focus on the extent to which the proposal represented a genuine break with the past. Second, and most important for this analysis, I will highlight the areas in which the 1963 proposal diverged from the earlier report.

One objective pervading the report is that of making assistance more equal to social insurance. While assistance still bore 'the taint of charity',[8] insurance was both felt to be and awarded as a right. Consequently, it is significant that the first paragraph of the proposed law is titled 'The right to Social Assistance'.[9]

The committee recognised that human needs are so varied that social insurance alone can neither embrace all cases of need nor give everyone receiving benefits full coverage of their requirements. Thus, substitution as well as supplementation of social insurance benefits would continue to constitute a major task of social assistance. It seems that those receiving assistance instead of, or in addition to, social insurance were the groups the committee had in mind when it argued for the establishment of an assistance scheme more in line with the principles of social insurance. With the statement 'Only when we get such a scheme can we truly claim that our National Insurance is completed',[10] the committee went even further, implicitly referring to assistance as a part of social insurance – a point of view not advocated elsewhere in the report.

Although the focus was clearly on present and potential insurance claimants, the proposed changes were meant to cover all recipients of assistance. This is implicit in the following statement: 'Those who receive assistance are not different from those in receipt of insurance, and should not, like those receiving poor relief, be made to feel inferior.'[11]

The enhancement of assistance was meant to be attained by various means. Traditionally, poor relief was given in kind as well as in cash. The committee maintained that a change to cash payments only 'would be in

8. Ibid.
9. Utkast til lov om sosialhjelp, 1953, p. 53.
10. Ibid., p. 16.
11. Ibid.

line with our insurance benefits and corresponds to the present understanding of what public benefits should consist of.'[12]

Similarly, in arguing for a stop to the traditional obligation to repay benefits whenever possible, the committee argued that 'the reason why people apply for assistance will in most cases not be very different from those for which they seek social insurance.'[13] Thus, in this area also the committee recommended that assistance practice should follow that of insurance. Although not explicitly expressed in the document, a change away from means-testing towards needs-testing in social assistance can also be traced here. Furthermore, the committee proposed the introduction of a right to appeal decisions made by the local authorities' assistance boards to a higher level of government.[14] Again, the committee used social insurance as the standard.

Another area in which the proposal diverged from existing assistance legislation was that of mutual obligation of maintenance between family members. The committee argued that the main objective of the existing rules was 'not to ensure the needs of the claimant, but rather to reduce spending on assistance.'[15] Here using the standard of civil law, the committee found it unreasonable that the assistance legislation should entail greater responsibilities than those found there. This meant that only obligations between parents and children and those between spouses would remain. Because these were covered by child and marital legislation respectively, the committee found no reason to include them in the new act. This is, as I see it, further evidence of a move away from the Poor Law towards a more stringent income maintenance scheme.

Further evidence of the desire for a split between income maintenance and other functions is found in the response to 'those who argue that people who receive social assistance are inferior persons, work-shy, given to drink, and criminals who should not be handled by society with kid gloves ... and whose existence justifies a social assistance scheme less desirable than social insurance.'[16] The committee acknowledged that such persons exist, but argued that 'the means society should employ to improve such persons or to protect itself against them are not those of a

12. Utkast til lov om sosialhjelp, 1953, p. 20.
13. Ibid., p. 24.
14. Ibid., p. 46.
15. Ibid., p. 28.
16. Ibid., p. 14.

social assistance act, but regulations in different acts aimed at all citizens of the type mentioned, and not only those who apply for social assistance.'[17]

Given the tone of the document as a whole, the recommendations for services required for this clientele were surprisingly harsh. The committee advocated more stringent provisions in the section of the vagrancy legislation relating to workcamps. Although the proposals advocated workfarms established by the authority in charge of social assistance, they recommended that the powers to refer clients to the camps should be covered, again, by legislation other than assistance legislation. The harshness of the proposal is somewhat disguised in this statement: 'Those who are referred to workfarms may turn the offer down, but when they do accept the help they must accept it in the form it is given.'[18]

It is difficult to interpret the significance of this apparent harshness in dealing with the more problematic assistance claimants. I see two possible interpretations. It can be seen as the result of a genuine desire to impose harsher measures on this particular section of the clientele. Because the proposal as a whole was much milder and extended clients' rights, this interpretation rests on the assumption that the more problematic clients were expected to form a small minority which could be further reduced by extensions in legislation relating to their particular problems. The above-mentioned focus on insurance-related needs makes this interpretation plausible. A different, and not mutually exclusive, explanation is that the proposals were a concession to the 'hawks' in social policy.[19] In this perspective, the enhancement for the majority was justified by stricter control for those not deserving of extended entitements. Again, this argument presupposes the expectation that such groups would form an insignificant minority of claimants.

Another question which received much attention in the proposal was the allocation of assistance expenditure among municipalities. Under the existing legislation, the local authority continued to be responsible for the cost of maintaining a pauper after he or she moved out of the municipality. Once the pauper had lived for two years in the new municipality without making any claims, the responsibility transferred to that munici-

17. Ibid.

18. Utkast til lov om sosialhjelp, 1953, p. 22.

19. A minority of the committee members consequently argued for the continuation of legislation giving the assistance boards the authority to use labour camps.

pality. Although practised even earlier, the principle of residence rights was first enacted in the 1845 Poor Law. Since that date it had remained more or less unchanged. Understandably, the application of this provision caused a lot of disputes between local authorities over the years. A majority of the committee proposed a change towards giving wider responsibilities to the original town of residence.[20] In effect this would have involved a growth in expenditure for municipalities with greater numbers moving out than moving in. Given the continued urbanisation in Norway in the 1950s, the proposal would have involved a shift of expenditure from the cities to the rural municipalities.

An obvious solution to this problem was that chosen by Britain in 1948. By making social assistance a national scheme, the financial responsibility was removed from the individual municipality. The committee debated this option and concluded as follows: 'There is a lot to be said in favour of the State taking over the responsibility of assistance as it has already done with social insurance. But the Committee realises that such a proposal will lead nowhere and that there is no prospect of the state taking on greater social assistance expenditure than what is already the case.'[21] The committee also stressed what it considered to be a positive aspect of keeping assistance local: 'Assistance is of a character that makes it of great importance that the scheme is managed by a local board responsible for accurate individual needs-testing as well as responsible for the expenditure.'[22]

The report gives no clue as to *why* it would be unlikely for the state to take on a greater financial responsibility for social assistance. At the time, the state reimbursed the expenses incurred by the municipality only in cases of vagrants and aliens. The report seems to suggest that the state should simply extend that responsibility rather than, as the earlier juxtaposition with social insurance might have indicated, effect a complete take-over. This apparent inconsistency in the argumentation might be a sign of the problems involved in breaking a long-standing policy inheritance whereby the very poorest were the responsibility of the local community. In the case of social insurance, by contrast, local schemes were being established with the hope that the state would take over the respon-

20. Utkast til lov om sosialhjelp, 1953, p. 41.
21. Ibid., p. 37.
22. Ibid.

sibility. Keeping in mind that Britain took a different route in this area, we will later look at the comparative evidence for possible explanations of why the option of a state take-over was ruled out.

Having presented the main recommendations in the proposal, I will return to a few key points in more detail while juxtaposing the 1953 document with the proposal that represented the next step in the legislative process.

The 1963 departmental response[23]

It took seven years for the Department of Social Affairs to submit its first proposal based on the plan submitted by the committee. After another three years the proposal on which the 1964 legislation was based was presented to the Storting. This latter scheme diverged very little from that put forward in 1960. Together, the two departmental proposals represented a contrasting socio-political approach to that embarked on by the committee that reported in 1953.

My review and analysis of the departmental plan will focus on the area where it diverged from the one submitted in 1953. For the purpose of this analysis, I will divide the comparison into four themes. First, the names chosen for the respective schemes will be seen to give an indication of the ideologies behind the proposals. Second, we will look at how the two proposals represented diverging ways of understanding the targeted clientele. This, in turn, will be seen to have influenced the recommendations for the types of services needed to cater for the clients. Thus, the third section will focus on service variation along the continuum of rights versus discretionary decision-making. The final theme is that of the changing relationship between income maintenance and counselling, or, as I see it, social work and money.

The names of the schemes

When social reformers set out to change welfare schemes, which traditionally carry a stigma, the choice of name for the new scheme tends to serve one of the following functions. First, when the scheme introduces

23. The 'Parliamentary Proposal to the Storting' (Ot.prp.) corresponds to the British 'Green Paper'.

no substantial changes, a new name serves as a mock reform. The changes enacted in 1948 exemplify such an approach. Second, when a scheme has undergone genuine changes, a new name will be used to emphasise the departure from the preceding service. For example, the term *sosialhjelp* (social assistance) in the 1953 proposal marked two major changes in relation to the existing scheme. First, social assistance was seen to be 'essentially different from "forsorg" [assistance]'.[24] Second, the committee proposed that 'the authority in charge of allocating social assistance will also provide advice in all cases of a social nature – also social insurance matters.'[25] Thus, compared with 'assistance', 'social assistance' gave a more correct picture of the proposed service. Furthermore, the committee felt that its choice of name was in line with international developments. In addition to the previously mentioned ILO report (1944), the Swedish reform and the British National Assistance Act were referred to as examples of legislation in the same direction.[26]

In the departmental response, the term 'social assistance' was replaced with 'social care' because it was felt that the latter gave 'a better description of the content of the proposed law.'[27] The reasoning behind this change was closely tied to the greater emphasis on advice and counselling in the latter scheme. The term 'social assistance' thus served as a generic term for the services covered by article 3,[28] while the term 'social care' comprises these services as well as the advice, counselling functions, and other support made available by the scheme.[29] The change of name thus heralded the shift away from the stress on income maintenance in the 1953 plan towards greater emphasis on extended service-delivery in the departmental response.

The perception of the clientele

Richard Titmuss claims that 'poor people's services will always be poor services.'[30] I will not attempt to question the degree to which that statement is

24. Utkast til lov om sosialhjelp, 1953, p. 16.
25. Ibid.
26. Ibid. The ILO report became known as the Philadelphia Declaration.
27. Ot.prp. nr. 56, 1962–63, p. 6.
28. Article 3 covered all the cash benefits of the scheme.
29. Ot.prp. nr. 56, 1962–63.
30. Titmuss [1968] 1979, p. 143.

universally valid. I will, however, start from the assumption that the nature of the targeted clientele is one of the determining factors when the nature and quality of a service is established. When I refer to the 'perception' rather than the 'nature' of the clientele, I do so because there are sources of error which might distort the policy-makers' understanding of the nature of the target group. When only sparse information about the group is available, any statements made should be checked for prejudice. A lack of information may, for example, lead planners to choose to focus attention on the section of the clientele towards whom they would like to target the scheme, and thereby implicitly make them representative of the group as a whole.[31] Thus, the perception does not accurately reflect the actual situation.

In this section I will focus on the extent to which the changing approach can be seen as a function of a changing perception of, and attitude towards, the clientele towards which the services were targeted. Changing attitudes may represent an adequate response to changing size and composition of the clientele. New socio-political ideologies can, however, develop independently of changes in the clientele. To understand why and how the divergence between the two proposed schemes came about, we must therefore see the changes in the light of the actual development of social assistance recipients.

I will first give an overview of the actual development of the target group in the period in question. Next follows an account of how the clientele was referred to in the two proposals. Together the two accounts form the basis for an analysis of the relationship between the subjective and objective elements which determine the policy-makers' perception of the clientele.

The (actual) size and composition of the clientele, 1946–1966

During the period 1946–66 there was a steady decrease in the numbers relying on social assistance in Norway; overall, the number of recipients fell by about one-third.[32] In 1966 approximately half the recipients also

31. A similar result may occur if the planners deliberately choose to redirect the scheme towards a specific section of the existing clientele.

32. The following account in based on the publications Fattigvesenet, 1945–47; Forsorgsvesenet, 1947–64; and Sosialhjelpsstatistikk, 1966. Each publication presents the statistics of social assistance/social care based on information gathered by the Central Bureau of Statistics and printed annually in the publication Statistiske Meddelelser.

received social insurance.[33] Before this no statistics concerning the composition of the clientele were available, though some of the annual reports contain interpretations of the changes occurring. Together with my own interpretations, these will be used to cast light on the developments underlying the numbers in Figure 6.1. In this way some of the more dramatic annual changes can be explained as effects of new social insurance legislation. The decrease caused by insurance occurred in two stages. Much of the decrease in the first decade can be explained by the continued establishment of municipal insurance schemes for elderly people, disabled people, tuberculosis patients, and in some cases single parents.[34] Thus, the sharp fall between, for example, 1947 and 1950 is explained mainly by the establishment of new municipal schemes: 'The municipal insurance schemes may bring about decreases in the number of recipients under the 1900 Poor Law by the introduction of new schemes, by the extension of existing schemes (like the Disability Pension in Oslo in 1947), or by the raising of benefit levels.'[35]

In 1950 the Central Bureau of Statistics carried out a small survey that showed the decrease in assistance to be greatest in the south-eastern parts of the country – the area with the greatest number of municipal pensions.[36] By leading the way in establishing alternatives outside the Poor Law, the municipal schemes became a major force behind the establishment of new state schemes. Towards the end of the period, however, municipal pensions were being replaced by the extension of national social insurance. The reduction following the 1960 enactment of the Disability Act would have been even greater were it not for the numerous municipal schemes for the disabled. Yet the decrease between 1960 and 1962, when the Act came into full effect, was substantial. In its 1962 report the department concluded that 'the marked decrease in the number receiving assistance over the last two years is first and foremost due to the introduction of the State Disability Pension as of January 1 1961.'[37] The establishment of other new schemes took large groups of clients directly out of social assistance. For example, with the enactment of the 1964 Child Care Act, 1,600 children were transferred from the

33. Sosialhjelpsstatistikk, 1966, p. 23.
34. See Chapter 3.
35. Forsorgsvesenet, 1950, p. 174.
36. Ibid.
37. Forsorgsvesenet, 1962, p. 5.

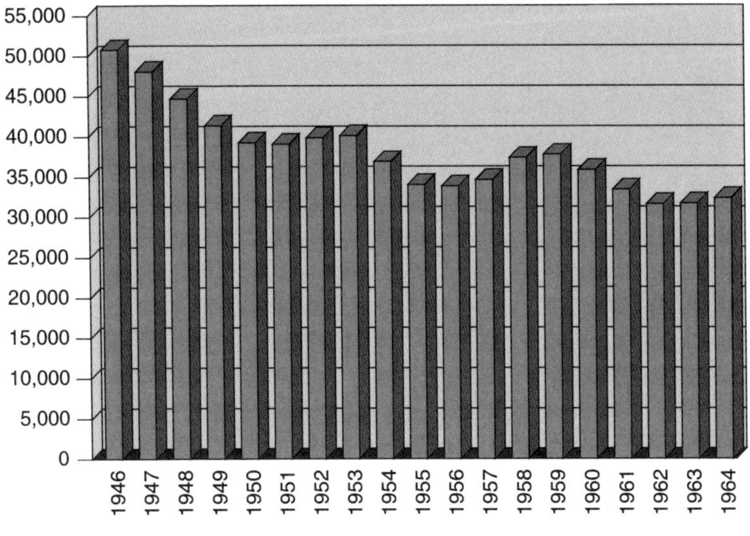

Figure 6.1. Heads of families receiving public assistance, 1946–1964. (Source: Historisk Statistikk, 1968, p. 578.)

responsibility of the assistance scheme. Moreover, the near-future outlook was for further reductions: a planned act covering social insurance for widows and mothers was expected to further reduce the number relying on assistance.[38]

The marked effect of the establishment of new legislation shows that alternative income maintenance schemes contributed greatly to the decrease in social assistance. Higher standards of living and minimal unemployment contributed in the same direction.

Without mentioning the changing composition of claimants, the above account indicates that the number of clients in need situations increasingly covered by social insurance formed a decreasing proportion of social assistance clients.

Because the departmental proposal will be seen to represent a shift away from social insurance thinking, it is of particular interest to see if this shift can be justified by changes in the nature of the targeted clientele. Traditionally, social assistance covers needs which occur in a limited

38. Seip 1994, p. 233.

time period. Social insurance, by contrast, is usually targeted at more permanent need situations. If one could document that typical insurance cases, such as the elderly and the disabled, constituted a decreasing proportion of the assistance clientele, the change of emphasis from 1953 to 1963 could be justified as a natural policy response. However, before 1966 no statistics were kept to break down the clientele according to need categories. I must therefore rely on my interpretation of the available statistics to find out if such a change actually occurred. By combining three variables in the statistics, I can get a picture of the clientele along these lines.

In the statistics I found the number of *new claimants* calculated for each year.[39] Immediately following the war there was a large increase in new claimants. This is explained by the high number of former 'Nazis and striped persons'.[40] Not surprisingly, these people had particular difficulties in finding work. The total number of new claimants remained fairly steady throughout the period. However, if we take into account the sharp decrease in the total number of assistance clients, we find that the new claimants constituted a growing proportion of the clientele; see Figure 6.2.

With the expansion of state and municipal social insurance, it was very unlikely that the assistance scheme would find its new 'recruits' in groups such as the elderly and the disabled. The stringent means test in insurance, whereby the poorest (i.e. potential assistance clients) were incorporated first, strengthens this interpretation.

The growing proportion of new claimants can therefore be seen as a sign of a shift in the nature of the clientele towards being less dominated by long-term need situations such as old age and chronic disability. The correlation between the decrease in the number of clients and the establishment of new insurance schemes supports such an interpretation.

In reviewing the 1953 proposal, I touched on the question of *rights of citizenship* in relation to the allocation of expenses among different municipalities. In the meagre statistics of the time, claimants from 'out of town' constituted one of the few specifications of the clientele. The statistics presented in Figure 6.3 give a further indication of the changing nature of the clientele in the period.

39. 'New claimants' are defined as those not having received benefits in the preceding five years.

40. Forsorgsvesenet, 1947, p. 350. The term 'striped' (*stripete*) refers to persons sympathising and/or collaborating with the occupying power.

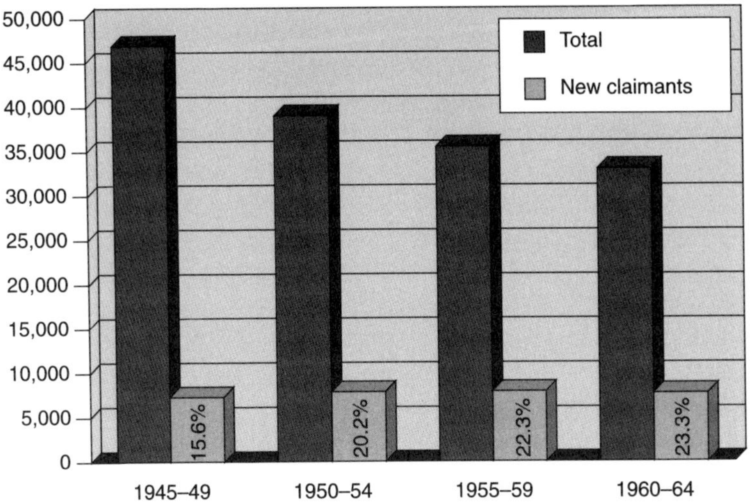

Figure 6.2. New claimants in relation to total numbers receiving assistance. Averages for given periods. (Based on material in Forsorgsstatistikk, 1964, p. 5.)

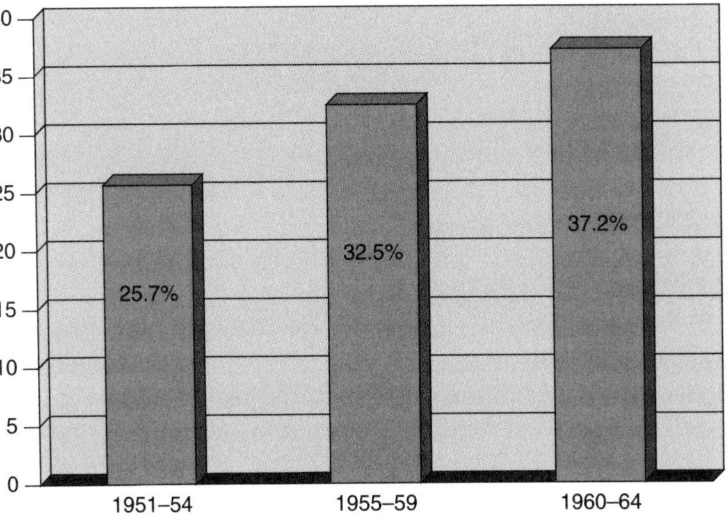

Figure 6.3. Numbers with right of citizenship in a municipality other than that where help was provided, as percentage of numbers receiving aid in their own community. Averages for given periods. (Based on material in Forsorgsstatistikk, 1951–64. Before 1951 the breakdown was not provided.)

The main reason for this increase, as the annual statistics repeatedly point out, was the greater mobility of the population. Inasmuch as different need categories differ with regard to mobility, this can also be seen as a shift in the composition of the clientele. We would, for example, expect elderly people and the disabled to be less 'on the move' than casual workers and people suffering from a combination of social problems, such as alcoholism, mental instability, and anti-social behaviour in general.

Starting in 1947 the statistics provide information on the relationship between 'decrease' and 'reduction', expressed in the term *gross decrease.*[41] In Figure 6.4 we see that the total number of individuals leaving the scheme increased. A great number of people leaving the scheme (decrease), in relation to the actual reduction in the number receiving assistance, can indicate increasing fluctuations in the clientele.

The fact that the gross decrease was larger than the overall reduction of the clientele is a further sign of increased fluctuations within the assistance population. In the annual statistics, the early post-war decreases are explained by the improved availability of work; with regard to the increase after 1950, new insurance schemes are often cited as the major cause.

In combination these three variables indicate a change in the composition of the clientele in this period: increasing numbers of new claimants, more people from 'out of town', and a gross decrease larger than the total reduction all point to a shift away from clients with long-term, unchanging need situations towards a more mobile, fluctuating clientele. As pensioners and disabled people tend to fall within the former category, this evidence suggests that the expansion of social insurance not only largely caused the reduction of assistance but also brought about a change in the composition of the clientele. By the early 1960s, therefore, assistance was less dominated by 'social insurance cases' than in the 1950s.

References made to the clientele in the two proposals

When the department in 1963 argued for a ten-year deliberate delay in presenting the proposal, it pointed to the 'expedience of implementing a

41. The gross decrease is calculated by subtracting the number of claimants in one year from the number in the preceding year, then adding the number of new claimants in the year. The result expresses the number of persons actually leaving the scheme in a particular year.

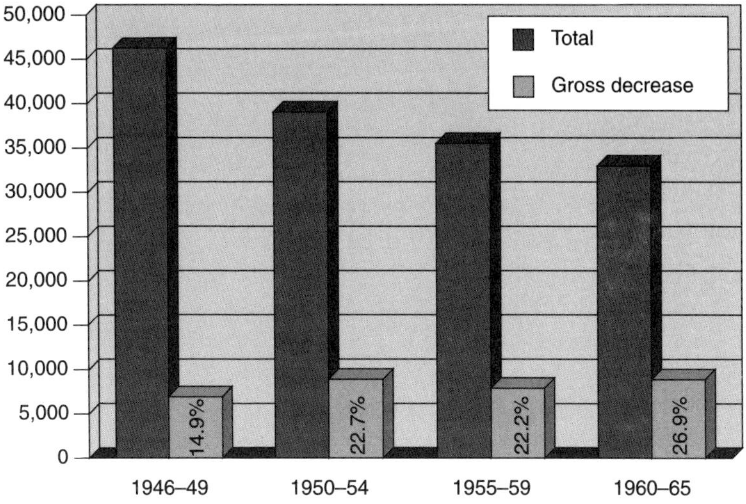

Figure 6.4. Gross decreases in relation to total numbers of claimants. Averages for given periods. (Based on material in Forsorgsstatistikk, 1947–65.)

number of social insurance schemes first'.[42] Thus, it continued, 'the Department, in contrast to the Committee, will be able to model its plan on the basis of a much more completed social insurance system. Naturally, this has resulted in a proposal diverging on many points from that of the Committee.'[43]

The statistical analysis presented above is based on material that was readily available to the policy-makers in 1963 as well as in 1953. It is surprising, therefore, that (with one exception) no reference to these figures is made in the proposals. If used, the material would have supported the department's interpretations. As this must have been known, we can only assume that the information was thought to be implicitly understood in the department's proposal. The only exception is an overview of the decrease in numbers since the Second World War in the 1953 plan.[44] Interestingly, the committee concluded that statistics breaking these numbers down did not exist. While the source referred to is

42. Ot.prp. nr. 56, 1962–63, p. 6. The most important of these was the Disability and Rehabilitation Act of 1960, but a number of other schemes also extended the coverage of social insurance during this period.

43. Ibid.

44. Utkast til lov om sosialhjelp, 1953, p. 38.

'Statistical Yearbook', the missing numbers could have been found in another report, also published by the Central Bureau of Statistics. This failure to use all the relevant statistical sources may be illustrative of the low priority given to this part of the project. By contrast, the complementary plans for social insurance employed detailed and thorough statistical material.

Referring to the lower numbers brought about by an advantageous expansion of the scope of social insurance, the committee concluded in 1953 that the main function of social assistance had been reduced to that of a 'safety valve for the needs cases which still do not come within the scope of insurance or where the help provided through insurance proves insufficient.'[45] It is significant that this realisation prompted the committee to recommend a scheme *as close to social insurance practice as possible.* Furthermore, this approach was adequate inasmuch as the clientele in 1953 was still strongly dominated by either recipients of insurance or groups for which insurance was generally accepted as desirable in the future.[46]

In its response the department pointed to the development of insurance in the period 1953–60 as the main reason why its 'proposal diverges from the Committee proposal on principal points.'[47] Still, it made no reference to how and to what extent the extension of social insurance had affected the scope of social assistance. It gave, however, a thorough account of what the department saw as 'the future need for social assistance.'[48] Because this was guided by 'what is left in spite of the expansion of the insurance system and remaining welfare schemes which has taken place',[49] I find it justifiable to see the following overview as an indication of how the department assessed the clientele at the time of writing.

As was the case in 1953, the scheme was defined in relation to social insurance. But while the committee used the complementary roles of the schemes to advocate a merging of the way needs were met, the department arrived at a contrasting conclusion from the same premises. As we shall see, the departmental proposal focused more on the differences

45. Ibid., p. 5.

46. Among the latter category, the disabled constituted the most important group.

47. Ot.prp. nr. 56, 1962–63, p. 6.

48. Ibid., p. 11.

49. Ibid.

between insurance and assistance. This is true both for the services and for the respective client groups. While I focus on the clientele in this section, I will return to the service in the following two sections.

The department categorised what it saw as the eight groups of clients, according to the cause of the need.[50]

a. Persons undergoing treatment for sickness, injury, or defect.
b. Persons who are permanently incapable of work.
c. Widows, divorcées, unwed mothers, and other women without means of support.
d. Elderly persons.
e. Unemployed persons.
f. Anti-social persons and psychopaths.
g. Vagrants.
h. Persons who have lost major assets as a result of accidents and the like.

Persons in categories a, c, d, and e were referred to uniformly as those whose full needs were not met by social insurance, for one reason or another. (In addition, social insurance did not yet cover certain categories of single parents.) Inasmuch as the department held out expectations of extended legislation to cover these groups in the near future, they were also referred to as 'social insurance cases'. This vague notion will become clearer, I hope, when I contrast the description of these groups with those in the remaining categories.

In the case of persons in category b (persons permanently incapable of work), the report makes an interesting distinction according to what caused the incapacity preventing work. Because the proposed Disability Pension covered only medical disabilities, substantial numbers were excluded from entitlement. The department also recognised that 'persons with only minor bodily disablements may have problems in obtaining sufficient incomes, for example when, in addition to the disability, they have an intellectual capability which is below average or are physically weak.'[51] Disabilities which are difficult to establish objectively, such as less serious neuroses and psychosomatic disorders, also fell outside the boundaries of disablement benefits. The department expected this group to form 'a substantial part of the clientele';[52] it was the only one for which ex-

50. Ot.prp. nr. 56, 1962–63, pp. 11–17.
51. Ibid., p. 13.
52. Ibid.

pectations about size were mentioned. Furthermore, the department expected such problems to increase in the years to come as a result of 'the work and living conditions in a modern urban industrial society'.[53] The strong distinction between physical and other causes of disability must be understood in the light of the proposed Disability Act, which was put forward simultaneously with the Social Assistance Act in 1960. Here the department further accentuated this distribution of responsibility between the two pieces of legislation.[54]

The other group which deserves particular attention in this analysis is that comprising those labelled 'anti-social persons and psychopaths' (category f). The proposal starts out by stating that 'numerically this group is perhaps not big, but each individual person represents an extremely difficult problem for his/her surroundings as well as for society as a whole.'[55] Thus, this group is discussed in the proposal in more detail than any of the others. 'Anti-social' is used as a collective term which includes the psychopaths: 'Characteristic of the psychopaths is precisely their antisocial attitude to life. They lack the ability to adjust to the prohibitions, demands and considerations – the entire system of norms – upon which an ordered society is based.'[56] The proposal goes on to expand on how this impairs their ability to live a normal life and, more important, to maintain themselves. While milieu is seen as the main reason for the problems of the group as a whole, psychopathy is also seen to be congenitally determined. The significance of this group will be further elucidated in the following two sections.

As we have seen, both proposals defined the purpose and the scope of the scheme in relation to existing and future social insurance. In 1953 the coexistence of the two schemes highlighted an important similarity: many of the claimants of assistance also received insurance. This led policy-makers to the conclusion that the two types of recipient should be treated in the same manner. A further reason for this decision may have been the knowledge that many of those dependent on social assistance, notably the disabled, were destined to enter future insurance schemes. Still, it is significant that the policy-makers concluded that all need categories covered by assistance deserved welfare similar to that enjoyed by

53. Ibid.
54. We will return to the relationship between the two proposals.
55. Ot.prp. nr. 56, 1962–63, p. 15.
56. Ibid.

social insurance recipients.

We must, then, consider whether the changes in the perception of the clientele as expressed in the 1963 proposal can be seen as a direct response to actual changes in the clientele. In 1963 the emphasis was on the difference between the two welfare institutions, despite the fact that a large proportion of assistance recipients were also receiving insurance benefits. (In 1966 this was true of half of those receiving assistance, and that proportion most probably was even greater when the proposal was being drafted in the early 1960s.) Still, my review of the statistics shows a move away from a dominance of 'insurance cases' in the years between the two proposals. The 1953 committee chose to stress equality – with insurance for all – because the need categories did not differ greatly; the department could have argued similarly, but did not. The disproportionate stress on some need categories over others according to an overview of the future need for assistance gives a first insight into the reasons why the emphasis was so different in 1963. The stress then was on need cases that were both outside insurance coverage and, most important, deliberately excluded from insurance. In the statement concerning category f ('anti-social persons and psychopaths') lies, in my view, the key to understanding the divergence. The scheme was targeted at, and designed around, a group which the department for specific reasons wanted to keep out of insurance. The 1953 scheme was designed according to the needs of the group then seen to be most dominant, and the same thing happened ten years later. But, for a variety of reasons, this had become a very different group, and thus the scheme also came to differ greatly. The changes cannot be explained by the changes in the clientele alone. To explain them I will first give an account of the nature of the proposed *services*. Later in the chapter I will turn to look at political and professional aspects outside the immediate proximity of the schemes in question, in order to see the development from a broader perspective.

Not surprisingly, changes both in the actual composition of the target group and with regard to which sections the reformers chose to emphasise came to have repercussions for the kind of services the policy-makers deemed suitable for the social assistance clientele.[57] In the following two sections, I will focus on how such changes can be traced in the two proposals.

57. This line of reasoning can, of course, be reversed in a 'chicken and egg' manner. We shall return to how changing ideas about servicing influenced the choice of groups to focus on.

Rights versus discretion

The use of means-testing in establishing entitlement to benefits follows from the subsidiary nature of social assistance. A means test may, however, be implemented in a variety of ways. The assessment of means can, for example, be carried out by evaluating the person's situation on the basis of a set of clearly defined rules. Alternatively, at the other end of the continuum, it may be entirely subject to the discretion of an official. If the latter is the case, the person's rights will be seen to be curtailed.[58] Both the 1953 and the 1963 proposal advocated a strong element of discretion in the schemes. They differed, however, with regard to the extent to which other measures should be taken to ensure the rights of the clients. These differences appear in the discussions on the questions of the right to appeal a decision, the extent to which clients are expected to repay benefits received, and the extent to which family members are made mutually bound to maintain each other.

The right to appeal[59]

I have already mentioned the significance of the wording of the first clause of the 1953 proposal.[60] Having chosen the term 'right to social assistance', the committee went on to discuss the extent to which this actually entails a right. In the sense that a right can be tested by a court

58. However, Pinker's notion of 'discretionary interpretation' in the case of a highly complex, rule-based system should be kept in mind. Beltram 1984, p. 35.

59. The differences between the two proposals have been inquired into by Terum (1987, 1996) and Andenæs (1992). While Terum stresses the differences with regard to entitlement, Andenæs argues that from a legal point of view the two proposals are not very different. I find both interpretations to be valid, and focus my comparison on the ideas expressed about the nature of discretionary assistance as compared with entitlement-based social insurance. Moreover, Terum (1996, p. 65) argues that the 1953 proposal manifested internal contradictions in the committees' proposals. On the one hand, they wanted to modernise assistance; on the other hand, they were not willing to legalise the scheme in the form of national standards. This argument presupposes that national scale rates were an option at the time. At this point, however, only Britain had introduced national scale rates, and this was made possible only by the full nationalisation of assistance. This was also the reaction of the local authorities when national scale rates were proposed for the first time in Norway in 1985 (Bernt 1989, p. 11). Only if the state paid the bill would the local authorities accept national rates. Such a nationalisation was not among the options in 1953.

60. See the section entitled 'The names of the schemes', earlier in this chapter.

of justice, the proposed scheme fell outside the definition. Therefore, to ensure the rights of the clients, the committee advocated the introduction of the right to appeal to a higher level of authority.[61] Again, social insurance was the yardstick against which assistance was measured: 'Because social assistance following the Committee's proposal will be made equal to social insurance, the right to appeal should be the same for the person claiming assistance and the insurance claimant.'[62]

While the right to appeal was extended beyond that of the existing Poor Law, the committee did not follow up its intention to make it equal to that of social insurance. The local board would be the first authority of appeal, and the ministry would be the second and last.

In the departmental response the tune changed, although the practical implications were similar. While the department approved of the right to appeal, it did not consider the two schemes to be of equal status: 'Social insurance is in a variety of ways fundamentally different from assistance. The social insurance schemes are a form of insurance designed to meet specific needs when certain established conditions exist.'[63] By contrast, 'assistance is based on an individual assessment with regard to need as well as with regard to the kind and extent of help provided.'[64]

This difference, the department felt, had to be kept in mind when deciding on the mode of appeal. The departmental proposal advocated substantial powers for the local Social Assistance Board as the first authority of appeal. The second tier was the regional commissioner. Arguing for this, the department stressed the desirability of choosing an appeal authority with 'the advantage of having personal contact with the applicant ... and of knowing his milieu and background.' This line of argument can be questioned on two points. First, with the way Norwegian social insurance was financed, the insurance (i.e. actuarial) aspect of the scheme was not much more than symbolic at the time.[65] Thus, both schemes were predominantly financed through general taxation. Also, like social assistance, social insurance entailed strong elements of discretion in the process of assessing need, for example in the case of disability benefits. Furthermore, it is difficult to see why there should be a lesser

61. Utkast til lov om sosialhjelp, 1953, p. 46.
62. Ibid.
63. Ot.prp. nr. 56, 1962–63, p. 52.
64. Ibid.
65. See Chapters 2 and 3.

need for a strong appeal authority in the case of a discretionary decision than in the case of a decision based on established rights. Surely the opposite priority could be argued. Second, the argument whereby a locally based appeal authority is preferred can be questioned. The other side of the coin of 'closeness' and 'personal knowledge' can be, in the case of a disadvantaged clientele claiming a stigmatised service, the experience of prejudice and negative attitudes. In the case of discretionary decisions concerning a clientele and a service of this kind, one could well argue the need for an appeal authority removed from the local community.

I will not claim that behind the argument lay a desire to actually curtail the right to appeal. However, the comparison with social insurance certainly indicates that the department was not willing to extend the right to the level of that scheme. And as the arguments are not convincing, an ulterior desire to limit the right is one possible explanation.

The duty to repay benefits

Since 1845 the Norwegian Poor Laws had included clauses regarding the duty of the recipient to repay benefits when he or she was able to.

Again, the committee's proposal in 1953 was influenced by the practice in social insurance. While social insurance is awarded without further conditions, 'assistance is regarded as a kind of loan or an advance to be repaid whenever possible.'[66] Arguing for a change, the committee stated that 'the reasons behind social assistance claims will in most cases be socially not very different from the causes behind social insurance claims. The principal rule should therefore be that social assistance benefits are not reclaimed.'[67]

The departmental response is another example of the turn away from insurance thinking. After first giving lukewarm support for a reduction in the practice of repayment, and thus the arguments behind this standpoint, it went on to argue for the introduction of loans as an alternative to grants in some cases.[68]

66. Utkast til lov om sosialhjelp, 1953, p. 24.
67. Ibid.
68. Ot.prp. nr. 56, 1962–63, p. 24.

Mutual responsibility of maintenance between family members

As I pointed out in the account of the 1953 proposal, the committee wanted to curtail this responsibility by replacing it with a system of warrants under separate legislation. The department supported the view of the committee on this point. But it also supported the view expressed by the Norwegian Social Welfare Association:[69] 'Even though the clauses on maintaining mutual responsibility to maintain have been abolished, one expects that the Social Assistance Board should consider the family situation when the question of aid arises. Such an approach becomes very important when assessing claims from old people living with well-paid, younger family members.'[70]

Geographical disparities

A fourth area which has bearing on the question of rights is that of geographical disparities in the awarding and measurement of benefits. Because social assistance in Norway is a municipal scheme, national legislation has proved to be insufficient to level out these dissimilarities.[71] While no attention was given to this problem in 1963, the 1953 proposal touched on it. Acknowledging that municipal self-determination might bring about social assistance 'of varying size and nature', the committee regarded this as 'to a great extent a natural consequence of the fact that natural, social and living conditions are very different in the various parts of the country.'[72] The fact that the report, here and in many other places, refers to municipal self-determination in highly positive terms makes me believe that its maintenance was given priority over the development of a uniform system. The somewhat naive statement above supports this conclusion. It is therefore not just through the wisdom of hindsight that I consider the problem of geographical disparity to have been deliberately played down.

---

69. Norges Sosialforbund, a subgroup within the national confederation of local authorities, concerned with social matters.

70. Ot.prp. nr. 56, 1962–63, p. 28.

71. Terum (1986) has carried out a survey showing strong disparities between municipalities.

72. Utkast til lov om sosialhjelp, 1953, p. 20.

Ten years later the department abstained from considering the problem. This was in itself a statement of priority.

Money and social work: A changing relationship

When I analysed the changing perception of the clientele, we saw a move towards focusing on those seen to be in need of more than income maintenance only. As we saw above, this change was reflected in a corresponding move away from rights towards greater stress on discretionary decisions. In this section we will look at the way in which this changing policy was put into practice. Both proposals considered the role of the Social Assistance Board in providing an advice and counselling service in combination with allocating cash and in-kind services. However, the suggestions regarding how the advice and counselling service should be implemented and what role it should play in relation to the other services differed greatly in the two proposals. It is in this area, I feel, that the differences between the sociopolitical approaches of the two proposals become most evident.

Assistance versus advice and counselling

In 1953 one of the reasons given for the change of name was the role given to advice and counselling. Clause 2 in the committee's proposal warrants this function of the law: 'The Social Assistance Board gives advice and counselling or provides other assistance to those who ask for it in order to obtain means for their maintenance.'[73] Compared with the existing law, this clause represented an extension. To stress this difference, the committee pointed out that 'the Board is supposed to give advice in all matters of a social nature.'[74]

When the committee's proposal is compared with the departmental response, however, what becomes important is the limitation expressed in the (1953) wording 'in order to obtain means for their maintenance'. I see this specification in the committee's plan as yet another attempt to steer the legislation towards income maintenance exclusively. The department felt, however, that clause 2 of the committee's proposal limited the scope of advice, not only to economic questions, but further to

73. Ibid., p. 52.
74. Ibid., p. 16.

economic questions regarding social assistance only. While the more general limitation follows from the committee's proposal, what the department saw as a limitation to only those questions dealing with assistance cannot be traced in the document. The main point is, however, that the department wished to extend advice to 'anybody who is in a position where he is in need of such assistance'.[75]

The department specified that this service should therefore be made available also to those who have problems 'of a more personal nature'.[76] A further sign of this changing priority of services is that while the 1953 proposal warranted material aid in the first clause and advice/counselling in the second, the order was the opposite in the department's proposal.

In the change towards focusing on advice and counselling, the allocation of material aid was also given a new function: 'Social assistance will first and foremost be awarded as a means to self-help, while assistance [as it was at the time] has been given as a means to maintenance.'[77] Behind this change of phrasing lay a stress on the virtues of paid work, not only as a source of maintenance, but also as a means of fostering self-reliance: 'The purpose of the various forms of assistance should not only be the more negative aspect of avoiding material need, but first and foremost the more positive end of enabling the individual to maintain himself and his family by his own means. Only when this has been attempted should more permanent assistance be considered.'[78]

In justifying the greater resources needed for this approach, the department argued that, in the long run, making clients self-reliant would be cost-effective.[79] We shall return to the optimism regarding rehabilitation that gave rise to this line of argument.

Social work and money

Naturally, the new focus on advice and counselling put different and increased demands on the workers who were to implement the scheme. As it was, social workers were singled out as the profession to fill the posts of officers in the social services. Thus, in the years that followed the enact-

75. Ot.prp. nr. 56, 1962–63, p. 20.
76. Ibid.
77. Ibid., p. 55.
78. Ibid., p. 6.
79. Ibid., p. 55.

ment of the law, we saw a dramatic growth in the number of social workers employed by local authorities.[80] Social workers were increasingly engaged in the combined role of allocating money to social assistance clients and at the same time carrying out the advice and counselling functions which came to be known as 'social treatment'.

Therefore, the Norwegian Social Welfare Association expressed in a statement to the committee the need for 'increased demands on the worker's education and experience'.[81] This was in line with the department's recommendation when it for the first time introduced the notion of 'social treatment' into social assistance. In the first instance, according to the departmental proposal, the client should be helped with advice and counselling. When this proves insufficient, it goes on, the workers should employ 'social treatment with the aim of reaching solutions which can give the individual client the ability to conduct life harmoniously and achieve a good relationship to family and society at large.'[82] This reduced economic aid to a last resort, 'only to be used after the present possibilities of making the client self-sufficient have been investigated and considered, and possibly in combination with social treatment.'[83]

In the proposal the term 'social treatment' is not further elucidated. In a statement printed in the proposal, the Norwegian Association of Social Workers gives its opinion of what 'social treatment' should consist of. It starts from the assumption that 'just about every social assistance client' will be in a situation where the feelings of inadequacy and failure dominate their perception of themselves. In the association's opinion only trained persons can avoid the danger of meeting such clients with 'moralistic attitudes and pressure'. Such attitudes would, it maintains, 'further increase negativity and defensive behaviour'. By contrast, 'the aim of social treatment is to enhance the client's self-esteem so that some of the defences can be abandoned for the benefit of a more constructive use of energy.'[84]

80. Terum 1982, p. 34.
81. Ot.prp. nr. 56, 1962–63, p. 21.
82. Ibid., p. 5.
83. Ibid., p. 19.
84. Ibid., p. 21.

The administration of the scheme

The administration of social assistance consists of two bodies. While the elected Social Board has the overall responsibility for the services, the daily running of the scheme is carried out by social service offices. In 1960, however, only 29% of Norwegian municipalities had established such offices.[85] In the countryside this percentage was even lower. In the 1953 proposal no attention was given to the need for the establishment of staffed administrations throughout the country. While there was a big dispute about the role of the board, the need for an expansion in the number of offices was generally agreed on in the responses to the departmental proposal. It was understood that the implementation of the scheme depended on the existence of social service offices for clients to approach in order to make use of the proposed services. Thus, the department proposed that all municipalities with more than 3,000 inhabitants should have established offices after a transitionary period. Also, the state would allocate money to cover part of the cost of employing a professional head in each office.[86] The department felt that the leader of each office should hold a qualification as a professional social worker.

The 1964 Social Care Act

According to the Act each municipality was obliged to elect a Social Board. This board, wrote Kluge in 1973, 'coordinates the administration of the social services, carries out social planning and provides general social services and help to individuals.'[87] To carry out the daily running of the services, each municipality was obliged to provide a Social Service Department, with the head of the office preferably holding a professional social work qualification. The social services offered two main forms of aid. According to clause 2,

> The Social Board gives information, advice and guidance to those who need such help either to become self-supporting or to overcome or adapt to a difficult condition of life.

85. Terum 1982, p. 33.
86. Ot.prp. nr. 56, 1962–63, pp. 50, 51.
87. Kluge 1973, p. 80. A new Social Assistance Act was enacted in 1991.

When the above course had been tried, clause 3 of the Act gave the board powers to supply the individual with material assistance:

> For those who are unable to secure their own income or who are unable to care for themselves, social aid may be provided in the following forms:
>
> a. Loan, guarantee for loans or contributions towards professional/vocational training, to start a business or towards different forms of assistance aimed at making the individual self-supporting.
> b. Paid work in a workhouse or in a sheltered workshop, where the client may or may not be residing.
> c. Stay in an old age home, nursing home or other appropriate institution.
> d. Private care (care in the family).
> e. Contributions or, in exceptional circumstances, loans towards maintenance.
> f. Loans or contributions towards other ends than those listed under letters a–e, to the extent that this is considered necessary.[88]

The politics of social policy

So far in this analysis I have not strayed far from the immediate proximity of the actual service in attempting to explain its development. Only in the case of the changing clientele have I touched on factors outside of the issues raised by the two proposals. Social policies are, however, the outcome of the interplay of many factors. Some of these do, at first sight, seem irrelevant to the development in question. An analysis restricted to a strict 'service orientation' can, however, easily overlook outside factors which contribute to, or perhaps even determine, the direction of a particular policy. In this section the focus will be on factors of this kind.

By extending the scope in this way, I hope to cast light on two questions, both of which are crucial to the understanding of the policy development outlined in this chapter. The first concerns the fate of the 1953 proposal. In normal procedure the committee's proposal would have been followed by a departmental response within a year. As a result of political responses to the committee's proposal, the departmental plan would typ-

88. Lov om sosial omsorg (Social Care Act), 1964.

ically differs on some points.[89] In this particular case the committee's plan was shelved for seven years. When the departmental response finally emerged, it proposed a scheme significantly different from that of the committee. The inactivity, in 1953 and in the following seven years, probably had a decisive impact on the development of social assistance in Norway. We must therefore attempt to understand the causes of this delay. The second question concerns the nature of the departmental proposal and, subsequently, the scheme enacted in 1964. The change away from 'insurance thinking' and towards social care and social treatment needs further elucidation. As we have seen, a changing clientele is only a contributory, and not a sufficient, explanation of this change.

To cast light on these questions, I was fortunate enough to meet four policy-makers who played key roles in the period. By centring the analysis in this section on these interviews, I also express the importance of individual social reformers in the shaping of policies.

The fate of the 1953 plan

In 1953 Rakel Seweriin began her term as the Norwegian minister of social affairs, holding this position for nearly two years. The timing is important. She took office in the third year of what turned out to be an interlude in the post-war reign of Einar Gerhardsen.[90] She served the last half-year of her term after he returned to office in January 1955. In February 1953 she received the proposal from the committee. When asked why she had failed to embark on preparing the departmental response, she stressed that she had feared resistance from the temperance movement.[91] In the first year of her term she had tried to enact a new intoxicant law, but felt forced to withdraw the proposal because of pressure from the temperance movement. There is no apparent evidence to explain why this movement should have objected to the proposal. (The

89. Usually the divergence between the two proposals relates to minor points only. This is due to the Norwegian tradition of composing a committee in a way which ensures the representation of the entire party-political spectrum as well as the interest groups affected by the legislation. Arntzen and Knutsen 1980, p. 63.

90. Einar Gerhardsen was prime minister of Norway in the periods 1945–51, 1955–63, and 1963–65.

91. At the time one-third of the members of the Storting belonged to this movement. The support did not follow party-political divisions. It was therefore both a strong and an unpredictable political force.

resistance might, however, become clearer when we later look at the movement's reactions to the proposal presented in 1960. What does become clear then is that there were no objections to the major points differentiating the two proposals.) One possible explanation for the delay would be a divided committee, unable to reach a consensus on the recommendations to be made. This was, however, not the case. Except for sustained disagreement from one member regarding all the points that involved a liberalisation of the scheme compared with the Poor Law, the committee appeared to be in full agreement about the central proposals.[92] I therefore turn to the role of the minister herself in the search for possible explanations for the delay.

Seweriin described the difficult relationship she had with Gerhardsen: 'I had a feeling that I would have to leave my post when Einar Gerhardsen returned to office.'[93] Soon after his return he offered her a position as a consultative minister with responsibility for 'family and consumer matters' in exchange for her ministerial post. Naturally, she considered this a demotion and never took on the job. When she finally left the department in the summer of 1955, she was 'relieved to be freed from the whole thing.'[94] With some bitterness she recalled that her suspicions of lacking support and trust from the prime minister were confirmed a few years later: 'In a radio interview I later heard Gudmund Harlem[95] say that he and Gerhardsen planned the future social policy in Gerhardsen's cottage in 1953.'[96] This was at a time when Gerhardsen was not the prime minister and *she* was the minister of social affairs. The secretary of the Labour Party, Haakon Lie, confirmed my interpretation that Seweriin was ruling with limited powers. While she had been given the post as 'a faithful servant', Gerhardsen replaced her to achieve more momentum in the ministry.[97] I am therefore left with the impression that the perceived lack of political support from the prime minister, together with the expected resistance from the temperance movement, largely explains

92. Esther Samuelsen joined the committee following the death of one of its appointed members.

93. Seweriin, pers. com. 14 August 1987. I interviewed her in her home.

94. Ibid.

95. Gudmund Harlem replaced her as minister in July 1955.

96. Seweriin, pers. com. 1987 (see note 93).

97. Haakon Lie is a former political secretary of the Labour Party. He is widely considered to be a very influential person in the party. I interviewed him in his home on 6 October 1995.

Seweriin's inability to act. However, as this interpretation depends on the recollections of a politician, then under great strain, trying to explain her inaction more than thirty years later, one should not exclude the possibility of an aberration of memory: The strong reaction of the temperance movement came later, with the plan to abolish the Sobriety Board in the 1960 proposal. While the committee's mandate included considering the question of administration, the proposal did not entail a recommendation to dissolve the Sobriety Board. The fact remains, though, that Seweriin's inability to carry the law through to enactment was the cause of the first postponement in this legislative process.

This does not, however, explain why the same proposal was shelved for seven years. To cast light on the fate of the 1953 plan, I now turn to the role of the minister who succeeded Seweriin in 1955.

The changing role and nature of social assistance, 1955–1964

The first post in Gudmund Harlem's long career as a cabinet member was that of minister for social affairs in the years 1955 to 1961. Thus, he was the person responsible for both the continued postponement in submitting a departmental response and the form this response took in 1960. Harlem's previous career is also important to this analysis. A trained physician, he spent 1946 in Britain studying the ongoing rehabilitation of war victims. In 1953 he became the first director of the newly established State Rehabilitation Institute.[98] Through his experience in Britain and his pioneering work for the institute, he became the standard-bearer for the campaign for rehabilitation in Norwegian medicine and, subsequently, the campaign for income maintenance. Underlying his faith in rehabilitation was a strong belief in the virtues of the work ethic: 'A person must be in paid employment if we expect him or her to function in society – this was such a strong conviction for me.'[99]

When he stressed *paid* work, he limited the significance of this to the West: 'I was therefore very puzzled by the British upper class. They seemed to function well in their lifestyle of idleness. I can only understand

98. Statens Attføringsinstitutt.

99. Harlem, pers. com. August 1987. I interviewed him in his office, where he was still working as a physician. He died later that year.

this to be a function of their great stress on hobbies – a good example is Charles Darwin.'[100]

The man who took over the Department of Social Affairs was thus a person who stressed the virtues of work. He also felt he had the means to enable many of those excluded from the workforce to enter or re-enter it. From the outset his rehabilitation plans were targeted at the physically sick and disabled. Therefore, the introduction of a long-awaited Disability Act became his first priority. A central element in this scheme was a rehabilitation allowance, which provided people with secure income maintenance while undergoing medical rehabilitation or professional (re)training. Only after one of the two had been attempted would a disability pension be considered.[101]

Only in relation to the above scheme did social assistance become interesting to Harlem. Thus, he explained the 1953–60 delay in the following way: 'I knew that Rakel [Seweriin] was aware of the potential resistance from the temperance movement. Personally, though, I wasn't very interested in doing anything with the Social Assistance Act before the Disability Act was ready to be submitted.'[102] The 1955–60 delay was therefore a result of priority not being given to the scheme. When the first departmental proposal was submitted in 1960, the timing as well as the nature of the assistance scheme reflected the development of services for the disabled. In the Green Paper for the latter scheme, which was presented to the Storting in 1960, the interconnection between the two schemes became apparent. In defining the kind of disabilities which were to be covered by the scheme, the department stated as follows:

> The definition covers all permanent or serious *medical* disabilities, organic as well as mental disease. Occupational disability caused by alcoholism, psychopathic constitution and similar problems fall, on the other hand, outside the scope of the scheme. Persons with problems of this kind will be helped by particular measures in a separate act on social assistance.[103]

This illustrates the fact that only when it was needed as a functional appendage to the implementation of a social insurance scheme did assistance become interesting to the minister. This raises interesting questions

100. Ibid.
101. Innst.O VIII, 1959–60, p. 2.
102. Harlem, pers. com. 1987 (see note 99).
103. Innst.O VIII, 1959–60, p. 3.

about the department's, and in particular Harlem's, perception of and attitude towards the assistance clientele. We know that the social assistance scheme, as proposed by his department, was very much geared towards 'treatment'. It is therefore valid to ask why the disability definition was not extended to include problems of a psychosomatic or social nature. While a rights-based and secure income maintenance service for those undergoing rehabilitation was seen to be essential in the case of the medically disabled, Harlem felt that the problems of the social assistance clientele called for a different approach: 'To give, for example, an alcoholic automatic income maintenance would be to further disable him, actually worsening his problem by giving him money to drink.'[104]

As we have seen, the department proposed a scheme very much targeted at dealing with the type of problems described above. I therefore see three possible interpretations of the department's perception of the clientele. One possibility is that it saw the clientele as consisting of a variety of problem categories, some requiring advice and counselling, others needing only income maintenance. If this was the perception, the stress on counselling and advice in the proposal can be seen as a deliberate prioritising of that part of the service, perhaps because this was seen to impose on the social services the greatest managerial challenges for the future. The second interpretation is that the department considered social assistance clients as being in need of advice and counselling *because* they were social assistance clients. If this was the case, a focus on counselling and advice would be a functional response to the problems the service was expected to deal with. The third interpretation is that the department felt it had the means (social work) to carry out social treatment. If this is true, it can be argued that the focus on social maladjustment resulted from a situation in which a solution was in search of a problem.

Inasmuch as Harlem's views can be seen as representative of those of the department at the time, his response to this line of reasoning should provide some insight into the prevailing perception of the clientele. In the interview I asked him if he at the time considered all social assistance clients as being in need of more than income maintenance alone. 'Sure, that's how I saw them' was his reply. He went on to substantiate this position by referring to a research project that he carried out in Oslo in 1945. By studying assistance clients he had come to understand that the

104. Harlem, pers. com. 1987 (see note 99).

inability to maintain themselves was not the real problem: 'This was only the expression of a deficiency. By giving money to the client this deficiency is maintained rather than dealt with – as long as you have the deficiency you also receive money.'[105] With Harlem's emphasis on social work in mind, we cannot, however, exclude the possibility that his interpretation was influenced by the aforementioned 'solution seeking a problem' syndrome.

This evidence supports the impression I got from reading the departmental plan. The policy-makers focused primarily on those clients for whom financial dependence was not believed to be the underlying problem, but merely a symptom of other deficiencies. Furthermore, the interview cast light on the way in which this perception manifested itself in the recommendations for the scheme. When we discussed the element of control in the scheme, Harlem again referred to experiences at the Rehabilitation Institute: 'We sometimes had the consent of the social security office to enable us to hold back money in case the clients didn't want to work. After a lot of hostility while the treatment lasted, we would afterwards receive letters expressing gratitude – "You were real devils, but God am I thankful now!" We had literally forced these people back onto their own feet.'[106] This prompted me to ask whether he saw the local social services as ideally some kind of 'social rehabilitation institute'. His reply: 'Yes, that's true. I also wondered what difference it made that we [the Rehabilitation Institute] were able to keep the clients in the house, and create a milieu, employing milieu-therapeutic methods.'[107] I feel justified in saying that behind the comparison lurks the workhouse.

Harlem expanded further on the relationship between social assistance and disability benefits. In his view, 'social assistance was a much better service than a disability pension which offered only income maintenance.' Furthermore, he claimed, this should also have had repercussions for the way complaints were to be dealt with: 'We dreamt about creating a true social rehabilitation system. Hence, there would be no need for an extensive appeal system; closeness to the problem was the key thing.'[108] Although he considered assistance to be a better service, social insurance was clearly given greater priority in the ongoing planning: 'We first

105. Ibid.
106. Ibid.
107. Ibid.
108. Ibid.

needed to find a solution to the problem of a new disability scheme; only then could we turn our attention to social assistance. In fact, we planned the entire assistance scheme on a one-day study trip to Sweden. By the end of that day we had decided the main features of the scheme – this must have been a record in speedy policy planning.'[109]

In 1960, then, two proposals were submitted, one for a Social Care Act and one for a Disability and Rehabilitation Act. Harlem was forced to withdraw the assistance scheme because of opposition from the temperance movement. As a consequence of the need for co-ordination, a new assistance board would take over many of the functions of the existing Sobriety Board and in effect make the latter subordinate to the main board. This caused a delay of two years in which a new committee was working to find a compromise on the question of administration. This was a blow for Harlem, because without the assistance element he could not implement a comprehensive rehabilitation system. Again, therefore, assistance was seen mainly as a functional addition to insurance, designed to cover the need cases which were deemed difficult to incorporate into – or deliberately keep out of – insurance.

It is significant that Harlem's optimism regarding rehabilitation extended beyond the need categories which he wanted to have covered by social insurance. The key difference is that in the case of assistance, money should not be allocated other than as a *component* of the overall treatment of the client. The above quotes regarding Harlem's evaluation of his findings in Oslo in 1945 illustrate his view that if only the 'deficiency' were eliminated, the client could become independent of public support. By contrast, in the case of, for example, medical rehabilitation, income maintenance and treatment were treated as two separate functions.

The role of social casework

In the review of the 1963 proposal we saw that social casework was given a prominent role in the scheme. This emphasis can be seen to have had one of two functions. I argued above that the new development in social casework provided new methods through which people suffering

109. Harlem, Kringlebotten, and Lund spent one day in Sweden to study the new assistance scheme being introduced there, which was along the same lines as the subsequent Norwegian scheme.

from social problems could be helped. If this was the starting point, the 1963 scheme can be seen as a legislative response to new methodology.

Alternatively, social casework can be viewed as a functional means towards an end stretching beyond the limits of social assistance. After studying the birth of the 1960–63 proposals in the light of social insurance plans and development, I feel that the latter interpretation is the more convincing of the two. (That is not to say, however, that the two are mutually exclusive.) Following this line of reasoning, social casework was the means by which Harlem could extend rehabilitation to embrace assistance clientele.

Responses to the 1960 departmental proposal

Given the divergence between the committee's plan and the departmental proposal, it was not surprising that the latter was subject to some political debate. We will therefore look briefly at the reception it received.

Bernt H. Lund, a central figure in the policy process in the period, pointed out a political manoeuvre that gives a clear indication of, first, the department's awareness of the magnitude of the changes and, second, the political controversy this might have been expected to cause: 'To present a departmental proposal to a public "hearing" is a breach of departmental custom.'[110] Usually the appointed committee would be in charge of obtaining statements from involved parties. In this case the department chose to take 'a second round' (by arranging a 'hearing' on the departmental proposal) – a move Lund saw as a way of avoiding the delay involved in appointing a new committee. The drastic changes in the departmental proposal compared with that of the committee, rather than the seven-year delay in itself, forced the department to carry out this unusual manoeuvre.

The 'hearing' resulted in fierce opposition, and the proposal had to be withdrawn. The temperance movement's objections to the declining powers of the Sobriety Board caused a further four-year delay in the legislative process. Kluge argues that the consolidation of the various boards

110. Lund, pers. com. August 1987. Harlem recruited Lund to study social work education in the United States and Canada in 1957. He later played a key role in the development of professional social work in Norway. 'Hearings' involve submitting drafts and proposals to those whose interests will be affected, asking for their opinions before final decisions are made. Arntzen and Knutsen 1980, p. 64.

into one joint board for social issues marks the major point of divergence between the committee's and the department's proposal.[111] Although this feature involved a major restructuring of the administration of the scheme, I disagree with Kluge's assessment on two counts. First, the 'Social Board' as proposed in 1953 was seen even then as a first step towards a co-ordination of the social services similar to what was taking place in Denmark at the time.[112] Second, I will argue that the changes I have analysed along the 'income maintenance versus social care' continuum signify a greater departure than those in the administration of the scheme.[113] The fact that this issue came to dominate the debate was more a result of the political power of the temperance movement and its opposition, based on moralistic ideas of what people need, than a reflection of its actual significance. By arousing a heated debate, the movement managed to dominate the political agenda. It is, of course, speculative to claim that, without the opposition of the temperance movement, other, more substantive issues could have entered the debate. As it was, however, the discussion in the Storting in May 1964 of the second departmental proposal entirely lacked stress on the major changes outlined above.[114]

Except for some last attempts by the temperance movement to stall the enactment, the parliamentary debate was highly consensual. The representatives from the various parties vied against each other in their praise of the scheme; Andreas Wormdahl of the Labour Party summed it up as a 'programme for human well-being'.[115] By employing social treatment, the law went further than to ensure income maintenance: 'This treatment is needed to give the individual client a harmonious pattern of life and a good relationship with family and society at large.'[116] Egil Aarvik,

111. Kluge 1973, p. 77.

112. Utkast til lov om sosialhjelp, 1953, p. 59. In Denmark the government gave the new 'Social Board' the responsibility of administering all municipal social services, thereby going even further than what was proposed in Norway in 1960.

113. This is not to say that I ignore the significance of the administrative changes for the then ongoing struggle concerning the distribution of powers between laypeople (elected boards) and professionals as represented by social services staff (Terum 1982, pp. 35–38).

114. The 1964 Act has been described as 'an act of compromise' (Kluge 1973, p. 78) because of the amendments instigated by the temperance movement. In the final version, the Sobriety Board was retained together with the Child Care Board.

115. Stortingsforhandlinger, 22 May 1964, p. 501.

116. Forhandlinger i Odelstinget nr. 63, 1964, pp. 501–2.

the chairman of the Storting's Social Committee, felt that ' "social care" is a beautiful phrase. It is genuinely different being subject to care and being left to others' assistance.'[117] Referring to the difference between insurance and assistance as regards the client's rights, the minister of social affairs, Olav Gjaerevoll, summed up the debate by stating, 'It is the spirit of the Act which is important and not the letter.'[118]

Conclusions

Norwegian social assistance underwent great changes during the first two decades of the post-war period. Due to increased prosperity and, more important, extensions and improvements of the social insurance system, a declining proportion of the population remained dependent on social assistance. In this process the composition of the clientele changed from being dominated by the elderly and the disabled to consist increasingly of 'remaining categories', that is, people suffering from problems not covered by social insurance.

However significant, the above changes did not in themselves justify the difference between the original 1953 proposal for a new social assistance scheme and the scheme ultimately implemented in 1964. The first plan for a replacement of the existing Poor Law was heavily influenced by 'insurance thinking' and aimed to give the clients extensive rights to a service aimed at ensuring their income maintenance. By contrast, the scheme which was finally enacted in 1964 was heavily influenced by social-casework ideology. From a comparative perspective, the weaving together of this kind of social work and the allocation of money for the clients' income maintenance represented the most significant trait of the new scheme.

I conclude that there were three factors contributing to the stress on treatment in the scheme that was eventually enacted. First, the period was characterised by strong optimism regarding the possibilities of rehabilitating into the workforce people suffering from various problems preventing them from maintaining themselves. Second, the development of social casework made it possible to rehabilitate people suffering from social problems. Third, the proposed rehabilitation measures were sup-

117. Forhandlinger i Odelstinget nr. 64, 1964, p. 508.
118. Ibid., p. 519.

ported by the (mistaken) belief that all clients were in need of social treatment. From this perspective, therefore, income maintenance alone was not only seen as inadequate but also seen to have a cementing effect on the clients' problems.

Of the above factors I consider the 'perception of the clientele' to be the most important. This prompts an analogy with the perception underlying the proposal for a new Poor Law in Britain in 1834. As the Webbs have pointed out, 'the architects of the 1834 act had never intended to subject the non-ablebodied to the full rigours of less eligibility; their mistake had been to assume that most paupers were able-bodied when in fact the majority of workhouse inmates were children or sick, disabled or elderly people.'[119] It was in full accordance with prevailing liberal ideology to label as many paupers as possible as able-bodied. I do not find it surprising that this way of thinking coloured the policy-makers' perception of the clientele. Juxtaposing this with the situation in Norway 130 years on, one similarity and one difference emerge. In both cases the perception of the clientele coincided not only with what the reformers wanted to see but also with what was best suited to the available remedies. The difference is equally striking. While the poor relief clients in 1834 were uniformly seen to be able-bodied, the opposite was the case in Norway in 1960. In both cases, however, I feel that objectives other than catering for the needs of the clients determined the services they were offered.

119. Pinker 1987, p. 1185.

Chapter 7
Cash and Care in the Norwegian Social Services

In the previous chapter I focused on the legislative process leading up to the enactment of the Norwegian 1964 Social Care Act. I will now turn to a study of some aspects of the institution responsible for implementing this scheme. While in Britain the income maintenance component is separated from the personal social services, in Norway the latter covers both functions. Thus, *social assistance is synonymous with personal social services in Norway.*

The chapter consists of two main sections. First I will look at how the local authority social services developed during this period. The focus will be on the process leading up to the administrative changes introduced with the 1964 legislation. Here I will attempt to analyse how and why social workers were given such an instrumental role in the implementation of the new scheme. In the second section the focus will be on the role of social workers in the personal social services after 1964.

Social assistance: From poor relief to social care

Social services under the Poor Law

As pointed out previously, the Norwegian Poor Law remained largely unchanged until its abolition in 1964. The main features of the administration of the scheme can be summed up in four points:

1. Based locally: Both the funding and the administration of the scheme were the responsibility of the local authority.
2. Dominated by laypeople. Throughout the period only a small minority of local authorities provided staffed social services.[1] Both the

1. Seip (1994) shows that in the 1930s the larger cities had already started to employ paid staff in the administration of poor relief.

assessment of need and the administrative decision-making were therefore in most cases the sole responsibility of the politically elected Poor Board.[2] The 1900 Poor Law gave instructions regarding the composition of the board; it was to consist of a vicar and as many members as the local council found appropriate.[3] It was the responsibility of each local authority to draft a plan for the Poor Law services. Some communities adopted the Elberfeld system, whereby each member of the Poor Board was allocated a number of paupers for whom he or she was made responsible. In such cases the plan often contained instructions urging the commissioner to be firm and exhort individual paupers to provide for their own income maintenance.[4]

3. Fragmented administration: With no staffed administration there was little coherence in the local authority social services. Sobriety work and child care were administered by separate boards.[5]
4. Emphasis on cash relief and benefits in kind: Although some local boards took on the task of attempting to 'reform' the poor by means of force or by setting a good example, the main function of the scheme was to offer a last-resort cash-or-kind benefit system.[6]

Professionally staffed SSDs: Departmental policy in its own right or (unintended) by-product of a political compromise?[7]

In this section I will discuss how and why social workers (in SSDs) were given a prominent role in the implementation of the 1964 Social Care Act.

As we saw in the previous chapter, the department presented two proposals, one in 1960 and one in 1963. While the 1960 proposal introduced the notion of 'social treatment', it did not expand on *who should implement it.* Only in the 1963 proposal were professionally staffed SSDs brought to the forefront. I will therefore begin the analysis by outlining

2. Norwegian: fattigstyre. (The name was changed to forsorgsstyre in 1948.)
3. Kluge 1973, p. 56.
4. Ibid., p. 57.
5. Before the enactment of the 1953 Child Care Act, the fragmentation was even greater, as child care was split between three boards. Ibid., p. 76.
6. The 1900 Poor Law did not distinguish clearly between cash benefits and benefits in kind. Clause 43 listed the different forms of help only in relation to where the pauper was being supported – in the home or in an institution.
7. I choose to use the British term Social Service Department (SSD).

the political/legislative developments in the period between the presentations of these two proposals.

The significance of the 1962 Report on the Reorganisation of Municipal Social Administration[8]

As we saw in the previous chapter, the 1960 departmental proposal had to be withdrawn due to strong resistance from the temperance movement. The movement objected to the proposed abolition of the Temperance Board. Its members realised they could stop the proposed legislation from being enacted by the Storting.[9] To find an acceptable compromise the department then established a commission to 'discuss the matter and present recommendations'.[10] In its terms of reference the commission was asked to 'find a solution which considered the municipality's need for the most efficient administration possible, the demands for further development of the quality and efficiency of social work, as well as the needs for quality and efficiency in the information service and casework aimed at the prevention and treatment of problems caused by alcohol.'[11]

Because the need for staffed administration and the professional qualifications of the staff were not discussed in the 1960 proposal, 'administration' in effect referred only to the work carried out by the members of the elected boards. The only reference made to such services is found in a clause stating, 'The local council *may* decide that the activities of the Social Care Board are to be administered by a social service department headed by a civil servant.'[12] As there was no exposition supporting this clause in the proposal, this statement is more likely a reflection of the fact that some municipalities had established such departments, rather than an expression of a desired area of growth.

---

8. Norwegian: Innstilling om omorganisering av kommunenes sosiale administrasjon. The committee was established in 1960 and presented its findings and recommendations on 23 January 1962. (I will refer to it in the text as the 1962 committee.)

9. Gudmund Harlem, from my interview in August 1987.

10. Innst. O VIII, 1959–60, p. 5.

11. Ibid.

12. Foreløpig utkast til Ot.prp. om lov om sosial omsorg (Preliminary proposal for Social Care Act), 1960, p. 122; emphasis added. The Social Care Board (sosialstyre) replaced the Poor Board (fattigstyre) with the 1964 Act.

The committee decided first to carry out a survey of the activities of the various welfare boards of the municipalities. A questionnaire was therefore sent to all Norwegian local authorities. Although the focus of the survey was on the boards, questions regarding the existence of SSDs and their staffing were included. Looking at the weight given to the two sets of questions, one is left with a feeling that those concerning SSDs were treated as being of lesser interest. Of particular interest to the committee was the role of the sobriety boards. The 'social work role' of these boards was mainly centred on measures to combat alcohol problems of individuals who had been reported to the boards.

The main finding of the survey was the *inactivity* of the sobriety boards in most municipalities. This led the committee to support the department in its desire to give more powers to the (proposed) Social Care Board. Still, the committee was forced to find a compromise acceptable to advocates of the prolonged existence of the Sobriety Board. Although the committee recognised the 'experience and insight' accumulated by the Sobriety Board and the Child Care Board, it felt that the lack of cases and subsequent inactivity on the part of the boards hindered the development of these services.[13] The solution, therefore, was to allow municipalities to keep the boards, but at the same time shift the balance of power and activity to the social care boards. This shift was ensured by a clause which stated that all clients with a combination of problems should be dealt with by the Welfare Board. If at least one member of the Sobriety Board or the Child Care Board considered a case to be of a combined nature, it would be transferred to the Social Care Board. The committee furthermore established close ties between the individual boards by proposing that at least one member of both the Sobriety Board and the Child Care Board should also be members of the Social Care Board.[14]

The way in which the committee constructed and argued a compromise in this delicate matter suddenly put both SSDs and professional social workers at the forefront of attention and importance. The starting point was the expressed desire to move away from a situation in which 'problems all concerning one family are being dealt with by different boards'.[15] Thus, the committee supported the 'principle of family treatment', which underlay the department's wish to amalgamate the

13. Innst. O VIII, 1959–60, p. 15.
14. Ibid., p. 18.
15. Ibid., p. 64.

boards.[16] It became important for the committee, therefore, to argue the need for this approach to social work.

The committee felt that the existence of SSDs would further 'family treatment': 'Even if we count on a considerable contribution from the laymen on the boards, one must expect the development of social treatment to be stalled unless more qualified professionals are employed in the social work of the local councils.'[17] Furthermore, by covering the whole field of social work, SSDs were expected to promote the intentions of the new legislation by being able to cater for people with widely varied problems and thereby counteract the problem of people falling through the cracks (i.e. between two or more boards) and consequently receiving no help.[18]

Having recognised the need for staffed SSDs, the committee went on to argue that the existing fragmentation also acted as a hindrance to the creation of such departments: 'The work-tasks within each board are too few to require paid help. It is only when the social work is seen as a whole that this need becomes apparent.'[19] Social planning was also considered to be suffering from the lack of SSDs: 'Where there is no office, it is the economic administration in the council which single-handedly prioritises and considers which of the many social tasks will be attended to.'[20] The committee did not perceive the opposite situation to be more favourable. Without the strength of a united Social Care Board, the municipalities *with* SSDs would in practice have to leave too much of the policy-making to their respective office directors. It followed, therefore, that the desired situation would be one with *a strong lay influence on the policy-making side, combined with strengthened SSDs employing qualified social workers to implement the scheme in a professional way.* A strengthening of the lay influence through the creation of a united board was therefore seen to be complementary to the objectives of the establishment of SSDs.

The survey found that while 56% of municipalities with more than 3,000 inhabitants had established SSDs, the figure was only 10% in the smaller municipalities.[21] Because Norwegian municipalities on average

16. Ibid., p. 16.
17. Ibid., p. 19.
18. Ibid., p. 17.
19. Ibid.
20. Ibid.
21. Innst. O VIII, 1959–60, p. 9.

are very small, this meant that only 29% of the total had established such offices by 1961.[22] This finding, coupled with the new emphasis on the need for such services, stimulated the committee to look for ways to promote their establishment. The role model in this case was Denmark, where a recently enacted Social Care Act contained a clause whereby local authorities with a specified minimum of inhabitants were requested to establish staffed administrations. On this basis the committee proposed the inclusion of a clause whereby all municipalities with more than 3,000 inhabitants were obliged to establish SSDs.[23] To achieve the combined effect of more SSDs and the employment of social workers, the committee proposed *state grants* to the municipalities towards covering a proportion of the wages of the heads of the departments.[24] In this connection the committee was pointing to the lack of qualified social workers in the country: 'We are, however, aware of the fact that the Church and Education Department is working on plans to considerably increase capacity in the schools educating social workers, and that it will therefore be possible to fill a considerably greater number of positions in local authority social work than is possible with the number of social workers available today.'[25]

These recommendations were all adopted by the department and included in the proposal which formed the basis for the 1964 Social Care Act. On one point, however, the department went further than the committee, making it a condition for paying 40% of the wages for the head of the SSD that the candidate was a qualified social worker or that he or she, if already employed, agreed to undergo training in social work and administration.[26] In this way the department created a very strong incentive towards the employment of professional social workers in the local SSDs.

This process of constructing an acceptable compromise features a number of actors and conflicting interests. As I feel that the key document in reaching a solution was that produced by the 1962 committee, I will

22. Terum 1982, p. 33.
23. Innst. O VIII, 1959–60, p. 20.
24. Ibid.
25. Ibid.
26. This was not made a specific condition in the final proposal, but Kluge (1973, p. 82) maintains that in reality it was a condition for receiving a state grant.

interpret the outcome on the basis of *its* line of reasoning and *its* conclusions.[27]

The committee was faced with satisfying, on the one hand, the need for efficiency and, on the other, the interests of the laypeople on the sobriety boards. The latter represented the *raison d'être* of the committee, and behind these interests was a strong and unpredictable political force.[28] As it was, the committee found that employing qualified social workers would enhance the efficiency of the service. The main advocate of the professional approach was the organisation for social workers themselves. In this organisation's response to the 1960 proposal, it argued that 'an uneducated person will easily fall prey to the temptation to use exhortation and pressure faced with an "unwilling" client. Experience shows that in very many cases this leads to resistance and negativity, rather than offering any help to the client.'[29] Thus, employing social workers was a necessary prerequisite to attaining the objectives of the proposed scheme.

This organisation was in its infancy at the time and had only 150 members. Thus, its potential for exerting political pressure was not comparable to that of the temperance movement. But meeting its demands turned out to be valuable in the pursuit of wider objectives – that is, producing arguments against the prolonged existence of the prevailing administrative structure.[30]

The SSDs and professional social work were brought to the forefront, therefore, because this area represented an important piece of the puzzle that policy-makers needed to solve. Three factors were of importance in achieving this compromise.[31] First, the existence of SSDs and social

---

27. In searching for factors explaining the emergence of the stress on the need for SSDs and social workers, I focus on the role of the 1962 committee because I feel that the main difference regarding this question is to be found between the two departmental proposals, not between the 1953 proposal and the two departmental responses. The latter interpretation underlies the conclusions of Ervik (1973), Terum (1982), and Kluge (1973).

28. The unpredictability follows from the fact that the temperance movement recruited members from various political parties.

29. Ot.prp. nr. 56, 1962–63, p. 21.

30. The Norwegian Association of Social Workers was established in 1959. While at first the only condition for membership was that the candidate should be working full time in social work, this was changed in 1965, when the completion of a 2½-year social work course became a requirement for membership (Tutvedt 1968).

31. The documentation of the lack of SSDs and social workers established by the committee's survey must be kept in mind.

workers was seen to be conducive to the implementation of both the general principle of 'social treatment' and the more specific principle of 'family treatment'. Second, the fragmentation of the administration into three different boards was seen to be holding up the establishment of SSDs. Third, it was argued that the establishment of SSDs would promote, and not curtail, the influence of elected laypeople on policy-making in the social services.

To solve the problem of administration, the department argued therefore that 'professional' and 'lay' interests were not in conflict. Moreover, it stressed compatibility by emphasising how the creation of SSDs would *further* the advancement of lay influence on policy-making in the local social services.[32]

The 1964 Social Care Act: A fillip to and course-setter for Norwegian social work

In the years that followed, the 1964 Act strongly influenced the development of professional social work. By becoming the major employer of social workers, the institution of social assistance both was influenced by the profession and at the same time formed much of the framework in which the new profession developed.

Creating work for social workers

As I have pointed out, the survey carried out by the 1960 committee showed that less than a third of Norwegian local authorities had established SSDs by that time. On this point the 1963 departmental proposal went further than the recommendation of the committee, stating that *all* municipalities were to set up SSDs.[33] In a later circular to the Act, however, this was somewhat modified, and a transitionary build-up period was accepted.[34] Furthermore, a clause was included to make the

32. This theme has previously been inquired into by Terum (1982). His starting point is that the 1964 Act represented a compromise between, on the one hand, 'lay ideology' and, on the other, 'treatment ideology'. The form that the compromise took, according to Terum, was a result of the struggle over the roles to be given to politically elected boards and staffed SSDs respectively.

33. Lov om sosial omsorg (Social Care Act), 1964, clause 10.

34. Øyen 1974, p. 20.

state support towards the salary of the leader of the office conditional on his or her education.[35] Although the clause did not specify that the leader should have a professional social work qualification, Kluge maintains that this was the intention.[36] As a result, the number of social work positions in the local authorities almost doubled in the period 1960–70. The proportion of *qualified* social workers in these positions also showed a marked increase, from 5% in 1960 to 40% in 1970.[37] In this period SSDs thus became by far the largest employer of qualified social workers. While only 9% of the candidates from the largest school of social work went on to work in local authority SSDs in 1960,[38] this proportion increased strongly following the 1964 enactment.[39]

Cash and care in the SSDs

In the previous chapter we saw how the combination of income maintenance and advice/counselling became an intended feature of the new personal social services in Norway. I will now turn to outline how these two functions were expressed and ordered in the Social Care Act itself. This will be followed by a discussion of how the particular arrangements came to influence the practice of professional social work.[40]

The various consultations leading up to the Act elaborated on the relationship between the two kinds of services. While these documents repeatedly referred to 'social treatment', this term was not used in the Act itself. We find it expressed, however, in clause 2 of the Act, which covered advice and counselling: 'The Social Welfare Board gives information,

35. Lov om sosial omsorg (Social Care Act), 1964, clause 11.
36. Kluge 1973, p. 81.
37. Terum 1982, p. 34.
38. Kluge 1960, p. 31.
39. I have no numbers from the late 1960s, but Terum (1982, p. 70) shows that in 1979 the proportion was 40%.
40. Like the 1900 Poor Law, the 1964 Social Care Act regulated the provisions of services in kind. While services such as home care and the allocation of places in old age homes became more integrated parts of the work as the local administrations developed, these tasks played a minor role at the time of enactment. Still, in 1974 Guttormsen and Høigård (1978) found that three-quarters of the clients approached the services with money problems (56.3%), alcohol problems (9.1%), or problems with housing (10.4%). The remaining 24% had a variety of requests, including municipal pensions, nursing home applications, and help to move. Of these requests, a third involved the need for material assistance (p. 126).

advice and guidance to those who need it in order to become self-reliant or in order to overcome or adjust to a difficult circumstance of life.' The warrant for the benefit side of the scheme is found in the next clause.[41] Of the different forms of help available, the most important and most frequent was 'e: grants, or in exceptional circumstances loans for subsistence'.[42]

'Cash' (or income maintenance) becomes interesting, in this context, only inasmuch as the allocation of it had an impact on the practice of social work. Because 'care' is more universally associated with social work, this part of the service is the dependent variable, on which the allocation of cash will be seen to have a decisive influence. This influence takes effect in a framework where the legal system itself, the characteristics of the target group, and the administrative setting all converge to create the particular practice of social work.

The first of these aspects is the *legal* component, as outlined above. As pointed out in the previous chapter, material assistance was, according to the departmental proposals, to be used only after advice and counselling had been attempted. Furthermore, financial assistance was to be used only in conjunction with advice and counselling. Neither of these objectives was spelled out in the Act. Still, I consider the ordering of the paragraphs to be a first indication of their underlying priorities. First comes advice, and then the cash follows. In a circular to the Act, it was furthermore stated that 'social assistance must not be seen in isolation, but as one of the means of help that the SSD can employ in its work with clients.'[43]

Because social workers are given an instrumental role in establishing the entitlement to assistance, the process leading to the allocation of aid will be seen to impinge on the nature of social work in the SSD. This influence is determined by the particular way by which entitlement is established. By definition, social assistance is a means-tested income maintenance system. There are, however, different methods by which both need and means are assessed. The Norwegian scheme has strong elements of discretion in establishing not only who is entitled to help but also what kind of help and how much help should be awarded. This particular arrangement has led scholars to inquire into the extent to which

41. See Chapter 6 for an outline of the major clauses of the Act.
42. Lov om sosial omsorg (Social Care Act), 1964.
43. Rundskriv nr. 3, 1980, p. 19.

social assistance as practised in Norway can be considered a right. In a legal evaluation of the legislation, Bull argues that 'nowhere in the act are expressions used to give a person in one of the need situations mentioned in the act a right to receive help or to indicate that the Welfare Board has a duty to give such help.'[44] Yet he argues that because the Welfare Board in many cases has a duty to pay benefits, it follows that the client has a corresponding right to benefits. In real life, however, both the complicated and time-consuming appeal system and the use of vague and elastic terminology in the text add to the feeling that social assistance is 'no proper right'.[45] Similarly, Kluge points out that 'the right is only subsidiary. The applicant must first have sought other solutions, e.g. maintaining himself by working, applying for social security etc.'[46] Finally, when the entitlement to cash benefits has been established, there is no national scale rate that can inform clients and SSDs alike regarding how much should be awarded. The vague notion of 'subsistence'[47] has led different municipalities to developed their own definitions, 'ranging from those including money for food only, to those covering all kinds of expenses.'[48]

Second, the *nature of the target group* has bearing on the work in the personal social services. As we saw in the previous chapter, it was the policymakers' expressed intention to move away from a situation whereby social assistance was a last-resort cash-relief system for the poor and towards a situation whereby any member of the community experiencing the kind of problems for which the new service was designed could approach the SSD for help. The extent to which this objective was achieved falls outside the scope of this study, however, and I will restrict my evaluation to quoting one of the civil servants assigned to implement the scheme. Writing in 1973, Kluge argued that in many municipalities 'the SSD never became the social service institution it was intended to be. Even today, many people who would readily visit the local insurance office find it difficult to approach the social service department of the town.'[49]

44. Bull 1981, p. 49.

45. Ibid. Andenæs (1992) has reviewed a number of factors that experts on social law have considered with regard to this matter. The picture is one of disagreement regarding the extent of entitlement to benefits in the Social Care Act.

46. Kluge 1973, p. 86.

47. Lov om sosial omsorg (Social Care Act), 1964, subclause 3(e).

48. Terum 1985, p. 4.

49. Kluge 1973, p. 91.

That the scheme never lived up to expectations must be understood in the light of the developments preceding the new legislation. As we saw in the previous chapter, the two decades leading up to the enactment had witnessed a narrowing of the assistance clientele. In particular the expansion of social insurance changed the nature of the clientele by incorporating large groups, leaving a small, heterogenous, poor, and stigmatised group behind. The very existence of this group as the main users of assistance in 1964 probably prevented more 'respectable' people from using it and thereby making it into the service institution it was intended to be. For social workers this meant being able to apply their social treatment methods to only the very poorest members of the population. According to Pinker, 'social services are used to impose sanctions as well as to confer benefits upon their clientele.'[50] The legal powers described above were well suited to fulfilling both of these functions. The composition and nature of the clientele make it a vulnerable target if the system is used to confer sanctions.

The *administrative* set-up added to this general impression. As we have seen, the Social Care Board was given the final say in individual client cases. This power was widely used, at least during the first decade of the new scheme. Social workers were expected to present applications for assistance to the Social Care Board. Even though professional social work ideology stressed the client's right to self-determination, there was no guarantee that this approach would be shared by the successor to the Poor Board.

With the 1964 Social Care Act, social workers were given the combined role of offering social treatment and assessing the client's entitlement to material assistance. The particular way in which this latter function was set out in the law gave social workers wide powers over their clients. The attendant assessment process and control functions were to have an impact on the relationship between clients and social workers. In sum, this created a setting which was bound to impinge on the practice of professional social work, on the nature and composition of the clientele using the scheme, and thus on the SSDs as a social service.

50. Pinker 1971, p. 144.

Conclusions

While the Poor Law was dominated by laypeople, and only the larger cities featured staffed offices, the development after 1960 was dominated by the establishment of local SSDs, even in the smaller municipalities. We found that this change could be only partly explained by the new focus on 'social treatment'. More important in creating the impetus for professional social work was the solution that this approach provided for the Department of Social Affairs in its struggle to find a compromise on the question of administration that would be acceptable to the temperance movement. Once the SSDs were established as the main employer of social workers, however, these departments and thus the Social Care Act proved to have a marked impact on the nature of professional social work in Norway. In particular the cash–care multifunctional nature of this service created a social work setting emphasising social control.

Chapter 8
British Social Assistance, 1948–1966

In this chapter we will follow the development of British social assistance from the introduction of National Assistance in 1948 to its replacement by Supplementary Benefit in 1966. I will focus on particular aspects of the British experience rather than attempt to give as broad a coverage of the events as in the corresponding chapter on Norway (Chapter 3). The themes of analysis arise from two sources. First, the coverage of British social insurance in Chapter 5 revealed the development of National Insurance (NI) to be the single most important factor in determining the *scope* (size) of assistance as well as the *composition* of the assistance clientele. In this chapter I turn to focus on the changing *nature* of British assistance in the period. The second set of questions are designed to cast further light on the reform of Norwegian assistance as outlined in the preceding chapters. By juxtaposing key variables in the Norwegian case with corresponding areas in Britain, the aim is to get a better understanding of the development of assistance in these two expanding and modernising welfare states.

The major difference between the assistance services in the two countries is that while Norway continued the tradition of a localised service combining cash and care functions, Britain departed from this path by abolishing the Poor Law and replacing it with a strictly income-maintenance-oriented *national* scheme in 1948. After briefly surveying the new service I will therefore give particular attention to the background to this decisive event, thereby venturing into the more distant past in search of understanding. The second part of the chapter explores the events leading up to the replacement of National Assistance by Supplementary Benefit.

The 1948 National Assistance Act

Like most of the post-war welfare legislation in Britain, the new assistance scheme was very dependent on the recommendations of the Beveridge Report. As the report discussed assistance as an integral part of public income maintenance, I will first present the scheme as Beveridge outlined it.

The cornerstone of Beveridge's income maintenance programme was, as we have seen, contributory social insurance. Universality in the sector of income maintenance as a whole was, however, dependent on the creation of an integrated assistance scheme 'available to meet all needs not covered by social insurance'.[1] While Beveridge stressed the importance of assistance as a 'part of social security'[2] by proposing a joint department to administer the two schemes, he also built incentives for the growth of insurance into the assistance scheme: 'It must be felt to be something less desirable than insurance benefits; otherwise the insured persons get nothing for their contributions. Assistance will therefore always be given subject to proof of needs and examinations of means.'[3]

Although Beveridge recognised a permanent need for assistance, it was only during the period of build-up towards subsistence-level insurance benefits that he envisaged the need for assistance in 'a considerable number of cases'.[4] After this, assistance would take on a limited role, 'much less than that of public assistance and of the Assistance Board at present'.[5] The groups for which this service would still be needed were then listed as four separate 'classes':

a. Persons failing to fulfil [insurance] contributions.
b. Persons failing to fulfil conditions for [insurance] benefits.
c. Persons with abnormal needs in respect of diet, care and other matters.
d. Persons in need through causes not suitable for insurance, e.g. some form of desertion or separation.[6]

1. Cmd 6404, para. 369.
2. Ibid.
3. Ibid.
4. Cmd 6404, para. 370.
5. Ibid., para. 371.
6. Ibid.

Benefits for these groups would be made available subject to a 'uniform means test'.[7]

The scheme enacted in 1948 followed Beveridge's proposals except for one major point. While he proposed the setting up of a joint government department to administer both assistance and insurance, assistance continued in fact to be administered by a separate board in keeping with the tradition of the Unemployment Assistance Board. Only with the 1966 enactment of the Supplementary Benefit scheme was a merged administration achieved.

Britain and Norway in 1948: Similar ends, different means

A comparison shows that the 1948 National Assistance (NA) scheme diverged from the simultaneously enacted '*forsorg*' scheme in three important ways. First, while the Norwegian scheme involved only a *reform* of the existing Poor Law, the British equivalent was *abolished* and replaced with a new system. Second, this change involved the setting up of a *national* scheme in Britain. In Norway, by contrast, the reformed Poor Law scheme continued to be financed, as well as administered, by the local authorities. Third, the enactment of NA resulted in a *separation of income maintenance services from other social services* in Britain. The latter continued to be the responsibility of the municipalities. In Norway the social services and last-resort income maintenance continued to be combined in the tradition shared by the two countries in their respective Poor Laws.

The three points of divergence become important because they represent not only the most significant differences between the two countries but also three important variables according to which social assistance/ social services differ between welfare states in general. In the words of Catherine Jones, 'remembering that all assistance systems are descended from nineteenth century poor relief arrangements, the obvious distinction to draw here is between those systems which have remained localized (*and* cash/care multifunctional) and those (i.e. the British) which have been centralized and divorced from anything other than a cash relief function.'[8]

7. Cmd 6404, para. 19.
8. Jones 1985, p. 113.

In spite of the differences, the two assistance systems also featured similarities strong enough to warrant further comparison. As we saw in the Introduction to Part Three, they both descended from Poor Laws which grew out of the same administrative and ideological roots. Furthermore, they were both given a mainly *transitionary role* in the immediate post-war planning. Eventually, they were both expected to be diminished in scope by expanding national insurance schemes.

While the last of the three themes outlined above will receive particular attention in Chapter 9, in which the practice of social work in the personal social services will be examined, I will start this chapter by outlining the background to the other two points of divergence.

Towards a national assistance scheme

A transfer of the responsibility for finance as well as for administration from local to central government necessarily implies changes in other aspects of a welfare scheme. In fact, this was probably the single most important departure introduced by the 1948 legislation. With this change Britain departed not only from Norway but also from the path taken by all other Western welfare states.

In the section on social insurance we saw that the 1946 National Insurance Act was a unification of existing schemes and a continuation of a long-established policy inheritance rather than a radical departure. As we shall see, this was also largely the case with the move towards a national social assistance scheme in Britain. The 1948 Act was the end result of a process which had started two decades earlier. Also before that time, Britain had historically had a Poor Law under strong central control.

The centralisation of assistance was closely tied to the development of the contributory unemployment scheme first enacted in 1911. The popularity of contributory insurance as a method of avoiding means-testing was outlined in Chapter 4. It is no surprise then that, in the years that followed, 'the Edwardian obsession with the undeserving and the deserving poor'[9] led a growing number of workers to subscribe in order to avoid the stigma associated with the means test. With the 1911 legislation, sickness benefits and retirement pensions also went over to the contributory

9. Deacon and Bradshaw 1983, p. 6.

system. By 1930, therefore, the great majority of workers drew contributory benefits in times of sickness, unemployment, and retirement.[10]

The onset of mass unemployment in the early 1920s put the insurance fund under great strain. The first attempt to curtail spending came in 1921 with the 'genuinely seeking work test'.[11] This resulted in great numbers being excluded from unemployment insurance and forced to rely on benefits from the Poor Law. The growth in poor relief for the unemployed was further encouraged by increasing acceptance of the scheme as a result of more generous treatment of the applicants, in particular by left-wing local authorities.[12] In spite of a tightening up of entitlement in 1921, continued high unemployment increased the pressure on the insurance fund throughout the decade. The government responded by extending Exchequer contributions to the scheme. While such transfers in 1921 accounted for 3–4% of government spending, this figure rose to nearly one-quarter in 1931.

In the years 1929 to 1935 this situation was to bring about major changes, not only in the relationship between assistance and insurance, but also in that between central and local government. A first step was taken with the 1929 Local Government Act. The main feature of this legislation was the removal of health care from the aegis of the Poor Law. For the able-bodied still dependent on the Poor Law, the Act involved centralising measures in two ways. First, the responsibility for poor relief was transferred from parish to county level. Second, the scheme was to be financed dually, by local rates and the Exchequer. Thane considers the latter a measure to achieve the combined aims of equalising entitlement and benefits, on the one hand, and of increasing Treasury control (over too-generous local authorities), on the other.[13]

With the 1929 Local Government Act, the term 'poor relief' changed to 'public assistance', and each county was directed to set up a Public Assistance Committee (PAC). In 1931 the PACs were given wider responsibilities with the introduction of Transitional Payments for the long-term unemployed. This scheme was financed from general taxation, but the PACs assessed claims for benefits. For the central government this reform was a further attempt to reduce spending on unemployment benefits after

10. Ibid., p. 7.
11. Ibid., p. 8.
12. Ibid.
13. Thane 1982, p. 188.

a period in which the long-term unemployed had been allowed to claim contributory insurance after their formal entitlements had been exhausted. For the claimants the change symbolised a return to reliance on poor relief.[14]

Because Transitional Payments and public assistance were financed from separate sources, the 1931 enactment involved a partial splitting up of the assistance clientele. While all assistance claimants approached the same office, the unemployed could claim a state benefit rather than local public assistance. In the section on Norway (Chapters 2 and 3) we saw that a transfer of groups from local to central financial and administrative responsibility brought about, without exception, an enhancement of welfare for the groups involved. This was not the case with the changes that followed the 1929 Act in Britain. According to Briggs and Deacon, 'To the unemployed the new PAC's were simply the old guardians writ large, and shortly to be armed with even greater inquisitorial powers.'[15] What lay in store for them was the household means test. Under this, the resources of each member of the household were regarded as being available to meet the needs of the claimant, whether or not they were related.[16] This development was anticipated by the labour movement: 'for the first time in history, the Poor Law received its strongest defence from the left.'[17]

The next step in this process occurred when the Unemployment Assistance Board (UAB) was introduced in 1934. For the central government the transfer of responsibility to the PAC turned out to be an inadequate device to curtail spending. During the three years in which the Transitional Payments scheme was in operation, Whitehall became increasingly worried that the local councillors were being 'over generous with the Treasury's money'.[18] The UAB became the instrument by which greater control of spending was achieved.[19] Originally the board was

---

14. Briggs and Deacon 1973, p. 43.
15. Fraser 1984, p. 188.
16. Deacon and Bradshaw 1983, p. 16.
17. Thane 1982, p. 188.
18. Briggs and Deacon 1973, p. 43.
19. In the literature there are various interpretations regarding the motivation behind the setting up of the board. George (1968, p. 73) describes it as a measure whereby the state relieved the local authorities of a burden which, with mass unemployment, had become too great for them. Briggs and Deacon (1973, p. 43) start out by referring to Millet's *The Unemployment Assistance Board* (1940), in which he sees

meant to take responsibility for the 800,000 people maintained on Transitional Payments as well as the 200,000 unemployed then in receipt of public assistance. The latter were, however, not incorporated until 1937. As it turned out, UAB rates were initially set lower than the benefits paid by most local authorities, and it was therefore impossible to transfer the 200,000 entitled to public assistance before this anomaly had been rectified.[20] The household means test also made a transfer from public assistance to the UAB far from attractive for the individual claimant.

For the remaining Poor Law services, this was another step in the long process of breaking them down 'from without'. With the 1934 and the 1937 changes, the Poor Law 'lost almost all its able-bodied males and became a generalised relief agency meeting a variety of residual conditions.'[21] For my analysis it is significant that this 'breakdown' led to the creation of new schemes representing a continuation of the principles of the Poor Law. By comparison, the establishment of pension schemes involved the creation of a real alternative to these principles.

Towards the end of the 1930s unemployment dropped drastically, and by 1940 the 'universalist demands of a total people's war' further contributed to a change in the role of the UAB.[22] As a result it dropped its association with unemployment and became the Assistance Board (AB). This change preceded and facilitated two important departures in the following year. First, the process of residualising the Poor Law was further advanced by the 1940 Old Age and Widow's Pension Act. With this piece of legislation responsibility for the supplementation of pensions for elderly people and widows was taken away from the Poor Law and placed with the AB. This decision symbolises a dramatic change of attitude towards the central relief agency from that which prevailed in 1935, when local authority poor relief was favoured by many over benefits from the UAB.

---

the change as 'essentially a Treasury measure, designed to halt the rise in the cost of unemployment relief by creating a buffer between the Government and the pressures for more generous benefits.' (The term 'buffer' refers to the independent status of the board.) In their conclusion Briggs and Deacon argue that 'the Board was a centralising measure above all else' (p. 61). These interpretations are, of course, not mutually exclusive. The point on which they converge – greater central control and responsibilities – becomes most important for this analysis.

20. Fraser 1984, p. 196.
21. Ibid., p. 197.
22. Ibid., p. 212.

Now the argument was suddenly that 'supplementation required by pensioners should be provided not by the Public Assistance Committees of the local authorities but by a national agency untainted by poor relief.'[23]

The second change came with the Determination of Needs Act in 1941. This enactment abolished the much-hated household means test and replaced it with a personal test. Immediately the number of people receiving benefits from the AB increased by a quarter of a million.[24] The literature gives no conclusive answer to why this happened in 1941. Fraser stresses the fact that it was the end of a process whereby the household means test had been less and less stringently implemented towards the end of the 1930s.[25] It could also be interpreted as a further step in what Titmuss described as the 'wartime trend towards universalising public provision for certain basic needs'.[26] In addition to these factors, the change in the composition of the AB clientele must have played an important role. With 'ten pensioners to every one man unemployed',[27] policy decisions would no longer be determined to the same extent by the fear of 'scrounging'.[28]

Having become the major assistance scheme, the AB continued to improve during the war. In addition to the elderly and widows, other people in wartime poverty, such as 'victims of the blitz, those in need of hardship allowances, evacuees, dependents of internees, foreign refugees', and others, were increasingly dealt with by the AB and not by the PACs.[29] The popularity of the AB was further enhanced in 1944 when the scale rates were improved.[30] This also involved a simplification of the scales; special additions were withdrawn, and the new uniform rate was set at a level high enough to meet the needs of those with the greatest hardships.[31]

This process of centralisation constituted a weighty policy inheritance

23. Ibid.
24. Fraser 1984, p. 213.
25. Ibid.
26. Titmuss, 'War and Social Policy' (1955), in Titmuss 1987, p. 109.
27. Fraser 1984, p. 213.
28. Traditionally, measures to avoid 'scrounging' had been targeted at the able-bodied. The changes around 1940 made the AB primarily concerned with non-able-bodied claimants.
29. Fraser 1984, p. 212.
30. Ibid., p. 213.
31. Deacon and Bradshaw 1983, p. 41.

which was bound to have an impact on the policy decisions made after the war. As Olive Stevenson points out, 'When the National Assistance Bill came before Parliament, central government machinery for the relief of need was already established.'[32] The need for a large-scale 'machinery' to administer assistance is further emphasised by the technical arrangement of insurance: a contributory scheme of insurance requires a substantial safety net beneath it.

This could, of course, equally well be argued the other way round: with a 'large assistance machinery' set up, a contributory insurance scheme became more feasible and acceptable. Like his proposals for social insurance, Beveridge's proposals for a *national* assistance scheme were therefore more a continuation of a trend than a break with the past. However, for the residual groups still relying on local authority public assistance, the 1948 enactment was a clear enhancement of welfare. They benefited from their incorporation into a centralised scheme which gave them clearer entitlements to better services. The limited number of residual groups, combined with the prolonged need for a large-scale assistance scheme, made this incorporation a natural one.

The development towards a national assistance scheme in Britain in the period 1929–48 represents, therefore, an interesting example of the interaction of the variables of, on one axis, central versus local welfare delivery and, on the other, residual versus institutional welfare. The first moves towards centralisation in 1929, 1931, and 1934 represented a change in the direction of a harsher, more residual welfare delivery. The subsequent alterations to this scheme, resulting from changes in the composition of its clientele caused by the war economy and war mentality, turned this strong, centralised machinery into a vehicle on the road to what became perhaps the most generally accessible assistance scheme in Europe.

Reform versus abolition of the Poor Law

We have seen that Britain and Norway took different courses of action with regard to the existing Poor Laws at the start of the post-war welfare state expansion. With the 1948 enactment Norway reformed the Poor Law and changed its name mainly in order to make it appear more

32. Stevenson 1973, p. 13.

humane and thus more accessible. The emphasis, though, was on an expanded social insurance which was designed to render the Poor Law 'superfluous' in the future. The reformed Poor Law continued to be 'localized and cash/care multifunctional'. Abolition of the Norwegian Poor Law appears not to have been seriously considered in the first post-war years. Only with the 1964 Social Care Act was the Poor Law officially buried.

To evaluate the extent to which the 1948 British legislation actually involved a break with the past, it is necessary to distinguish between two major groups covered by the National Assistance Act. The first consisted of those covered by the Assistance Board. As we have seen, the coverage of this scheme was greatly expanded during the war. In 1948 these groups accounted for approximately two-thirds of the clientele of the newly established assistance scheme. For these groups – the elderly, widows, long-term unemployed, and those suffering from war injuries – the 1948 reform involved little change. Through the AB, nationally financed and scaled benefits had been offered for almost a decade. Furthermore, these benefits were provided subject to a uniform test of means, without recourse to further investigation into the personal life of the claimant. The administrative structure of the new scheme was also modelled on that of the AB. Glennerster puts this in the wider picture of British incremental reform when he argues that, 'with a typical British passion for using any existing machinery that happened to be lying around, the drafters of the National Assistance Act absorbed the essentials of the old Public Assistance Board into their new structure.'[33] He goes on to argue that this was equally true on the policy-making level: 'the six members of the Public Assistance Board were transferred on July 3rd, 1948, to the National Assistance Board.'[34] Also, the day-to-day running of the new scheme was carried out by much the same staff: '1500 Relieving Officers of local authorities joined the new N.A.B., and the employees of the old Public Assistance Board simply moved into the new administration.'[35]

The remaining one-third of the clientele experienced, however, much greater changes in 1948. During the debate on the National Assistance Bill, Aneurin Bevan, then minister of health, referred to the recent break-

33. Glennerster 1962, p. 4.
34. Ibid., p. 6.
35. Ibid., p. 4.

down of the Poor Law and concluded as follows: 'However, there will still remain, after all these things have been done, 400 000 persons on outdoor relief and 50 000 in institutions. There thus remain, after we have bitten into the main body of the Poor Law, these residual groups which have to be provided for.'[36] These 'residual groups' were those still serviced by the remaining Poor Law, financed and administered by the local authorities. While the non-able-bodied continued to be the responsibility of the municipalities after 1948, the remaining 400,000 were swept up by the new national scheme. As this was largely a continuation of the AB, the change in effect implied an incorporation of the local authority poor relief clientele into a scheme originally designed to free large groups of 'deserving' clients, such as the elderly and widows, from the stigma of the Poor Law.

One question remains, though: *Why* were these 'residual' groups incorporated and not, as in Norway, left to diminish? Although we can only speculate, the best answer is probably to be found in the momentum created by the need to establish a new assistance scheme. Unlike Norway, Britain decided to create a permanent, national assistance scheme as a necessary adjunct to a contributory social insurance programme. While the Norwegian assistance scheme was allowed to continue in relative obscurity, the developments described above put social assistance high on the political agenda in Britain. The fact that assistance was not divided into two tiers must furthermore be understood in the light of the shared experience of poverty and Poor Law dependency of large segments of the population in the 1920s and '30s, together with the solidarity brought about by the wartime experience and the consequent stress on universality. But as we shall see later, the stress on equal treatment of the entire assistance clientele was short-lived. In the late 1950s, the British party which had introduced it was the first to switch to advocating a new division at the bottom of the welfare hierarchy.

In summary, the 'breakup' of the Poor Law followed different patterns in the two countries. In both the main factor was the growth of various social insurance programmes. In Britain these were supplemented by alternative national assistance schemes for groups which represented typical 'insurance cases' (elderly people, widows) and which insurance did not cover, or did not cover sufficiently. In Norway the pioneering

36. A. Bevan, Hansard, 24 April 1947, 1603.

schemes for the corresponding groups were established in the municipalities. Although these schemes (see Chapter 2) featured 'assistance characteristics' such as tax-financing and means-testing, three aspects combined to make them direct precursors of national insurance schemes. First, they were called, and considered to be, municipal *insurance* schemes. Second, they were established in expectation of, and as a means of exerting pressure to effect, eventual state take-over. Third, because the state schemes were financed through general taxation rather than individual contributions, the extent of 'take-over' became a political rather than, as in Britain, a practical question. The significance of this comparison is that while the British schemes outlined above preceded and pointed towards an *alternative assistance scheme*, the developments in Norway laid the foundation for the expansion of social insurance coverage and, subsequently, further 'breakdown' of assistance from without.

Thane argues that 'unemployment dominated the history of the Poor Law [in the inter-war years] as it dominated everything else; it led at last to its abolition.'[37] The evidence presented above suggests that this argument needs qualification. While it is true that unemployment paved the way for a *national* assistance scheme in 1948, there is reason to believe that the *nature* of this scheme would have been different had it been the unemployed that made up the majority of its clientele in the period of reform during and following the Second World War. Even at this stage, it was concern for the elderly together with other 'deserving' groups that dominated the public debate on assistance in Britain. In the following two decades the growing dependency on NA among the elderly led to its abolition. That is the theme of the next section.

From National Assistance to Supplementary Benefit

In the chapter on social insurance in Britain (Chapter 5), we saw that the NI scheme failed to reduce the scope of assistance for two main reasons. First, the continuing sub-subsistence level benefits were inadequate to 'float' NI recipients off dependency on assistance for supplementation. Second, the implementation of the contributory principle excluded individuals and groups for whom it was difficult to establish a sufficient record of contribution. In combination, these factors brought about a

37. Thane 1982, p. 185.

composition of the assistance clientele very different from that of the corresponding scheme in Norway. The very groups that in Norway contributed most to the reduction of assistance in the 1950s accounted for most of the dramatic *growth* in assistance in Britain in the same period. Beveridge stated that insurance should not leave out any risk 'so general or so uniform that social insurance can be justified'.[38] But this vision was not translated into reality. Between 1948 and 1962 the number of claimants increased from 1.5 million to 2.5 million.[39] This compares with a reduction from roughly 44,000 to 31,000 heads of families receiving assistance in Norway during the same period.[40]

As we saw in Chapter 6, there are no statistics available to provide conclusive evidence of the changes in the composition of the Norwegian assistance clientele before 1966. In that year approximately one-half of the claimants also received social insurance benefits. These were, however, spread over a wide variety of insurance schemes, of which 'other schemes', including a variety of occupational pensions, constituted the largest group. If we turn to our major group of interest, we find that recipients of old age pensions represented 14.4% of the total number of people receiving assistance. The evidence presented in Chapter 6 furthermore suggested that this percentage had decreased in the period 1948–66.[41] The far-better statistics available for the British equivalent are perhaps indicative of the differences between a unified, national scheme and one which continued to be run entirely by the local authorities.

In Chapter 5 we saw that over three-quarters of the weekly NA allowances were paid to people over pension age in 1965. Moreover, this percentage had increased in the period 1949–65.[42] While recipients of old age pensions from National Insurance constituted 48.2% of the clientele in 1949, this percentage had increased to 59.9 by 1965. I can therefore conclude that the main function of the British NA was to provide supplementary benefits in order to give NI pensioners enough money to subsist. Thus, I see an increasingly diverging composition of the assistance clientele in the two countries.

In the chapter on Norwegian assistance (Chapter 6), we found that the

38. Cmd 6404, para. 308.
39. Glennerster 1962, p. 2.
40. See Figure 6.1.
41. See Chapter 6.
42. See Table 5.2.

changing size and composition of the clientele had a marked impact on the development of the service. Turning now to analyse the corresponding service–clientele relationship in Britain, my hypothesis is that the differences outlined above largely explain the continued divergence between the assistance schemes of the two countries. In addition to the growth in size, particular attention will be given to reactions to the increasing dominance of 'insurance cases' during the period. Given that a service better than that of the existing NA was desired for these groups, policy-makers were in principle left with the choice between two alternative options. The first involved a singling out of groups for which an improved income maintenance service would be provided – in other words, a *continued breakdown of assistance 'from without'*. Alternatively, a less targeted approach would involve the *improvement of the entire assistance scheme.* When we study the inter- as well as intra-governmental changes of policy along these lines, the emphasis will be on the different consequences for the residual 'non-insurance-type' clientele, that is, the group of NA recipients most similar to the dominant clientele in the Norwegian scheme.

Conservative policy

In the period 1951–64 Britain was ruled by Conservative governments. In Chapter 5, I outlined the recommendations of the Phillips Committee presented in 1954. The findings of this 'carefully chosen'[43] group provided the Eden and Macmillan governments 'with a relatively inexpensive way to raise [pensioners'] standard of living'.[44] By elevating NA benefits instead of improving the level of national insurance, the Conservatives followed the second of the two options outlined above. While this approach had continuing detrimental effects for insurance,[45] it was also the main reason for the gradual enhancement of NA as an income maintenance scheme. In particular, the major increases introduced in 1959 can be ascribed to this policy.[46]

When the Conservatives adopted the *selective route* (i.e. assistance rather than non-means-tested insurance) to solve poverty in old age, they claimed to do so for reasons other than economy. In the White Paper that

43. Glennerster 1962, p. 2.
44. Webb 1975, p. 428.
45. See Chapter 5.
46. Deacon and Bradshaw 1983, p. 102.

preceded the 1959 improvements, they proclaimed a new standard for assistance: 'The time has come when it is right to move to a higher standard, so giving [the elderly] *a share in increasing national prosperity.*'[47] In his influential 1962 study, Tony Lynes analyses the extent to which this expressed aim was translated into practical politics. He concludes that the 1959 changes, in spite of the substantial increases, were 'less than half of what was needed to give those on assistance the same share of national income as they received in 1948.'[48]

Labour policy

During the 1950s the Labour Party changed its policy with regard to assistance. In 1951 its election manifesto maintained that NA had become a 'humane' scheme. Four years later, then in opposition, the party argued for the improvement of NI in order to 'remove the last taint of "public assistance"'.[49] Webb considers this change of attitude to be partly a result of the party's role changing 'from that of outgoing government defending its record (in 1951) to that of critical opposition', but also considers the changing size and composition of assistance to have had a decisive impact on the policy. Towards the end of the 1950s, the party's hostility towards NA grew proportionately with the number of old age pensioners relying on it. In 1959 this resulted in a position whereby the party criticised the NAB, not only for providing the elderly with inadequate income maintenance, but also for deterring large numbers from applying: 'The living standards of more than half of our old age pensioners are a national disgrace. About a million are driven by poverty to seek National Assistance and another 500 000 would be entitled to receive it.'[50] The latter part of this statement refers to the growing evidence of the problem of take-up, in particular among the elderly. That this line of reasoning led the Labour Party to direct its attention towards NI must, according to Webb, be understood as a rejection of means-tested benefits as a solution to poverty in old age.[51] Faced with a growing 'float-over'

47. Cmnd 782 (1959), referred to in Lynes 1962, p. 16; emphasis added.
48. Lynes 1962, p. 46. Lynes uses national average earnings as a measure of 'national prosperity'.
49. Referred to in Webb 1975, pp. 411, 412.
50. Ibid., p. 412.
51. Ibid.

from insurance to assistance, the party therefore adopted a policy along the lines of the first option outlined above: strengthening NI's ability to meet the needs of the elderly. When we turn to look at the programme this resulted in, the emphasis will again be on the groups for whom assistance would *still* be the major source of relief.

The Income Guarantee

While Labour's long-term solution of the problem of poverty in old age was to abandon the flat-rate principle and introduce earnings-related pensions,[52] a complementary scheme was proposed for the already old. The programme was first proposed at the 1957 Labour Conference as 'some kind of national minimum income during the transitional period – in other words to revise the present conditions and standards of the National Assistance Scheme.'[53] Soon after this a study group was established to inquire into the whole area of 'Security in Old Age'. The group was chaired by Richard Crossman and included a group of academics: Richard Titmuss, Peter Townsend, Brian Abel-Smith, and, later, Tony Lynes.[54] The work of the group finally resulted in the policy pamphlet *New Frontiers for Social Security,* released in 1963. While the emphasis was on the new system of superannuation, the Income Guarantee was also for the first time given a detailed presentation. The scheme represented what turned out to be a compromise between the two options for solving the crisis in the assistance–insurance relationship: 'It has always been assumed that there are only two alternative ways of dealing with the problem [of existing pensioners]. Either there must be an all-round flat rate increase in the retirement pension to take all pensioners off National Assistance [option one], or alternatively we should increase the rates and coverage of National Assistance [option two]. Both alternatives are unacceptable.'[55] The solution was found in selecting the group for which assistance dependency was unacceptable and targeting it with a scheme that was neither assistance nor insurance – or, as Webb puts it, 'To provide selective benefits without recourse to a detailed and stigmatising means

52. See Chapter 5.
53. Referred to in Webb 1975, p. 415.
54. Ibid.
55. Labour Party 1963, p. 17.

test.'[56] A further reduction of stigma was envisaged by paying the benefits through the post office rather than through the NAB.[57]

The 'residuum' under the Income Guarantee

While the proposed scheme offered an escape from NA for the groups targeted – the elderly and widows – my interest is mainly in those *remaining in assistance* after the proposed reform. Not surprisingly, given the overall focus on the elderly at the time, *New Frontiers for Social Security* failed to explore this issue fully. The only mention given is short enough to be quoted: 'As a result of our proposals, the National Assistance Board will gradually cease to supplement inadequate National Insurance benefits, and so revert to its original purpose of providing a 'safety net' for those who do not qualify for National Insurance. This will mean for those still on National Assistance *more generous treatment and greater care and attention from the staff.*'[58] I added the emphasis to highlight the resemblance to the ideas expressed in the proposal for the 1964 Norwegian Social Care Act.[59] As in Norway, the reformers in Britain were faced with the problem of how to deal with the few who remained after alternative schemes had, or were thought to have, freed the majority of 'insurance types' from assistance. For reasons of comparison, I will therefore explore what kind of a service the above statement suggested.

As it happened, a pamphlet evaluating and making recommendations for changes in the NA scheme was published a year before *New Frontiers for Social Security*. To establish the relevance of Howard Glennerster's *National Assistance: Service or Charity?*, we must turn our attention to individuals involved in the process of policy-making. I have already mentioned the presence of four academics in the study group. In his diary, Richard Crossman makes it clear that they had a decisive impact on the nature of the proposed reforms. He refers to a conversation he had with one of the other members of the study group, Harold Wilson. After discussing how to present the proposals, as a working party report or as an executive policy statement, Wilson proposed to 'have the first three chapters as a Party statement, with an appendix signed by Titmuss, Abel-

56. Webb 1975, p. 422.
57. Ibid., p. 425.
58. Labour Party 1963, p. 19; emphasis added.
59. See Chapter 6.

Smith and Townsend. We shall get all the kudos for their research and they will be responsible for all the detailed figures.'[60]

In his pamphlet Glennerster advocated a change towards more active 'advertising' of the services of the NAB to mitigate the problems of 'take-up'. His main concern, though, was with the attitudes and training of the personnel manning the local NAB offices. He saw prejudice and a division of clients into the 'deserving' and 'non deserving' as inherent features of a system in which 'discretion plays such an important part' and 'officers are haphazardly recruited and poorly trained'.[61] On the assumption that a client tended to get better treatment from the NAB if he or she had the backing of a social worker, Glennerster concluded that training NAB officers in social work techniques would greatly alter their perception of and attitudes towards the client: 'He should therefore be acting in very much the same way as the Younghusband second grade social worker.'[62] This reasoning was faulty, because it ignored the difference between the role of a social worker, who is free to act as an advocate for the client, and that of an NA officer who, with or without social work training, was first and foremost accountable to the NAB and whose role was therefore bound to include strong elements of control over the client/claimant.

In the chapter on the Norwegian assistance scheme (Chapter 6), I argued that the introduction of 'treatment' ('care and attention') could be seen from one perspective as an extension of the paternalism of the Poor Law. This rests on the assumption that the scheme was targeted at the 'residuum', that is, groups in need of more than 'money alone'. Glennerster confirmed in an interview that this is a fair description of the group for which his proposals were targeted: 'At the time we saw the assistance clientele to consist of two groups. On the one hand there was the unproblematic pensioner who collected his weekly allowances. On the other hand there was the "problem family" who failed to feed their children "beyond Wednesday" and who, in spite of rent allowances, managed to work up rent arrears.'[63] It was this group that Glennerster and the study

60. Crossman 1981, p. 581.

61. Glennerster 1962, p. 16.

62. Ibid.

63. Glennerster, pers. com. 6 July 1988. Knowing that Glennerster had later worked closely with the 'Titmuss Group', I arranged an interview on 6 July 1988 to establish his links with the working party at the time of the publication of his pamphlet. The relationship was closer than expected; at the time of writing he was research assistant to the group, working particularly closely with Titmuss and the

group had in mind when they proposed a new 'caring' NA. As we saw, this was also the prevailing perception of the clientele among the architects of the simultaneous reforms of assistance in Norway. Glennerster was also directly influenced by social caseworkers in his work on the pamphlet: 'It was a result of cooperation with caseworkers in the voluntary sector who shared the experience of not getting understanding for their ideas among the NAB officers.'[64]

If my inference is correct, the 'young Fabian' Glennerster belonged to a tradition very similar to that in Norway.[65] In the Fabian movement also, the attitude towards the 'residuum' had changed, but continued to include a strong desire for paternalistic control. In the Minority Report to the 1909 Poor Law Commission, the Webbs proposed the setting up of 'punitive labour colonies or similar institutions' for the 'heterogenous residuum'.[66] In the early 1950s Brian Abel-Smith expressed similar, although less draconian, views: 'The social casualties and the old must have financial help with no slur attached, but we should not hesitate to use strong curative measures against any shirkers and slackers in the community.'[67]

In both countries paternalistic attitudes took a much more humane form in the early 1960s. What appears to have been ignored in both countries, though, is the truth in Titmuss's statement 'poor people's services will always be poor services.'[68] From targeting the reformed assistance scheme at the 'residuum', continued stigma was a more likely outcome than 'more generous treatment'. While in Norway this largely became reality, the British process took a decisive turn when the Income Guarantee failed to become realised. This development has been thoroughly documented by Webb, and since I am mainly concerned with the results of the failure, I will give only a brief overview of these events.[69]

---

other academic members. He confirmed that he consulted with Titmuss while writing the pamphlet. Furthermore, he agreed with the suggestion that his proposal for change of assistance can be seen to represent the ideas underlying the phrase 'greater care and attention' in *New Frontiers for Social Security*.

64. Ibid.
65. Glennerster's article was published in the series *Young Fabian Pamphlets*.
66. Referred to in Thane 1982, p. 90.
67. Abel-Smith 1953, p. 15.
68. Titmuss [1968] 1979, p. 143.
69. Webb 1975.

The abandonment of the Income Guarantee

When the Wilson government took office in 1964, the Income Guarantee was high on the agenda of proposed welfare reforms. The interaction of several factors led, however, to its initial postponement and eventual abandonment.

In the early 1960s NA fell into growing disrepute. The findings of Cole and Utting released in 1962 highlighted the problem of non-take-up of assistance among the elderly.[70] From a wider perspective, Webb argues that 'perhaps the most important thing revealed by these findings and their discussion in Parliament, was the degree of ignorance about the effectiveness or the defects of the National Assistance system and the way in which potential clients perceived such a service.'[71] Criticism of assistance took on a new dimension with the discovery of widespread *family poverty.*[72] With that, the problem could no longer be solved by ensuring the departure of pensioners from NA.

The problems of implementation were exacerbated by coinciding political, administrative, and economic factors. Politically, the Wilson government was under great pressure to enact the new income maintenance schemes soon after taking office in 1964. This must be understood in the light of the emphasis put on the scheme as a popular reform. As early as 1957 Crossman noted this in his diary: 'Everyone knows I am cooking this wonderful vote-winner.' Revealing apprehension, however, he added, 'I hope to God it is.'[73] Administratively, the scheme, which was popular in the Labour Party while it was in opposition, 'could also embroil a future Minister in delay, considerable expenditure of staff and financial resources as well as the expenditure of influence in winning co-operation between different government departments.'[74]

Due to its extravagant promises while in opposition, the governing Labour Party was 'on trial' in its attempts to put the economy right.[75] Not surprisingly, therefore, the scheme was postponed in 1965.[76] Once

70. Cole and Utting 1962.
71. Webb 1975, p. 429.
72. The most important study in this connection is Abel-Smith and Townsend 1965.
73. Crossman 1981, p. 581.
74. Webb 1975, p. 430.
75. Ibid., p. 434.
76. Ibid., p. 440.

delayed, 'other commitments were entered into; consequently, if the administrative issues were to be resolved and the money earmarked, the scheme would have to be delayed for several years.'[77]

At this point, the above factors combined to force the government to make immediate changes in assistance: reforms had been promised, new evidence made reform even more pressing, and the opposition was ready to remind the government of its earlier promises. But the new evidence of poverty in general and NA in particular rendered the creation of an alternative scheme for the elderly an insufficient reform. The pressure on the government to act fast contributed to a move away from a selective, targeted approach to one which dealt with NA as a whole.

Referring back to the options for reform, Labour went through a transitional period between 1957 and 1965 in which it advocated the breakdown of assistance 'from without', only to return to reform 'from within' in 1966. The two approaches had different outcomes for assistance as a whole, but I am primarily interested in the different consequences for the non-elderly section of the clientele. I speculated above about the outcome of the proposed Income Guarantee for the 'residuum'. I now turn to give a short overview of the service into which they were swept by the wave of reform in 1966.[78]

The 1966 Social Security Act

Perhaps the greatest reform introduced by this legislation was the consolidation of social security as was first recommended by Beveridge in his report. This took two forms. On the national level all public income maintenance was administered by one unified body, the Ministry of Social Security. For the individual claimant the change meant that there were no longer separate offices for social insurance and assistance. For the assistance clientele as a whole, this implied an enhancement of welfare because they were no longer forced to approach a separate office in order to claim their means-tested benefits. According to Jones, this reform therefore brought about a reduction in the 'stigma by association'

77. Ibid., p. 449.

78. The existence of the new powers under section 1 of the 1963 Children and Young Persons Act *might* have contributed to the government's willingness to include the 'problem families' also; by that time a residual alternative for groups such as these had been established. See next chapter.

attached to the unit through which a stigmatised service had been administered.[79]

Although the distinction between pensioners and other claimants, as proposed in the Income Guarantee, was introduced in the form of Supplementary Pension and Supplementary Allowance, the scheme was generally referred to by the generic term Supplementary Benefit. Compared with what would have resulted from the combination of the Income Guarantee and a reformed NA (as outlined by Glennerster), Supplementary Benefit involved a double enhancement for the 'residuum': In addition to being 'kept together' with the more 'deserving' groups in assistance, they benefited from the reduction in stigma brought about by the administrative merger of assistance and insurance. Furthermore, while assistance in Glennerster's proposal would have involved a merger of income maintenance and other welfare (social work) functions, the separation of cash allocation and social work, as introduced in 1948, was maintained in the 1966 scheme.

As in 1948, the 'residuum' benefited from a reform not primarily targeted at them. In 1948 they were swept along on the post-war euphoria and optimism about their forthcoming disappearance. The attempts to improve the image of the service in 1966 through the change in name, greater emphasis on rights at the expense of discretion, and efforts to better inform the public about the services available were mainly an outcome of the focus on NA caused by the revelation of, first, old age poverty and, later, poverty among families.

When Webb argues that Supplementary Benefit failed to reduce stigma, he makes an omission in not comparing it with the likely outcome of the alternative plans for the Income Guarantee, and in not distinguishing between sections of the clientele according to the way that they would have been segregated in these plans.[80] While it can be argued that the 'higher status group of pensioners'[81] suffered from still being lumped together with the 'problem families' and other 'undesirable' groups, these latter groups of clients profited from a higher level of welfare than that intended for them by the Crossman group.

79. Jones 1985, p. 109.
80. Webb 1975, p. 465.
81. Ibid., p. 462.

Conclusions

The findings in this chapter can be summed up in three points. First, we found that the 1948 nationalisation of assistance represented the culmination of a process rather than a radical break with the past. Second, the description of the 1948 National Assistance Act as a fundamental change of policy needs qualification. For the two-thirds of the clientele (mainly the elderly and the disabled) who were previously the responsibility of the Assistance Board, the change could not be described as dramatic, given the enhancement of this scheme in the period 1940–48. However, for the residual one-third still covered by the local Public Assistance Committees, the reform involved a major enhancement of welfare; they were included in a system in which the rates were set to meet the needs of the elderly and the disabled. Third, during the 1950s it was realised that both the size and composition of NA were unacceptable. Faced with the problem of reforming the scheme, the policy-makers were left with the choice between two alternative strategies. They could either enhance the scheme for all NA recipients, or single out the groups for which a better service was desired and create a two-tier assistance scheme. While the Conservatives in the 1950s followed the selective course of attempting to enhance the status of NA by giving its recipients 'a share in national prosperity', the Labour Party changed its policy several times. After the abandonment of a proposal involving a two-tier system, the party was rushed into creating a scheme which did not differentiate to the same extent between the various need categories covered. In this process the 'residuum' were 'swept along' and profited from being administratively grouped together with large, deserving groups in the Supplementary Benefit scheme. For the 'residuum', therefore, the 1966 reform involved an enhancement of welfare by political default.

Chapter 9

British Personal Social Services: From Specialisation to Unification

Joan Cooper entitled her study of the process leading up to the 1974 reorganisation of local authorities *The Creation of the British Personal Social Services 1962–1974.*[1] To a Norwegian observer the title appears to be somewhat misleading. Compared with the Norwegian development outlined in Chapter 7, the British case featured a wide array of personal social services before this period. As we will see, the difference between a process of *creation of new services*, as in Norway, and one of *unification of existing services*, as in Britain, becomes an important factor when comparing developments in the two countries.

In this chapter the first section outlines the early development of local authority personal social services following the 1948 National Assistance Act. In the second section the emphasis will be on the process of co-ordination of services in the 1950s. This leads naturally to an analysis of the relationship between money and social work in the period leading up to the 1963 Children and Young Persons Act. The fourth section follows the change from co-ordination to unification as outlined by the influential Seebohm Committee.

The creation of specialised services to replace the welfare element of the Poor Law

In Chapter 7 we saw that the Norwegian personal social services were largely dominated by laypeople in the pre-1964 period; by that year only one-third of the local authorities had established staffed social service departments. Furthermore, the services continued to be multifunctional

1. Cooper 1983.

in offering a combination of cash and care. The service moreover covered a wide variety of groups and problems, with material want as the main common denominator. Following the post-war legislation, Britain took a different route than Norway with regard to both the function of local authority services and their staffing and administrative structure.

The most decisive piece of legislation in creating this divergence was the 1948 National Assistance Act. By transferring the responsibility for all financial assistance from the local authority to the state, the Act not only broke with a tradition dating back to the Poor Law of 1388[2] but also established British social assistance as a unique case in European welfare development.

Having transformed the nature of residual relief, the Act went on to outline the future role of the local authorities as deliverers of welfare services. Section 3 of the Act specifies the main responsibility to be the provision of residential care for the aged infirm and other groups in need of such care. The welfare services under the National Assistance Act were organised in *welfare departments.* Jordan and Marshall both consider these services to represent the continuation of the Poor Law tradition in local welfare.[3] Parker points to the continuation of giving priority to 'indoor' over 'outdoor' relief: 'Local authorities had a *duty* to provide residential accommodation while merely having the *power* to give grants to voluntary organisations providing domiciliary meals and recreational activities.'[4] In addition to providing for residential services, the Act outlined the responsibilities of local authorities towards the handicapped. Although the local authorities had had some duties in this area before 1948, these were greatly expanded by the Act. In contrast to the services targeted at the elderly, this area of social work saw an increasing emphasis on the client's independence through work-training and measures to counteract isolation.[5] Finally, the Act assigned the counties the duties of rehousing the homeless and providing shelter for vagrants.[6]

A second set of services to be provided by the local authorities were set out in the 1946 National Health Service Act. Local *health departments*

2. Fraser 1984, p. 31.
3. Jordan 1974, p. 81; Marshall [1965] 1985, p. 144.
4. Parker 1965, p. 109.
5. Ibid., pp. 135, 136.
6. Ibid., p. 140.

were set up to provide health visitors, domestic workers, and home nurses, as well as domiciliary services for the mentally ill.[7]

A third set of services were provided by *children's departments* as set out in the 1948 Children Act. The work of the new departments was divided between, first, ensuring that children 'who have not the benefit of a normal home' were taken into care of the local authority and, second, building homes and, preferably, providing foster families for these children.[8]

Thus, out of the Poor Law there grew a range of services, divided according to the groups targeted. Furthermore, specialised and distinct professional groups developed within each of these departments. Before 1948 the provision of health care, education, shelter, and financial aid all rested, not just with one authority (the Public Assistance Committee), but also with one category of worker (the relieving officer).[9] Following the 1948 legislation these officials were offered the choice between working for the National Assistance Board (i.e. continuing their function of relieving financial distress) or joining the Health Department to work with the mentally ill.[10] Although the professionalisation of British personal social services had started much earlier,[11] this process was greatly accelerated by the post-war legislation. But one problem shared by all the departments in the years that followed was the shortage of trained workers. Another shared challenge was to prove decisive for the development of services leading up to their unification in 1970: with separate departments divided according to groups and not needs, co-ordination became crucial to meet the needs of the clients. We shall return to this, but first I will address the decision that gave Britain a unique position in European social assistance.

The division of cash and care: An expression of a principle?

In the British literature one finds several references to the *principle* of a division between cash and care functions as established by the 1948

7. Ibid., p. 68.
8. National Health Service Act, 1946.
9. Mays, Forder, and Keidan 1971, p. 223.
10. Ibid., p. 257.
11. In the first half of this century, housing remained the only service that was not professionally staffed. Cooper 1983, p. 15.

National Assistance Act.[12] These texts share an emphasis on the experience of means-testing in general and the household means test of the 1930s in particular, as a major catalyst of the Labour Party's desire to separate the provision of services from income maintenance. Stevenson refers to 'the hatred – a word not too strong – of the governing party for the old Poor Law.'[13] Pinker argues that 'more than any other consideration, it was the memory of the hated Poor Law means test which impelled the legislators of the National Assistance Act in 1948 to separate social work from discretionary means-testing and make the central government responsible for financial support.'[14] There is, however, evidence to suggest that these interpretations need qualification.

To analyse this, it is necessary to distinguish between two aspects of the 'principle'. First, I will inquire into the motivation behind the *establishment* of the separation of functions; second, the later development will be analysed to trace the extent to which the separation was established as a principle in British social policy.

The direct cause of the division was the creation of a *national* assistance scheme. As we saw in the previous chapter the setting up of a national scheme proved to be the culmination of a process starting in the late 1920s, rather than a radical departure from established policies.[15] Once National Assistance was established it would have required the setting up of corresponding national personal social services to maintain the pre-1948 cash–care multifunctional nature of assistance. There is no evidence to suggest that this was discussed in the political process leading up to the enactments of that year. This suggests that the separation of functions could have been a natural by-product of the creation of a national assistance scheme more than an intentional decision in its own right. The lack of attention given to welfare services compared with income maintenance in this period lends credence to this interpretation. Moreover, local authorities were given wide powers to exercise means-testing in assessing claimants for means-tested benefits in kind: 'In assessing the ability of residents to contribute towards their own maintenance, local authorities were to use the same means test that was applied by the National

12. Hill and Laing 1979; Jones 1985; George 1968; Pinker 1990.
13. Stevenson 1973, p. 13.
14. Pinker 1990, p. 50.
15. Still, from a historical perspective the transfer can be viewed as a break with the past.

Assistance Board.'[16] This appears to contradict the interpretations that give the departure from means-testing prominence in explaining the motivation behind the separation of functions.

This is not to argue, however, that the final step towards a national assistance scheme was not facilitated by Labour's attitude towards the existing Poor Law. Furthermore, the evidence presented above does not *exclude* the possibility of a deliberate separation on principle. If this was the case, it should be evident in the debates preceding the enactment.

Presenting the National Assistance Bill at its second reading, Aneurin Bevan, the minister of health, made a distinction between two ways of dealing 'with the whole residual problem'.[17] While the government wished to make assistance national, it argued that welfare should be a local responsibility: 'Where the individual is concerned, where warmth and humanity of administration is the primary consideration, then the authority which is responsible should be as near to the recipient as possible.'[18] As was pointed out in the debate that followed, Bevan clearly contradicted a statement he had made when the 1940 Old Age and Widows Bill was discussed in Parliament. At that time he had strongly opposed the transfer of responsibility to assess entitlement for old age and widows' pensions from the local authority to the state. He had argued then that the 'personal relationship which necessarily must exist between those who are giving assistance to the old people and the old people themselves is so essential a part of the effective and humane administration of assistance that people are frightened that this is to be revolutionised and that old people are now to be passed under the control of officials over whose conduct there is no effective local check.'[19] In the debate that followed the second reading of the NA Bill, Bevan invited the scorn of the opposition by not acknowledging the contradiction. The point is not to ridicule a politician for having changed his mind, but rather to ask the interesting question why he should have argued so differently on the two occasions (while not changing his attitude towards the question of assistance).

As the debate provides no answer to why Bevan and the Labour Party changed their position, we have to speculate. One possible interpretation is that the Labour Party saw in the new National Assistance scheme the

16. Parker 1965, p. 107.
17. Hansard, 24 November 1947, 1603 (vol. 444).
18. Ibid.
19. Hansard, 29 February 1940, 1604.

prospect for the more 'humane and effective administration' that it considered to be absent in the Unemployment Assistance Board (UAB) in 1940. As we saw in the previous chapter, the UAB and later the Assistance Board gained in popularity and accessibility following the inclusion of the elderly and widows in 1940. In view of this it appears likely that Labour's attitude changed, first with the legislation it opposed in 1940, and later with the scheme debated in 1947, which was the party's own proposal to abolish and depart from the Poor Law.

For the present analysis, however, it is most important that the debate was more about assistance than about social services, and it was the transfer of responsibility for the social services that Labour advocated. As I have argued, it would have taken a transfer of assistance from local to central government to retain the combined cash–care agency of the Poor Law. This was never debated in Parliament.

On the basis of the evidence presented, I am left with the impression that the separation of money from social work was less of an issue of principle in 1948 than it has since been interpreted (or taken for granted) to have been. Still, it cannot be ruled out that it later became an important principle among all or some of the groups involved in the shaping and delivery of welfare. The extent to which this was the case will be addressed as we turn now to look at the process eventually leading to the first departure from the 'principle' 15 years after its establishment.

Emphasis on the need for co-ordination in the 1950s

In the chapter on the Norwegian personal social services (Chapter 7), we saw how the changing perception of the nature and needs of the assistance clientele influenced the services targeted at them. Furthermore, we found that, with perceptions changing rapidly according to the notions of the day, the timing of new legislation became a crucial factor. Thus, for example, if the Norwegian assistance scheme had been reformed according to the proposals of the early 1950s, it would have assumed a very different nature from that of the scheme finally enacted in 1964.

It is from this same perspective that I turn now to analyse the changes in the relationship between money and social work in Britain. My hypothesis is that changing perceptions of the clientele were equally important in the British development. Also, similar perceptions appear to have prevailed in the same time periods. Timing of legislation therefore becomes an important factor in explaining the different paths taken by the two countries in this area.

Handler's distinction between a pathology theory of poverty and a structural theory is helpful in describing the changes in the perception of the assistance clientele in Britain during the 1950s. The structural theory takes as its starting point that poverty originates in the conditions under which people live: poor housing, education, lack of adequate jobs and income, bad health – these all become central factors not only in explaining poverty but also as areas to target in alleviating poverty. By contrast, the pathology theory explains poverty in terms of individual character defects or family pathology.[20]

In the immediate post-war period the structural theory dominated in Britain. In income maintenance this found its expression in a 'crude universalism.... Contemporaries found it difficult to reconcile the idea of these broad assistance services with anything but standard benefits for all persons eligible by a common test of need.'[21] This philosophy was complemented in the personal social services: 'It was not considered that a general class of persons might exist who might have a need for general social work and there was little appreciation that the needs of potential clients might not fit easily into a number of separate categories defined in a limited number of statutes.'[22] My analysis of the return of the pathology theory takes as its point of departure the 'discovery' of the 'problem family'.

The problem family

This concept originated in the work carried out by the Pacifist Service Unit (PSU) during the Second World War. In its attempts to help families with rehousing, it found that the problems of many families had little to do with wartime conditions. These problems were only an additional stress for families already overwhelmed by financial, housing, and emotional problems.[23] In his analysis based on work in the PSU, Stephens makes the distinction between the 'problem families' and the rest of the

20. Handler 1973, p. 5.
21. Jackson and Valencia 1979, p. 5.
22. Ibid., p. 6.
23. Brown 1982, p. 168.

'submerged tenth' of the population. While the majority of the poor are seen to be able to gain from improved education, social security, housing, and health services, 'the problem families do not respond automatically to improved social conditions; their peculiar characteristic is the inability to make the best of their circumstances and to profit by the facilities and services which are available to them.'[24]

The work of the PSU continued after the war under the aegis of the Family Service Unit (FSU). This organisation became instrumental, not only in helping these families, but also in influencing the course of the debate regarding the *statutory* social services. In its work with the 'problem family', the FSU furthermore introduced the notion of prevention into social work. It should be noted that none of the immediate post-war legislation paid attention to preventive work. This emphasis was gradually adopted by the statutory services, and by the mid-1950s most children's departments had embarked on preventive work.[25]

In 1951 Dr Bowlby published his book *Maternal Care and Mental Health*. In this study he stresses the importance of the first two years of life for a person's mental health in later years. In this early period, he argues, even the worst-functioning family is to be preferred to an institution. This study contributed to an emerging emphasis on the family in general and on preventive work with the 'problem family' in particular.

As we have seen, the social services were divided according to needs, and were highly specialised at this time. Thus, the change of emphasis away from the individual and towards the family in the social services naturally led to a call for co-ordination between the services to meet the needs of the family. As early as 1950 the Home Office issued a circular requesting local authorities to appoint co-ordination officers. The work proved difficult, however, as the experience of specialisation, together with growing professional awareness in the individual departments, brought about administrative as well as professional in-fighting. The children's departments were in the forefront both in focusing on the family and in emphasising preventive work. Incidentally, these were also the departments with the greatest proportion of trained social workers. This imbalance added to the problems of establishing closer co-operation between the different local authority personal social service departments.

24. Stephens 1943, p. 2.
25. Jackson and Valencia 1979, p. 11.

To prevent families from breaking up, workers in children's departments realised the need to help with material resources. For example, a kettle could help when the gas was shut off; a loan or grant could prevent eviction in cases of rent arrears. Consequently, the departments spent more and more time trying to obtain these resources from voluntary organisations as well as from the National Assistance Board. The latter proved to be bureaucratic and slow in meeting urgent needs.

Eventually the emphasis on prevention, together with the realisation of the importance of ready material resources in successfully carrying out preventive work, brought about demands from social workers that they be given the power to allocate financial assistance.

Money and social work in the 1960s

The developments outlined above pointed towards a reconsideration of the separation of money from statutory social services as enacted in 1948. The first decisive move in this direction resulted from the work of the Committee on Children and Young Persons (1960) under the chairmanship of Lord Ingleby.

The Ingleby Committee

The main objective of the committee was to inquire into the operation of the juvenile courts and the custodial institutions for children. A second task was added as an afterthought:[26] to inquire into whether local authorities should 'be given new powers and duties to prevent or forestall the suffering of children through neglect in their own homes.'[27] In its consideration of this question the report discussed the work already carried out by statutory and voluntary services in the field. Referring to the FSU the committee praised the preventive work being done with problem families.[28] While pointing out that local authorities under the 1948 Children Act had no powers to give material help in cash or kind, the committee referred to the changes in the work of the departments after that date:

26. Ibid., p. 12; Handler 1973, p. 58.
27. Cmnd 1191, p. 10.
28. Ibid., p. 14.

> Nevertheless, an increasing part of the work of local authorities' children's departments now consists both in helping to rehabilitate the homes of children in care so that the family can be reunited, and in forestalling the need for children to come into care by taking measures, in co-operation with the other community services, to keep the family in being wherever this is in the best interest of the children.[29]

The committee furthermore encouraged the attempts to create greater co-ordination between the different social services. (The report made special reference to the 1959 Younghusband Report, which reviewed the problem of co-ordination in social work.)[30] From there the report went on to endorse the power to allocate assistance as a measure to further and facilitate the work already being carried out. The committee recommended that the scheme to prevent 'suffering of children through neglect' should provide for

> a. the detection of families where help is needed;
> b. the co-ordination of information (investigation) and diagnosis of the problem;
> c. the provision of appropriate assistance; and
> d. arrangements for making the services known to the public and for advice as to where individuals can apply for help.[31]

The 1963 Children and Young Persons Act

Section 1 of the Act stated as follows:

> It shall be the duty of every local authority to make available such advice, guidance and assistance as may promote the welfare of children by diminishing the need to receive children into or keep them in care under the Children Act 1948, the Principal Act or the Principal Scottish Act, or to bring children before a juvenile court; and any provisions made by a local authority under this subsection may, if the local authority think fit, include provision for giving assistance in kind or, in exceptional circumstances cash.[32]

With this enactment the power to give money was reintroduced into British statutory social work. In an article in *Child Care*, N. Taylor sums

29. Ibid., p. 11.
30. Ibid., p. 15.
31. Ibid., p. 20.
32. Children and Young Persons Act, 1963, section 1.

up the development from a social work perspective: 'So we have moved full circle in a fairly short time. Social work grew out of meeting material needs ... [but] recently we have moved away from this concept.' During those early years money 'was considered to endanger the case-work relationship', while 'now we are faced with a new situation, the power to give money.'[33]

It should be noted here that the Act fell far short of re-establishing the relationship between money and social work as it had existed before 1948. The number of cases in which the power could be exercised was, as we have seen, very limited. The significance of the enactment lies in the break with an established practice. As such, the process leading up to the enactment provides an opportunity to discuss whether the separation of the two functions had developed into a principle. Although I argued that it did not originate as a decision on principle, this did not prevent it from gaining such a status later. Taylor's statement about the belief that money could 'endanger the case-work relationship' can be seen as an indication that it had done so by the time she was writing. In pursuing this question, I will examine, in addition to the role of social workers, the responses to the proposal of the Labour Party, which had been responsible for the 1948 separation.

If this was seen as an issue of principle in the party, then one would expect there to have been, from the Labour benches, either opposition to the proposal or arguments justifying the departure from the principle. When the Bill was debated in the Commons on 27 February 1963, there were no critical comments along these lines from the Labour benches. On the contrary, the strongest advocates for the new powers were to be found among the Labour representatives. Mr MacColl wanted to go even further: 'I do not like the limitations of the cash grants. It is necessary to have power to give them, and I do not see why it should be regarded as exceptional to give them. In many cases it is necessary to spend money quite liberally in rehabilitating families. If we lack the money we cannot begin to carry out constructive social work which is done by bodies such as the Family Service Units.'[34] This was the voice of a party in opposition calling for more spending on welfare and not one defending, or even considering, a principle. In the Standing Committee Ms Bacon raised further

33. *Child Care*, 1962.
34. Hansard, 27 February 1963.

criticism of the Bill. She wanted all the 'mays' changed to 'shalls' in order to make it a duty for local authorities to give assistance.[35] The impression that the debate was more about public spending than principles of social policy is strengthened by the Conservative Mr Brooke's reply to Mr MacColl. He argued that the words 'exceptional' and 'may' were there to avoid imposing on local authorities a duty to provide cash at the expense of the taxpayer, money which should be provided by the National Assistance Board.[36]

Although much of the demand for powers to give assistance came from social workers, the unconditional and strong support from social work circles is still surprising. A survey of the three most important social work journals in the period 1954–64 reveals no articles opposing the reintroduction of money into social work.[37] The articles in favour were, however, numerous. In 1963 the president of the Association of Children Officers, Brook Willes, wrote that 'this will give statutory authority to the work which has been carried out over the past years by officers of children Committees whose every endeavour has been to prevent the break up of families. Clause 1 of the Bill will find its place in the social history of our country.'[38]

Some wanted to go even further than the proposals of the Bill in establishing close ties between social work and income maintenance. Sommerville Hastings advocated the setting up of family care departments in every local authority and went on to argue that 'at the birth of a child the family care department should be notified and a social worker should visit the household. It might be desirable to make the payment of family allowances dependent on the willingness of the mother to accept visits from the family care worker when required.'[39] The main significance of this article lies in the fact that it triggered no response.

On the basis of the evidence presented above, I conclude that the separation of money and social work neither was established according to a principle nor gained the status of one (among those traditionally seen to be most in favour of the split) in the years to follow.

---

35. Standing Committee (on 1963 Children and Young Persons Act), Official Report, 1962–63.

36. Ibid.

37. The journals are *Child Care, Social Service Quarterly*, and *Social Work*.

38. *Child Care*, 1963.

39. *Child Care*, 1960.

Towards a unified personal social service

In the outline of the developments that led to the 1963 Children and Young Persons Act, we saw a move away from specialisation towards co-ordination of services. We now turn to follow the continuation of this process after co-ordination was found to be an insufficient solution to the problems facing the social services.

The Seebohm Report

In 1965 a committee under the chairmanship of Frederick Seebohm was appointed to 'review the organisation and responsibilities of the local authority personal social services in England and Wales, and to consider what changes are desirable to secure an effective family service.'[40] The recommendations of the committee were later largely implemented in the 1970 Local Authority Social Services Act. The greatest significance of the report is in its plan for a unified department to bring together the different local social services that had developed independently after the war. As we have seen, the specialisation of these departments brought about demands for greater co-ordination. By the time the committee reported in 1968, the separateness of the local departments had been allowed to develop to a point where co-ordination was no longer a sufficient means of achieving a needs-oriented, rather than group-oriented, service.[41]

Again the family was the unit around which the service was to be developed. The terms of reference equated a personal social service to a 'family service'. This was a continuation of the policy that had developed since the early 1950s. The focus on the family started out as a more extensive approach compared with the individualistic approach of the existing services. When the term 'family' became a controversial issue in the days of the Seebohm group, it was, however, the *limitations* of the approach that gave rise to debate.

The exponents of a family service, to be constructed largely 'as an extension of children's departments', found their strongest allies in the Labour Party subgroup known as the Longford group.[42] The main critique of this position came from an *ad hoc* group consisting of people from

40. Cmnd 3703, para. 1.
41. Cooper 1983, p. 84; Cmnd 3703, para. 79.
42. Cooper 1983, pp. 58, 59.

social administration and social work backgrounds. This group found the Longford proposals for a family service to be too narrow. They argued that, by focusing on the family, the proposals excluded large numbers of people, in particular elderly and handicapped people whose needs were then being met by the local health departments. With this in mind Richard Titmuss, who was the dominant figure in the *ad hoc* group, proposed a service 'created and organised around the services to be provided rather than around categories of clients or particular fragments of need.'[43]

It was up to the Seebohm Committee to find a meeting point between these two positions. The compromise reached hinged largely on rhetoric. The committee retained the term 'family' while stretching its definition to include virtually everybody.[44]

The policy of one large department providing universal coverage was also seen to facilitate a desired escape from the historical associations with poverty. In doing so, it was hoped, the overriding objective of increased accessibility could be achieved. The Social Service Departments (SSDs), as implemented after 1970, thus embraced all statutory social services including personal health but excluding medical and nursing services, which were assigned to the National Health Service. (Probation was also kept out and maintained its traditional autonomy.) Each SSD was to be organised as an area office serving populations between 50,000 and 100,000 people, and employing 10 to 12 social workers. Yet social workers made up only 10% of the workers in the new service. The other groups were non-professional social care workers, such as those employed in domiciliary, day care and residential services, and day service officers working with the mentally handicapped. The new personal social service thus became much more than a 'social work department'. Its responsibilities included 'the physically handicapped, the mentally handicapped, the mentally ill, and the frail elderly'.[45] Services included 'community care, day care, and residential care'.[46] The large size was strongly advocated by Titmuss as a measure to create career opportunities for social workers, to give the departments political weight, and to reduce problems of confidentiality.[47]

43. Ibid., p. 63.
44. Cmnd 3703, para. 32.
45. Ibid.
46. Ibid.
47. Handler 1973, p. 105.

The report also discussed the relationship between money and social work. The question raised was whether to extend the powers then restricted to children's department work under section 1 of the 1963 Children and Young Persons Act. The committee argued the case for 'an additional power enabling social service departments to give financial help in families where only adults are concerned.'[48] That this recommendation failed to be implemented in 1970, Pinker argues, must be understood in the light of the Treasury's hostility towards giving social workers the power to allocate money.[49]

The Scottish example

The personal social services in Scotland developed along different lines from those of England and Wales. As I have chosen to follow the English example in this analysis, I will touch on this difference only inasmuch as the Scottish developments can be seen to have influenced the path chosen in England. With the 1968 Social Work (Scotland) Act, the power of the local authorities to give material assistance was expanded compared with the 1963 Children and Young Persons Act. While the latter limited the granting of material assistance to families with children, section 12 of the Scottish Act had no such limitation. In a similar way to that of the Ingleby Committee, the Kilbrandon Report, published in 1964, advocated the co-ordination of services for children in difficulty. As in England, this approach was later expanded to include a wider definition of 'family', as well as to replace co-ordination with unification.

Richard Titmuss was once more instrumental in the shaping of policies. Judith Hart, who had been one of his students at the London School of Economics, became the parliamentary under secretary of state for Scotland in 1964. She included Titmuss in an advisory group whose brief was to further develop the policies outlined in the Kilbrandon Report.[50] Titmuss's advocacy of a unified and comprehensive service received greater support and enjoyed a speedier enactment process in Scotland than in England and Wales. Cooper argues that this difference can be explained largely by the fact that in Scotland one minister was in charge

48. Cmnd 3703, para. 604.
49. Pinker 1990, p. 51.
50. Cooper 1983, p. 39.

of all the areas affected by the proposed legislation.[51] Furthermore, she attributes the extended power to allocate money in Scotland to its lower population density: 'Individuals living in remote or isolated circumstances might, it was argued, more effectively and easily be helped in kind or, in an emergency, in cash, and be helped less expensively through the pump-priming of local community initiatives than through the highly organised services more commonly available in densely populated urban areas.'[52]

Because of its open-ended nature section 12 proved to be difficult to negotiate with the Treasury. This perception of its being open to excessive use by social workers was strengthened in its two years of operation before the English and Welsh legislation was ready for enactment. By then, Cooper argues, there was widespread criticism of 'giving a cheque book to social workers'.[53] This last point raises an interesting comparative observation. In Norway, where social workers have continually exercised the power to allocate assistance benefits to their clients, it has been said, albeit jokingly, that a safe way to save money on a benefit budget is to employ social workers to allocate it. By contrast, British social workers spent two decades advocating, mainly on behalf of their clients, more benefits from statutory and voluntary bodies. Although the Treasury's fear was most likely exaggerated, this British tradition could, at least in the short run, have led to very generous allocations by the social workers.

Treasury hostility is also the most likely explanation of the rejection of extended powers to allocate money in the 1968 Health Services and Public Health Act: 'No arrangements under this section shall provide for the payment of money to old people.'[54]

Summary

Two main themes have been analysed in this chapter. First, after the abolition of the all-purpose Poor Law in 1948, the British personal social services developed from a high degree of specialisation in the early stages

51. Ibid.

52. Cooper 1983, p. 50. This, incidentally, could equally well be a description of the average Norwegian municipality. However, this was never used as an argument in the Norwegian debate.

53. Ibid.

54. Health Services and Public Health Act, 1968, para. 43.4.

towards a unified service in the late 1960s. In the 1950s the fragmentation of services led to calls for greater co-ordination between the different departments. This process was closely linked to an increasing interest in the family, both as a source of social problems and, consequently, as the group to be targeted for their solution. The fragmentation had, however, gone too far for co-operation between existing bodies to be a feasible solution. In 1968, therefore, the Seebohm Committee proposed the setting up of a unified and comprehensive family service.

Second, coinciding with this development was that regarding the relationship between the social services and income maintenance, or money and social work, as I have put it. Here I first questioned the understanding of the 1948 division of money and social work as a decision on principle. Rather than being a reaction to the hated means test of the Poor Law, the separation was first and foremost a natural by-product of the setting up of a *national* social assistance scheme. The emphasis on families and prevention in the 1950s brought about a renewed debate about the desirability to give local authority social workers the power to allocate money to clients in particular circumstances, for example when the breakup of a family was threatening. The Ingleby Committee recommended that such powers should be given. In the period leading up to the 1963 Children and Young Persons Act, I found no fundamental questioning of the reintroduction of money into social work. On the contrary, the Labour Party (as the party responsible for the 1948 split) and the social work organisations (as supposed upholders of the principle) proved to be the most outspoken advocates of the new powers being given.

Part Four
Conclusion

Chapter 10
Conclusion

In this study I have attempted to analyse the unequal development of services targeted at the poorest and most vulnerable segments of the population in Norway and Britain. The main hypothesis for the study was as follows: The unequal development of social insurance caused the size and composition of the social assistance clientele in the two countries to differ. The respective social assistance schemes were therefore designed to cater for the needs of different groups.

In this chapter I will first present the main findings regarding variation in my dependent variable: social assistance and personal social services. The findings are then summarised using the indicators of residuality outlined in Chapter 1. Having established the major differences, I will evaluate possible explanatory factors. Finally, the findings and conclusions will be discussed in relation to theories and models of welfare.

Summary of main findings: The contrasting developments of British and Norwegian residual services

Welfare programmes targeted at the poor were the topic of Part Three. I have distinguished between social assistance and personal social services. While assistance covers the successors of the income maintenance component of the Poor Laws, personal social services are defined as the modern-day version of services offered as adjuncts to the allocation of poor relief in former times. Together, these two sets of services are (in both nations) the modern heir to the multipurpose Poor Law.

Social assistance

The development of social assistance was analysed in Chapter 6 (Norway) and Chapter 8 (Britain). In the first two post-war decades, Norway continued its approach of breaking down the Poor Law 'from without' through the successful extension of social insurance. The scheme introduced in 1964 continued in the Poor Law tradition of a cash–care multifunctional, localised service. The emphasis in the programme was on care rather than income maintenance, and professional social workers were employed to offer the modern form of care: 'social treatment'. In assessing entitlement to assistance, social workers, together with politically elected lay representatives of the Social Boards, were given wide discretionary powers by legislators. From the client's point of view, assistance could not be *claimed*, and it was therefore difficult to describe assistance as a *right*. Furthermore, the service was highly selective – in effect, it was targeted at the poorest and least 'deserving' segments of the population.

Britain, by contrast, started out by abolishing the Poor Law and changing the nature of assistance as early as 1948. In the years to follow, the failure of insurance to incorporate and contain the groups for which it was designed brought about continued pressure for reform of the assistance scheme. Reforms were, however, not targeted at the clientele for which assistance was originally intended. Around 1960, therefore, attempts were made to create a two-tier assistance system – one level for the traditional assistance clientele and a better service for the 'deserving' claimants, in particular the elderly and the disabled. These attempts failed, however, and the result was an enhanced service for the entire assistance clientele, introduced in 1966. Therefore, except for the changes in 1948, when there appears to have been a deliberate aim to enhance welfare for all, the ensuing elevation of assistance can, from the perspective of the residuum, be described as 'institutionalisation by default'.

Cash and care in the personal social services

In Chapters 7 (Norway) and 9 (Britain), I analysed the development of the personal social services in the two countries to explore what happened to the care (or control) element of the cash–care multifunctional Poor Law in the reformed programmes. The emphasis was therefore on the extent to which social workers were responsible for the provision of cash to their clientele. In Norway the two sets of services were kept together, and professional social workers increasingly took on the role of providing care, in the form of social treatment, as an adjunct to the provision of cash. In Britain the two functions were separated with the nationalisation of social assistance in 1948. Later, in 1963, British social workers in the personal social services were again empowered to provide material benefits and cash to their clientele, albeit on a more limited scale than in Norway.

From the outset after the war, the British personal social services covered much wider need categories than their Norwegian counterparts. The different departments, which were eventually unified into one Social Service Department (SSD), comprised services for the elderly, the disabled, and children, as well as more traditional Poor Law clientele for whom material want played a central role. In Norway, by contrast, the continued cash–care multifunctional nature of the service ensured that the clientele were defined as, and in effect limited to, those seeking help for reasons of material need. Jones describes the personal social services as the 'first aid service' of the welfare state.[1] As regards income maintenance, the Norwegian scheme can better be described as a 'last-resort' service, to be used only in the absence of any other solution to the problem.

Also, the Norwegian 1964 Act covered the provision of services targeted at a wider segment of the population than the poor only. Unlike the personal social services in Britain, these services were in their infancy in Norway at the time of enactment in 1964. The focus on the provision of last-resort cash relief within the combined service, along with the ensuing stigma of the service, probably curtailed the expected widening of the catchment areas of need to be met by the services. A decade later, the overwhelming majority of clients of the Norwegian social services had material problems.

Degrees of residuality

In Chapter 1, I outlined the variables by which social assistance and personal social services would be compared. The following summarises

1. Jones 1985, p. 172.

the main findings of the comparison with reference to the indicators in Table 1.1.

The central/local dimension

This study was inspired by the observation of the stark contrast between the nationalised British social assistance scheme and the Norwegian scheme, which had remained local in the tradition of the Poor Law.

During the period of this analysis, the divergence continued as the income maintenance part of British assistance was further centralised and, in 1966, the administration of assistance was merged with that of National Insurance.

The nature of the legislation

In Britain assistance was legalised and codified with the abolition of the Poor Law in 1948. Throughout the period of analysis, British social assistance was allocated according to nationally established rules that gave claimants access to non-discretionary benefits awarded after a test of *need.* The result was an income maintenance system by which people could make *claims* when they found themselves in any one of its defined need situations. The much later reform in Norway did not result in similar legislation. Instead, the 1964 reform introduced a framework legislation leaving considerable discretion to the local authorities in charge of implementing the scheme.

The decision-makers

In Britain administrative officers carried out the day-to-day casework and made decisions concerning eligibility on the basis of established criteria. In Norway the decisions were made at two levels. First, the laypeople in the local Social Care Boards continued to have a say in individual cases. Second, the new scheme was designed to be administered by professional social workers. The main influx of this group into social assistance took place after the introduction of the law. Both social workers and laypeople were allowed considerable discretion in deciding both eligibility and the level and nature of benefits provided.

Cash and/or care

With the nationalisation of assistance in Britain in 1948, the provision of cash was separated from the personal social services, which continued as a local responsibility. This entailed that the administrators focused exclusively on material problems by assessing claims for last-resort income maintenance. In Norway the tradition of cash–care multifunctional services continued after the abolition of the Poor Law in 1964.

Target groups

In Britain elderly and disabled people continued to dominate the clientele of the social services. Also, an increasing proportion of the population received benefits during the period studied. In Norway, by contrast, while the number of assistance clients decreased, there was an increase in the proportion of able-bodied poor, many of whom suffered from complex social problems (the 'residuum').

With reference to the index of residuality set out in Chapter 1 (see Table 1.1), we can therefore conclude that the Norwegian assistance scheme continued to feature strong similarities to the Poor Law and can thus be described as a service with strong residual traits. By contrast, the British assistance scheme proved more successful in escaping the residual model out of which it, like its Norwegian counterpart, originally grew. While the British welfare state ended up with a large welfare residuum served by a not-so-residual service, Norway continued to offer a highly residual service to a small and decreasing minority relying on public income maintenance.

Towards an understanding of divergence

During the course of this study, I have touched on several possible explanations of the unequal development of the residual services. It is now time to sum up the contribution of the various (explanatory) factors outlined in Chapter 1. I will start by discussing factors which I will argue offer only partial explanations and conclude with a discussion of the factor which I consider to be the most important.

The attitudes towards poverty and dependency

Throughout this study normative issues, such as policy-makers' perceptions of the social assistance clientele and corresponding measures advocated, have been central to the analysis. We have seen that, in Norway, the Poor Law tradition of social control, lay influence, and local autonomy remained much more intact than in Britain. This observation calls for an inquiry into national differences with regard to ideas about self-help, the distinction between the deserving and the undeserving, and, ultimately, the perception of the needs of the poor and how to meet them.

It is possible, for example, that the provision of unilateral material aid on the basis of entitlement, regardless of the cause of the need, was a more dominant and widely accepted norm in British society, and that this explains the greater modernisation and legalisation of social assistance in Britain.

In a recent study Lars Inge Terum highlights the importance of normative aspects in his analysis of what he describes as the resistance towards the modernisation of Norwegian post-war social assistance.[2] He puts particular emphasis on the strength of the ideas of self-help and the value of work, as a source of both income and self-worth, within the Labour Party. The party's resistance to legalising social assistance in the form of nationally established scale rates (thereby reducing discretion and local variation) is understood as 'resting on the view of *work* and a fear of undermining the *work-ethic* in society'.[3]

By applying an explicitly normative perspective, Terum provides new and valuable insight into the political background to the lacking modernisation of Norwegian assistance in the post-war period.[4] I will, however, discuss the extent to which the normative perspective adds to our understanding of why Norway in this particular period modernised, or escaped the tenets of the Poor Law, to a lesser degree than Britain.[5]

---

2. Terum 1996.
3. Ibid., p. 234.
4. In discussing modernisation he focuses on two aspects, legalisation and professionalisation. I will restrict my discussion to aspects concerning the former.
5. Terum's discussion (1996, pp. 209–18) of the Labour Party's attitude towards work is wider, and he discusses the role of paid labour in general, not only in relation to the non-working. On the other hand, he argues convincingly that the introduction of legal rights to social insurance benefits was made possible by the normative understanding that everybody would choose to work if they had the choice.

Terum's conclusion concerning the influence of the work ethic on the legalisation of social assistance is suitable for comparative testing: if the Labour Party's attitudes towards work and non-work blocked the legalisation and modernisation of assistance in Norway, a different outcome in a country with an equally influential labour party can be understood only if the two parties viewed these normative questions differently. Terum alludes to such a comparative position by referring to various indications of the strength of the work ethic in Norway compared with other countries,[6] and notes that normative questions concerning poverty relief are more prevalent in Norway than in countries such as Germany and Britain.

The material presented in my study allows me to discuss the usefulness of this perspective for an understanding of the formative twenty-year period after the war in Britain and Norway.[7] As in Norway, the developments in Britain in this area of welfare were also mainly the outcome of Labour politics.[8] We can therefore compare the attitudes of two similar political parties. My assertion is that the perception of, and the attitudes towards, the able-bodied poor were more similar than different in the labour parties of the two nations.

To discuss this we need to distinguish between attitudes towards social assistance and attitudes towards similar social groups in the two countries. The debate concerning social assistance in the 1960s was indeed of a different flavour in the two countries. Following the growing awareness of the number of elderly people, disabled people, and widows relying on

---

6. He refers to the European 'Work Orientation 1989', in which Norwegians proved to be more oriented towards work than, for example, Germans and the British. This is tentatively interpreted as being connected to the strength of lay movements, not least the labour movement, in Norway. The Norwegian labour movement is emphasised as an upholder of ideas about diligence, work, and social cohesion. Moreover, it is seen as being more concerned with ensuring that its own do not fall into poverty than with helping the already-poor out of poverty. This suggests that the solidarity of the Norwegian labour movement does not extend to the marginal poor. Ibid., pp. 217–18.

7. Terum argues that in particular the resistance towards legalisation in the 1980s (rather than the period discussed here), when the number of recipients increased sharply, is best understood by applying the normative perspective. Ibid., p. 20.

8. Labour introduced National Assistance in 1948. It was also Labour that planned the Income Guarantee in 1963 and introduced the Supplementary Benefit scheme in 1966.

National Assistance for their livelihood, the debate concerning minimum income reform in Britain was increasingly about material poverty, shameful treatment of elderly people, and, in effect, the need for an enhancement of social assistance as an income maintenance programme. In Norway the concern was with those who, in spite of full employment and a universal social insurance system, still relied on social assistance.

While the debates concerning social assistance were different, the evidence presented in Part Three documents that the attitudes towards the *able-bodied* poor, or those considered to be *socially maladjusted* poor, were very similar in the two countries. The distinction between the deserving and the undeserving poor was in both countries detectable and in both cases defined in relation to behaviour and the virtues of self-help through work. To highlight this similarity, I need to return briefly to the discussion of Britain in the early 1960s, as outlined in Chapter 8. During those years, one reform and one proposed reform illustrated attitudes in the Labour Party similar to those prevailing in Norway.

Labour's proposed Income Guarantee involved measures for the residuum different from those advocated for the remaining clients of National Assistance. The Labour Party's plans for the former groups differed little from those simultaneously made for the entire social assistance clientele in Norway.[9] If introduced, the residual appendix to the Income Guarantee would have involved a return to welfare more in line with the doctrines of the Poor Law for the undeserving poor in Britain, and, as a consequence, residual policies in the two countries would have converged.

The Income Guarantee was, however, never implemented, and the residuum were swept along into the social security of the 1966 Supplementary Benefit scheme. The re-creation of a new bottom 'division of welfare' was instead introduced, on a smaller scale, in the social services with the 1963 Children and Young Persons Act. With this Act the material needs of the poorest families increasingly became a concern of the personal social services, and a different world of welfare was created for (large numbers of) families with a combination of social and economic problems. In his analysis of the implementation of the provision of cash (Section 1) of the 1963 Act, Bill Jordan describes how a new category of income maintenance clients was created by the Supplementary Benefit

9. Glennerster 1962.

Commission and other agencies making referrals to the personal social services:

> Social workers' willingness to do preventive work, their anxiety to take earlier referrals of client's problems, to forestall by intervention rather than to wait for disaster, has encouraged other agencies to identify large numbers of 'welfare cases', and to send them to social service departments for all their needs. They see 'welfare cases' as specially needy people who cannot make proper use of ordinary provision.[10]

The reintroduction of cash in the English personal social services was the end of a process that started with the 'discovery' of the 'problem family' in the late 1940s. The subsequent focus on the family in general, and preventive work targeted at the family in particular, resulted in demands that social workers be given powers to allocate cash as a preventive measure.

In Norway similar developments can be traced. Although there was no reference made to 'problem families' as such, the understanding of social and material problems underlying this term was very much shared by the policy-makers behind the 1964 scheme. Here the clients were mainly seen to be suffering from 'social disabilities'. In rehabilitating them, money was seen to be insufficient in itself. On the contrary, the minister of social affairs feared that the allocation of cash without accompanying casework would be directly harmful to the client. The Norwegian plans in the early 1960s went further than the Ingleby proposals by referring to money as a 'therapeutic means'. Still, a critical assessment of the application of the powers given to British social workers in 1963 suggests that in practice the 1963 scheme shared important similarities with its Norwegian counterpart.

What the two countries shared was an emphasis on a non-structural understanding of poverty in the 1960s. While this involved (and indeed resulted from) a return to 'pathology theory' in Britain, this theory was never seriously challenged in Norway, where the poorest continued to be kept in a separate world of combined cash and care/control.

In Britain, therefore, two debates were running simultaneously in the late 1950s and early '60s: one concerning social assistance, which was predominantly about the needs of the elderly, and one concerning the

10. Jordan 1976, p. 161.

'problem family' and other problematic poor, which was about social treatment and social control. In Norway there was only one debate concerning social assistance – the latter of the two. The debate about the elderly was conducted elsewhere, for example in the struggle over the benefit level of the old age pension. That debate had similarities to the British social assistance debate.[11] The difference was that, in Norway, this did not change social assistance.

With regard to the crucial period 1945–66, therefore, it is not different attitudes towards the poor that explain the unequal development or modernisation of social assistance in Norway and Britain. Divergence must be attributed more to the different groups for which social assistance was designed. In Norway these were increasingly the residuum; in Britain they were increasingly the elderly and widows. The importance of normative issues was due to circumstances particular to Norway rather than particular norms prevailing in Norwegian society. The normative perspective therefore offers only a partial understanding of the development in Norway in this period.

The timing of reform

The comparison above illustrates the importance of the timing of legislation. We have seen how the prevailing understanding of the causes of, and remedies for, poverty changed in both countries from a structural theory in the early post-war years to a pathological understanding in the late 1950s and early 1960s. The main difference is that while the UK abolished its Poor Law and introduced social assistance in the early period, Norway legislated in the later. An early proposal (1953) for reform in Norway was influenced by the structural theory. However, the proposal was shelved, and the following ten years of gestation paved the way for the enactment of assistance in a different socio-political climate, in which poverty was seen more as an expression of social maladjustment than economic want in itself. Conversely, in Britain policy-makers attempted in the early 1960s to divide social assistance into higher and lower tiers. But this proposal was never enacted.

11. If we were to follow the definitions used by Eardley et al. (1996), the old age pension in Norway would be considered a social assistance programme, at least until 1957, when the means test was lifted. From this perspective it can be argued that, in the case of the elderly, the two countries had constructed two different schemes.

Moreover, in both countries the size and the composition of the assistance clientele changed during the period between the early post-war years and the 1960s. I will return to how this change influenced the different paths taken.

Individual policy-makers

In the final section below, I will address the wider political issues. Let us now pause to look at how individual policy-makers influenced the paths taken. This perspective has been charted in various parts of this study. One area open to influence from individuals is the timing of reform. In the UK Beveridge's achievements included bringing social assistance to the core of social reform plans during the war and reserving a place for it in the early post-war legislation. As we saw in Chapter 8, even though centralisation had already come a long way, the inclusion of assistance in the Beveridge Plan facilitated the nationalisation of assistance at a crossroads where this was possible.

In Norway a key politician played the opposite role, contributing to the delay of the abolition of the Poor Law for a decade. Rakel Seweriin, the minister of social welfare, had neither the necessary political will nor the support of her prime minister when the first proposal was submitted to her in 1953. Her inability to push it through contributed to delaying the Norwegian legislative reform from the time of the early post-war structural understanding of poverty to a different climate in the 1960s. This illustrates that policy-makers can play an important role, either by living up to the responsibility bestowed upon them[12] or by failing to achieve what could be expected of them.

Policy inheritance

The choices made at one crossroads will influence the path taken later. In both countries the Poor Law influenced the choices made when it was abolished and replaced with assistance. Most important, while Britain had a long tradition of a centralised system of poor relief, local autonomy in general and local responsibility for poor relief in particular were

12. The inclusion of social assistance as a national programme was not part of the terms of reference given to the committee chaired by William Beveridge. Cmd 6404, para. 2.

equally well rooted in Norway. From this perspective it is of little importance, however contradictory it may seem, that centralisation as a key factor in the institutionalisation of British assistance was originally introduced to implement the harsh residual Poor Law with a maximum of efficiency.[13] The events in the 1930s shortened the step towards full nationalisation further, albeit with a different clientele than that targeted by Edwin Chadwick a century earlier. Still, the administrative structure and trained officers were in place to take on a changing clientele and new roles.

Because Britain at the outset had a more repressive Poor Law than Norway, the breach with the policy inheritance was greater, although the machinery changed little.

Social insurance

The four factors discussed above all contribute to our understanding of the unequal development of social assistance in Norway and Britain. However, whether individually or combined, they still offer only a partial explanation.

A recurrent aspect in the discussions above is the importance of who the clients of assistance are. I have discussed two aspects concerning the target groups: size and composition. These cannot be viewed independently, and the composition or the nature of the clientele is the more important one. The main distinction is between individuals who are perceived as deserving of unilateral support and those met with suspicion of fraud or with fear of undermining their ability to be self-reliant through the allocation of cash with few strings attached. If the 'deserving' group increases in size, the problem is not only moral, but also one of increasing political significance as a question of redistribution. If the 'undeserving' group increases, this is more likely to be perceived as a moral question, and more a concern of expenditure than of redistribution.

The unequal development in the size and composition of the assistance clientele can result from changes in two main alternative sources of maintenance. The first is paid employment. During the first twenty years after the war, both Norway and Britain enjoyed low levels of unemploy-

13. Margaret Thatcher therefore followed an old tradition when she centralised power in order to implement liberalist policies in the 1980s.

ment. In both nations wages were such that few working poor were entitled to assistance. Differences in the labour market are therefore not a decisive factor in creating divergence in the numbers and composition of those relying on social assistance.

The second alternative is social insurance benefits. Social insurance was created in both nations to replace the Poor Law for the majority of people in need. On the basis of this understanding, I have devoted half of this book to the study of the unequal development of social insurance in the two countries. The main comparative points were summarised at the end of Part Two. Below, I will briefly use this evidence to discuss the unequal influence of social insurance on the size and composition of the social assistance clientele in the two countries.

The British system of social insurance, as laid down in the 1946 National Insurance Act, was based on the Beveridge Report. The system followed the contributory system of financing, whereby the insured persons were the main source of funds. This was combined with the flat-rate principle: the insured were to pay equal contributions and receive equal benefits in return. This combination proved detrimental to the development of the level of social insurance benefits. In the relative hardship of the early post-war period, no minister was willing to pay the political cost of the necessary raising of contributions and the unreasonable burden this would put on the lowest paid workers. With unexpected inflation, the pension benefits, already set very low in 1946, failed to reach subsistence level.

Although Norway had a similar long-term ambition, it started out much slower than Britain in its post-war reform of social security. While Britain took a much greater initial leap towards universality with the 1946 National Insurance Act, Norway continued its incremental expansion of social insurance based on its first old age pension, established in 1937. The major difference between this scheme and its British counterpart was that while Britain adhered to the contributory principle, Norway followed a mainly non-contributory road, creating a system of 'people's insurance' paid for mainly through tax revenues.

The system of financing proved to have a decisive impact on the divergent development of coverage and benefits experienced in the two nations.[14] In Britain the contributory flat-rate approach impeded the

14. In Chapters 2 (Norway) and 4 (Britain), I analysed how the two nations arrived at very different systems of financing social insurance.

achievement of full universality, first through the exclusion of non-contributors and later through increasing spillover to social assistance due to the inability to raise the level of benefits.

In Norway the choice of the taxation principle allowed for the incorporation of new groups regardless of their ability to contribute towards the cost of the programmes. The extension of social insurance was therefore a political, rather than a practical, question. Although Britain took the greater initial first step towards universality, in the long run the British universality proved to be limited to a very low level of benefits, thereby causing increased selectivity. In Part Two I concluded that, as a result of these developments, social insurance in Britain retained strong elements of the residual model of welfare, while the Norwegian system developed into an example of the institutional model (also incorporating elements of the industrial achievement model of welfare).

Mainly as a result of the developments in social insurance, the assistance clientele continued to grow in Britain in the 1950s and early 1960s. Between 1948 and 1962 the number of claimants increased from 1.5 to 2.5 million, and the clientele was increasingly dominated by groups which, according to Beveridge, should have been sufficiently covered by social insurance. While, for example, recipients of old age pensions from National Insurance constituted 48.2% of the clientele in 1949, this figure had increased to 59.9% in 1965.

In Norway we witness a contrasting development. During the period 1946–64 the number of people receiving assistance in Norway fell from 50,000 to 32,000. As this decrease, in addition to full employment, was largely caused by the successful extension of social insurance coverage, a contrastive development in the composition of the clientele in the two countries also emerges. Although less conclusive evidence is available for Norway than for Britain, available statistics suggest that the clientele was less dominated by 'insurance cases' at the time of the abolition of the Poor Law in 1964 than when the first proposal for reform was presented a decade earlier.

I have focused on social insurance because the development of this set of income maintenance programmes did not determine changes in social assistance, but rather the size and composition of the clientele for whom social assistance was designed in the two countries. This in turn strongly influenced the divergent development of social assistance. The main lesson to be learned from this discussion is, however, that there is no one factor that can explain the divergence of social assistance within the expanding welfare state. What I hope to have achieved, though, is a presentation of the relative value of different explanatory factors for a better understanding of the unequal development in these two countries in this crucial period of the history of welfare.

Future studies of minimum income schemes need to pay more attention to the interrelationship between the extent of poverty, the composition of the poor, the perception of these groups, and the political and popular ideas about the appropriate measures for the alleviation of poverty. Poverty requires unilateral transfers. To gain acceptance for entitlement to such transfers, with few strings attached, the popular perception of the recipient is crucial. If the person is old and physically disabled, such acceptance comes easier than if the person is, for example, young, single, male, and able-bodied. With small variations, this is probably true in most societies.[15]

The welfare paradox

My focus has been on services targeted at the residual groups for whom both nations reserved a separate form of income maintenance even after social insurance, fulfilling the visions of the 1940s, had successfully expanded to cover all the needs for which it was intended. In defining these social groups, both countries emphasised their need for more than just cash. The consequent stress on social control and guidance bore in both nations a strong similarity to the notions of the 'undeserving poor' that prevailed in the era of the Poor Laws. The extent to which these attitudes found their expression in practical policies, however, differed greatly in the two nations. Here we found the seemingly contradictory situation in which Norway, which in overall terms was more successful in escaping the legacy of the Poor Law through the creation of a close-to-universal social insurance at a high level of service delivery, was in fact the country that maintained residual services most in line with the administrative and ideological tenets of the Poor Law. To express this in terms of the models set out in Chapter 1, Norway had greater success in achieving institutional welfare while maintaining a small assistance scheme and personal social services more in line with the doctrines of the

15. Article 12 of the Soviet Constitution of 1936 stated that 'he who does not work, neither shall he eat' (quoted in Barker 1985).

residual model. It is now time to qualify further the notion of this apparent contradiction. To do so, let us return briefly to the theoretical models discussed in Chapter 1.

Models of welfare

In his analysis of Norwegian post-war welfare development, Tvede concluded in 1983 that 'Norwegian social policy has today few or no similarities to the residual model'.[16] In this perspective the existing assistance scheme was seen as a system designed to be 'flexible and able to meet acute problems arising from non-standardised need situations'.[17] A similar understanding is evident in Esping-Andersen's stress on the limited scope of social assistance in the Nordic countries as a feature of the well-developed 'social democratic welfare regime'.[18] Conversely, the greater reliance on assistance in Britain is, in this perspective, a sign of its liberal regime type. By focusing on the internal division of the British and the Norwegian welfare states, I have found not only that the nature of the 'sub-regimes' of social assistance differs from the 'total welfare state' regime types, but also that the sub-regimes do not co-vary with the regimes in Esping-Andersen's 'worlds of welfare': the Norwegian social democratic, or institutional, model features a more residual, or liberal, sub-regime of assistance than its British liberal, or residual, counterpart.

The models developed by Titmuss, as applied by Tvede and (indirectly) Esping-Andersen, portray a one-dimensional picture in which the expansion of institutional welfare results in a reduction of residual welfare delivery. While this is numerically true, the internal divisions of the welfare states escape attention.

While, in the case of Esping-Andersen, the one-dimensionality results from his focus on pensions and the welfare state as a unitary system, Titmuss's approach must be understood in the light of his sharp distinction between the economic and the social markets. For Titmuss the developed welfare state, and thereby institutional welfare, necessitated a rejection of the values of the economic market.[19] In this rejection he

16. Tvede 1983, p. 95.
17. Ibid., p. 104.
18. Esping-Andersen 1990.
19. It is tempting to view this rejection in the light of Titmuss's transformation from an insurance man to a scholar and advocate of social welfare. Indeed, his

ignored not only the voluntary sector but also the means by which the incorporation of economic values into social policy could enhance, rather than undermine, the welfare state. In Norway we saw how the increasing emphasis on market values through the growth of earnings-related pensions secured the continued enhancement of this scheme as a real alternative to the welfare offered through the private and occupational insurance market. While Titmuss appears to view the 'handmaiden model' as little more than a more developed form of residual welfare, my evidence suggests that the strength of the Norwegian institutional model is its incorporation of elements of 'handmaiden welfare'.[20]

Titmuss's writing must furthermore be understood in the light of the particular British experience about which he wrote. Even before the war, Britain had a much stronger tradition of private and occupational income maintenance programmes. While Beveridge appears to have maintained the role of market values in social welfare through continued reliance on the insurance principle, his intention in doing so was to limit the scope of public insurance, and in this way ensure room for the continued growth of the private insurance sector. In effect, therefore, the particular arrangement of British contributory pensions decreased, rather than increased, the emphasis on market values *within* public welfare.

Furthermore, this rested on a British tradition of separating economic policy from social policy. The labour movement contributed to this, not only by securing its vested interests in the occupational welfare sector, but also through a more direct hostility towards public welfare measures. Perhaps the best example of the latter is the opposition to family allowances in the 1940s. Hilary Land writes that 'sections of the Labour movement opposed family allowances on the grounds that they would restrict trade union freedom in wage bargaining'.[21] In Norway the labour movement took a much greater interest in, and through corporate channels played a much greater role in, the development of public welfare. While this has contributed to the strength of the Norwegian institutional

---

normative basis played an instrumental role in his assessment of social policy. While this transfer to normative science was a healthy reaction to the ideas of dead ideologies prevailing in the social sciences of the 1950s, Titmuss's 'commitment to welfare' opened up new scientific pitfalls.

20. Correspondingly, Tvede (1983, p. 97) describes the Norwegian model as 'institutional-handmaiden'.

21. Hilary Land in Hall et al. 1975, p. 228.

model, the British experience resulted in a gradual residualisation of social insurance through low coverage and insufficient benefits. The other side of this coin was, as we have seen, a greater emphasis on the services aimed at alleviating poverty. The institutionalisation of British assistance in the 1950s and '60s was therefore both a result of the failure of insurance and a continuation of the preoccupation with the poor in the Webb tradition of the Fabian intellectuals who filled the vacuum left by an inactive union movement in the shaping of Labour's social policy. We can therefore conclude that Britain, in my period of analysis, moved in the direction of a residualised institutional model of social insurance and an institutionalised residual model of social assistance.

While the Titmuss models are helpful in describing the differences in the social assistance and personal social services in the two countries, they are less helpful in highlighting the differences in the development of social insurance. On this side of the equation, Mishra's distinction between the 'differentiated' welfare state and the 'integrated' welfare state provides a more helpful framework. In accordance with the first of these models, the British approach has been limited to 'correcting the tendencies of a market economy'. The Norwegian example, by contrast, has followed the integrated, or corporatist, model, which 'recognises the need to harmonise the economic and the social within society as a whole'.[22]

Furthermore, the distinction between selective and universal services has played very different roles in the building of the welfare state in the two countries. In Britain, soon after the war, universality was seen as an end in itself. One way of understanding this is through the symbolic importance of the means test, in particular the household means test of the 1930s, as an embodiment of the repressive 'welfare' that the post-war welfare expansion was aimed at eradicating. The universality of the 1940s was, however, built on shaky foundations, and it fostered more selectivity in the long run. In Norway the more pragmatic approach allowed a continued element of means-testing as a factor in achieving greater redistribution through welfare – that is, a greater integration of economic and social policy. When we assess the role of universality and selectivity in relation to institutional and residual welfare, we must therefore consider the particular ways in which they were implemented. In

22. Mishra 1984, p. 106. He also describes the differentiated model as the 'Keynes–Beveridge' approach. As we have seen, British social policy diverged little from the principles laid down by Beveridge and condoned by the labour movement.

Norway the means test was maintained to exclude the *top earners*, as a means of elevating the level of the pension before the ultimate aim of universality was achieved. Selectivity therefore became an instrument in the achievement of institutional welfare in the long run. Conversely, the premature British universality fostered selectivity and a gradual residualisation of welfare.

The social division of welfare

In his seminal article 'The Social Division of Welfare', Titmuss highlights the division between social welfare on the one hand and fiscal and occupational welfare on the other.[23] This highly politically motivated article was an attack on those who argued that the provision of welfare benefited the poor only and impoverished the middle class. By defining social services by their *aims* rather than by the administrative and institutional devices employed to achieve them, he shows that more services are offered through fiscal and occupational welfare. Moreover, they are redistributional in favour of the better-off. Two aspects of this article are of interest to my analysis. First, Titmuss raises, but chooses not to answer, the most important question in relation to the public services. Having recognised that fiscal and occupational welfare are allocated according to merit, he asks 'whether and to what extent social service dependency benefits should be related to occupational and income achievement'.[24] Judging from his rejection of market values in public welfare, my guess is that his answer would have been that such criteria should not be employed in the allocation of benefits.

The evidence concerning pensions suggests that the inclusion of such considerations has contributed to the growth of, and political support for, public welfare in Norway.[25] Social policy (perhaps in any society) can do little more than modify the existing inequalities. The role of social policy is determined by whether policy-makers accept this fact and allow policy to reflect these inequalities, thereby playing an active role in modifying

23. Titmuss 1974. In the following I will use the term 'public' instead of 'social' because, like Sinfield (1978, p. 130), I feel that 'social does not denote public provision sufficiently clearly'.

24. Titmuss 1974, p. 52.

25. Britain also introduced earnings-related pensions, but their scope was curtailed by the 'contracting out' arrangements. See Chapter 4.

them. This was the Norwegian approach. Alternatively, they can choose to keep to the straight and narrow path by not allowing pure welfare to be tainted by the inclusion of market values. If this solution is adopted, social policy can become little more than an adjunct to society, and, though 'pure', it allows market forces to reign elsewhere, outside the societal control to which social policy could otherwise contribute. Human nature suggests that, when able, people will tend to save for a rainy day; the crucial question for the development of the welfare state is whether this takes place within the welfare state or in the marketplace. The purity of British social insurance has contributed to its residualisation.

While the Norwegian development resulted in an integrated welfare state, this achievement has drawn attention away from the residual world of social assistance. Conversely, in Britain a preoccupation with the alleviation of poverty was allowed to continue as a main social policy objective. This leads us to the second aspect of the social division of welfare. While it was important in the 1950s to highlight the divisions between public and non-public welfare, the development since calls for analysis of the *social divisions within public welfare* also.[26] The other side of the institutional coin in Norway is a much stronger division along these lines. Attention was drawn to the expansion of social insurance, while assistance was relegated to obscurity and expected to vanish in the process. The success of insurance in incorporating large parts of the assistance clientele strengthened this tendency and left the field open to professionals and civil servants who 're-created' the Poor Law under the more humane disguise of 'social treatment' in 1964. Resulting from this was a *strong social division between assistance and insurance.*[27] But divisions have also been encouraged within insurance by the inclusion of a strong earnings-related element. Here fiscal and occupational channels played a comparably modest role in Norway.

In Britain, by contrast, the main division was increasingly, as Titmuss pointed out, between the public on the one hand and fiscal and occupa-

---

26. Titmuss's article set the agenda for British studies into social divisions of welfare for the years to follow. Reisman (1977, p. xi) argues that 'the model was used thereafter to justify a moral indictment of the fiscal and occupational systems of welfare: a seal was set upon the division between the ethics of work and the ethics of welfare which was to last for another twenty years.'

27. Leibfried and Tennstedt (1985) arrive at a similar conclusion in their study of the '*Spaltung*' of the German welfare state. Here, a much larger assistance scheme (*Sozialhilfe*) has made the cleavages clearer.

tional channels on the other. This was both a product of, and further facilitated by, the residualisation of public welfare: following Beveridge, public welfare was restricted to acting as a safety net above which fiscal and occupational channels offered 'standard security'. Once this relationship had been established, it facilitated the growth of private pensions and thereby tapped from the public sector economic and political resources, first through the need for private schemes to supplement the inadequate benefits of the 1940s and '50s and, later, through the system of 'contracting out' from the state earnings-related programmes. The other side of the coin is, however, a much less socially divided *public* income maintenance in Britain.

This difference is perhaps best understood with reference to the terminology of Peter Baldwin. In his view the nature of the Scandinavian solidaristic model is to be found in the breadth of the *risk groups*, including both urban industrial workers and the agrarian middle class.[28] The poor in this perspective benefited in the Scandinavian model from 'clinging to the coattails of the advantaged.... The middle classes arranged things first and foremost for themselves, the unfortunate were beneficiaries of a comparatively successful trickle-down.'[29] The choice of a tax-financed system of social insurance further facilitated this inclusion, and only political will determined which group(s) to include. Baldwin focuses exclusively on the development of pension systems in his study, and therefore discusses the social divisions of only the higher echelons of the welfare state. My evidence, therefore, complements the picture presented by him: As we have seen, not all of 'the needy' managed to cling to the coattails of the middle class in Norway (or in any of the Scandinavian countries). Those included were mainly the 'deserving poor' – widows, elderly people, and disabled people.

This had very different consequences for the undeserving residuum in the two countries: In Norway, they were left in a very small remainder group, uniformly regarded as undeserving of entitlement after the solidaristic model of insurance had taken care of the deserving. In Britain, by contrast, it was the deserving poor who were devoid of coattails to hang on to. For the residuum, however, this meant that they found themselves in a larger risk group, where they could benefit from sharing the lot of the deserving.

Sinfield argues that studies of the social division of welfare, if carried

28. Baldwin 1990, p. 289.
29. Ibid., p. 298.

out cross-nationally in basically capitalist societies, 'will advance the understanding of not only the welfare systems but also the class structure of these societies'.[30] While I feel that my analysis has cast light on the former, I will be more cautious in drawing conclusions about the overall class structure from my evidence. I feel, however, that the unequal development becomes more intelligible if seen in relation to the internal divisions within the working classes in the two countries. In Britain the early experience with self-help schemes through Friendly Societies reflected and strengthened the divisions between the skilled, well-organised, and 'respectable' sections of the working class on the one hand and the casual, unorganised and 'rough' sections on the other. Both the unions' support of the contributory principle from 1911 onwards and their fear of 'scroungers' should be viewed in this light.

In Norway the much later industrialisation ensured that self-help schemes did not have time to develop before public welfare was put on the political agenda, as in Britain, towards the end of the 19th century. This facilitated a more united working-class drive for welfare, which in turn prevented existing divisions within the working classes from developing to the degree experienced in Britain. The inclusion of a strong earnings-related element, together with the smaller role played by private and occupational schemes, furthermore enabled a greater incorporation of the middle classes into public welfare in Norway.

Lastly, the other side of the corporate relationship also differs greatly in the two countries. In Norway the major influence has been a relatively co-operative industrial capital. Corporate management has furthermore been facilitated by a strong national employers' organisation, creating channels for collective bargaining. In Britain, by contrast, financial capital (or 'the city') has dominated a relatively weak and less organised industrial capital in policy-making.[31] In addition to providing fewer corporate channels, the city has strong vested interests in non-public welfare through its involvement in the private insurance industry.

Stigma and the accessibility of services

One measure of the residual nature of social assistance and personal social services is the extent to which approaching these for help alters the

30. Sinfield 1978, p. 132.
31. See, for example, Ingham 1984.

status of the individual client. Furthermore, the status of the client is itself an independent variable: low-status clients will reflect low status and low standards on the services exclusively used by them. According to Titmuss, 'separate state systems for the poor, operating in the context of a powerful private welfare market, tend to be poor standard systems.'[32] My findings allow me only to speculate about the clientele's experience of approaching services. A more conclusive assessment would depend on empirical interview evidence. For my period of analysis, no such material exists for either country. I am therefore forced to start with the other side of the equation, the status potential of services, and infer from this. Pinker argues that 'social services are used to impose sanctions as well as to confer benefits upon their clientele.'[33] In the Poor Law, the relationship between the two functions was clearly complementary: through imposed negative sanctions in the form of lost citizenship rights and resulting stigma, the expenditure on benefits was curtailed. In the post-war successors to these services, both countries have explicitly set out to eradicate the imposition of stigma. Still, the memory of the Poor Law is long lived, and in both countries it has proved difficult to escape the 'stigma by association'[34] directed at services that are seen by the general public as its descendants. Commenting on the British post-war experience, Spicker concludes that 'the stigma of pauperism, which had seemed to be the result of a conscious policy, has proved greatly resistant to abolition.'[35]

Selective social services are by their very nature less accessible than universal services. While, from one perspective, selectivity is an administrative means of targeting the services to those whose needs are greatest, it adds to the individual client's potential resistance to approaching that service, for example through the imposition of a means test. This is, of course, true of only those welfare schemes traditionally associated with stigma. A service that enhances the recipient's status, such as a competitive and means-tested scholarship, is itself enhanced by its selective nature. We also need to specify which client categories we are concerned with when we assess a service according to its stigma potential and

32. Titmuss [1968] 1979, p. 143.
33. Pinker 1971, p. 144.
34. Jones 1985, p. 109.
35. Spicker 1983a, p. 27.

resulting level of accessibility.[36] If a service is exclusively targeted at the poorest and most stigmatised sections of the population, this does not necessarily mean that the service is less accessible to these groups than a less selective service would be. I believe that the experience of stigma and the effects it has on a person's actions involve thresholds and watersheds. The first visit is likely to be the most difficult. Therefore, if an individual or a family has a history of assistance and social work dependency, perhaps stretching over several generations, the resistance towards seeking benefits and exposing oneself to the related stigma will probably decrease. This argument does not lend support to theories of 'cultures of poverty'; it is just a statement concerning human adaptability. The main test of accessibility is therefore the extent to which people generally feel able to approach these services in situations of need.

Pinker argues that 'if we are genuinely concerned to reduce the incidence of stigma in social welfare, we ought to give much more serious consideration to the proposition that the most anonymous forms of social provision tend to be the least stigmatising, and the most personal forms of social service are likely to be the most humiliating for the beneficiary.'[37] The continued 'personal' nature of assistance in Norway is the factor that contributes most to its lack of accessibility compared with its British counterpart. A final point can be made from the Norwegian evidence. The departure of the 'deserving' clients (elderly and disabled people in particular) through their incorporation into social insurance is, seen in isolation, likely to have increased the stigma of assistance, even compared with the Poor Law. Although the nature of the service is less stigma-imposing, the composition of the clientele could have outweighed this improvement.[38] This suggests that the most important factor in determining the extent of stigma of a service is the nature of its clientele: A service targeted at the poor will be associated with poverty and hence stigmatised by the public at large. This conclusion corresponds to that made by Spicker in his study of stigma in the social services.[39]

36. While Jones (1985) and Titmuss refer to the 'acceptability' of a service, I choose to use the term 'accessibility' because it highlights the obstacles which potential clients need to surpass to seek and get assistance.

37. Pinker 1971, p. 151.

38. The more 'humane' social treatment, from the client's point of view, can be seen to impose stigma of a nature similar to the explicit impingement of freedom and status in the personal contact between helper and client in the Poor Law.

39. Spicker 1983a, p. 124.

Contradiction or paradox?

I began this study by asking whether the comparative evidence presented above could be described as contradictory. The notion of a one-dimensional relationship between residual and institutional welfare, on which the understanding of a Norwegian contradiction hinges, is, I believe, an inherent feature of Titmuss's models as they have been employed by him and in later attempts to describe welfare state variation through the use of typologies. The contradiction is, moreover, valid only if we deny that the two forms of welfare can coexist. In Norway we have seen not only that residual and institutional welfare coexisted but also that the circumstances which made one possible also to a large extent explain the other. Thus, the apparently contradictory features of the welfare states constitute not a contradiction but a paradox – something which appears contradictory at first sight.

So far I have treated social insurance as the independent variable and social assistance as the dependent variable. Albeit with more caution than the above conclusion, it can be argued that the evidence presented here also indicates that the preservation of 'residual welfare' may further the development of universal welfare programmes operating according to the tenets of the institutional model. The evidence of my investigation into the prolonged existence of Norwegian assistance in its particular form suggests that the scope and nature of social assistance may have contributed to the expansion of institutional welfare through pensions. In the 1960s, when Gudmund Harlem, then the Norwegian minister of social affairs, argued for the establishment of a separate treatment and income maintenance system for the socially disabled, this was both a reflection of his ideas of what could serve these people best and a means of excluding them from the insurance-based disability scheme, thereby allowing that scheme to offer income maintenance in accordance with the doctrines of the institutional model. The maintenance of a residual system in Norway therefore appears to be both a functional means and a political means in the development of institutional welfare. It was political in that it would have been more difficult to find acceptance for a high-level disability scheme if such a scheme had given access to need categories who were perceived by the general public as being less deserving, and for whom entitlement to benefits would have involved easier access to money to be 'wasted on alcohol and bad management'. This is probably particularly true of a system such as the Norwegian one, a system funded primarily through general taxation and in which the presence of strong rights based on social citizenship called for clear demarcation of which groups should be included.

Any assessment of the relative success of the policies of these two countries depends on which services are in focus. From the perspective of the majority of old age pensioners and disabled people, including those with no work record, the Norwegian development features greater enhancement of welfare than its British counterpart. If we look at the assistance side, the opposite is true. The British welfare residuum profited from services featuring less residual traits compared with those offered to equivalent groups in Norway. If we put the comparison to the utilitarian test and look for 'the greatest happiness for the greatest number', the conclusion is twofold. In the area of assistance, the more residual welfare in Norway does 'less harm', as it covers only a small minority of the population. With regard to public income maintenance as a whole, the Norwegian experience has also proved more successful in providing welfare on a high level to the vast majority of those depending on the state for their maintenance. It should be made clear, though, that this is an assessment of the nature and quality of income maintenance and personal social services only. I have *not* studied the total welfare of the recipients of any of the three forms of welfare under scrutiny. For example, it is possible that, at the top end, fiscal and occupational welfare, together with public provision, provide a total welfare in Britain which adds a different dimension to the picture I have drawn by focusing on the public arena alone. Similarly, at the bottom end it is possible that housing, education, and other services alter the configuration and that the total welfare of the Norwegian residuum might prove better than that of its British equivalent.

At the beginning of the period studied, the two countries shared a belief in the gradual phasing-out of assistance. Towards the end of the period, only Norway had reason to retain some of that optimism. Today no Western country expects that economic development and extended social insurance coverage will make social assistance obsolete in the foreseeable future. On the contrary, the fear of spiralling social security expenditure and its negative effects on economic performance has contributed to a renewed acceptance of, and interest in, selective forms of income maintenance. The fact that young people account for much of the often-dramatic increase in social assistance dependency over the last two decades has led to renewed questioning of the extent to which benefits should be awarded in the form of entitlements with few strings attached. Faced with such challenges, at least six Western European countries are already experimenting with US-style workfare programmes. To some, this symbolises a return to the forced labour of the depression years; to others, it is an adequate method to meet the needs of an assistance clientele with few options in the labour market, and who have not internalised the values of self-help and the shame of dependency. Again, therefore, the target group is shaping the face of last-resort income maintenance. To understand these ongoing developments, we need to return to history to understand how the present welfare programmes were chiselled out. This book is a first attempt, covering only two countries. Future contributions will surely highlight aspects other than those focused on here. My hope, though, is to have contributed to the development of a new field of comparative welfare studies.

References

Official documents

Britain

Children and Young Persons Act, 1963.

Cmd 6404, 1942. Social Insurance and Allied Services (Beveridge Report), London, HMSO.

Cmd 6405, 1942. Appendix to the Beveridge Report: Memoranda Submitted by Organisations and Individuals, London, HMSO.

Cmd 9333, 1954. Phillips Report.

Cmnd 1085, 1959. Appendix to Annual Report of the National Assistance Board.

Cmnd 1191, 1960. Report of the Committee on Children and Young Persons, London, HMSO.

Cmnd 3703, 1968. Report of the Committee on Local Authority and Allied Personal Social Services, London, HMSO.

Hansard, 1942–66.

Health Services and Public Health Act, 1968.

National Health Service Act, 1946.

Standing Committee (on 1963 Children and Young Persons Act), Official Report, 1962–63.

Norway

Fattigvesenet, 1945–47. Central Bureau of Statistics.

Fellesprogrammet, 1945.

Foreløpig utkast til Ot.prp. om lov om sosial omsorg, February 1960. Oslo, Ministry of Health and Social Affairs.

Forhandlinger i Odelstinget, 1964.

Forsorgsvesenet, 1947–64. Central Bureau of Statistics.

Historisk Statistikk, 1968.

Innst. O VIII, 1959–60. Innstilling om omorganisering av kommunenes sosiale administrasjon. Utvalg oppnevnt 18. november 1960. Oslo, Ministry of Health and Social Affairs, 1962.

Lov om sosial omsorg, 1964.

Ot.prp. nr. 56, 1962–63. (Regarding Lov om sosial omsorg.)
Rundskriv nr. 3, 1980. Oslo, Ministry of Health and Social Affairs.
Sosialhjelpsstatistikk, 1966. Central Bureau of Statistics.
Stortingsforhandlinger, 1964.
Stortingsmelding nr. 58, 1948. Om Folketrygden.
Utkast til lov om sosialhjelp, 1953. Innstilling den ved kongelig resolusjon av 15. desember 1950.

Books and articles

Abel-Smith, B. 1953. *The Reform of Social Security*, London, Fabian Research Series, No. 161.
Abel-Smith, B. 1964. *The Hospitals, 1800–1948: A Study in Social Administration in England and Wales*, London, Heinemann.
Abel-Smith, B. 1983. 'Assessing the Balance Sheet', in H. Glennerster (ed.), *The Future of the Welfare State: Remaking Social Policy*, London, Heinemann.
Abel-Smith, B., and P. Townsend. 1955. *New Pensions for the Old*, Fabian Research Series, No. 171.
Abel-Smith, B., and P. Townsend. 1965. *The Poor and the Poorest*, London, Bell & Sons.
Addison, P. 1975. *The Road to 1945: British Politics and the Second World War*, London, Jonathan Cape.
Alber, J. 1982. *Sozialwissenschaftliche Theorien der Entwicklung des Wohlfahrtstaats*, Frankfurt am Main, Campus.
Andenæs, K. 1992. *Sosialomsorg i gode og onde dager*, Oslo, TANO.
Arntzen, J.G., and B.B. Knutsen. 1980. *Political Life and Institutions in Norway*, International Summer School, University of Oslo.
Ashford, D.E. 1986. *The Emergence of the Welfare States*, Oxford, Basil Blackwell.
Baker, J. 1979. 'Social Conscience and Social Policy', *Journal of Social Policy* 8 (April).
Baldwin, P. 1990. *The Politics of Social Solidarity: Class Bases of the European Welfare States 1875–1975*, Cambridge, Cambridge University Press.
Barker, P. (ed.). 1985. *Founders of the Welfare State*, London, Heinemann Educational.
Beltram, J. 1984. *Testing the Safety Net*, London, Bedford Square Press.
Bernt, J.F. 1989. *Rett til økonomisk sosialhjelp*, Bergen, Det juridiske fakultets skriftserie, nr. 23.
Berthaud, R., and J.C. Brown. 1981. *Poverty and the Development of Anti-poverty Policies in the United Kingdom*, London, Heinemann Educational.
Beveridge, Lord. 1953. *Power and Influence*, London, Hodder and Stoughton.
Bowlby, J. 1951. *Maternal Care and Mental Health*, report for the World Health Organization.
Briggs, A. 1961. 'The Welfare State in a Historical Perspective', *European Journal of Sociology* 2: 221–58.
Briggs, E., and A. Deacon. 1973. 'The Creation of the Unemployment Assistance Board', *Policy and Politics* 2(1).
Brown, M. 1982. *Introduction to Social Administration in Britain*, London, Hutchkinson & Co.
Bull, E. [1968] 1976. *Norsk Fagbevegelse*, Oslo, Tiden norsk forlag.
Bull, S. 1981. *Sosialhjelpen. Sosialomsorgens vern mot fattigdom*, Oslo, Universitetsforlaget.

Cole, D., and J. Utting. 1962. *The Economic Circumstances of Old People*, London, Codicote.

Cooper, J. 1983. *The Creation of the British Personal Social Services 1962–1974*, London, Heinemann Educational.

Crossman, R. 1981. *The Backbench Diaries of Richard Crossman*, London, Hamish Hamilton and Jonathan Cape.

Deacon, A., and J. Bradshaw. 1983. *Reserved for the Poor: The Means Test in British Social Policy*, Oxford, Basil Blackwell and Martin Robertson.

De Swaan, A. 1988. *In Care of the State*, Oxford, Polity Press.

Eardley, T., J. Bradshaw, J. Ditch, I. Gough, and P. Whiteford. 1996. *Social Assistance Schemes in the OECD Countries*, Vol. 1, Synthesis Report, University of York.

Ervik, A. 1973. 'Den Sosialpolitiske Prosess', *Sosialt Arbeid.*

Esping-Andersen, Gøsta. 1990. *The Three Worlds of Welfare Capitalism*, Cambridge, Polity Press.

Flora, P. 1983. *State, Economy and Society in Western Europe, 1815–1975: A Data Handbook*, Vol. 1, Frankfurt, Campus Verlag.

Flora, P., and J. Alber. 1981. 'Modernization, Democratization and the Development of Welfare States in Western Europe', in P. Flora and A. Heidenheimer (eds), *The Development of Welfare States in Europe and in the United States*, New Brunswick, N.J., Transaction Books.

Fraser, D. 1981. 'The English Poor Law and the Origins of the English Welfare State', in G. Mommsen (ed.), *The Emergence of the Welfare State in Britain and West Germany*, London, Croom Helm.

Fraser, D. 1984. *The Evolution of the British Welfare State*, London, Macmillan.

George, V. 1968. *Social Security: Beveridge and After*, London, Routledge and Kegan Paul.

Glennerster, H. 1962. *National Assistance: Service or Charity?*, London, Young Fabian Pamphlet No. 4.

Gough, I., J. Bradshaw, J. Ditch, T. Eardley, and P. Whiteford. 1997. 'Social Assistance Variation in OECD Countries', *Journal of European Social Policy* 1.

Guttormsen, G., and L. Høigård. 1978. *Fattigdom i en velstandskommune. En undersøkelse av sosialomsorgen i Bærum*, Oslo, Universitetsforlaget.

Hall, P., H. Land, R. Parker, and A. Webb. 1975. *Change, Choice and Conflict in Social Policy*, London, Heinemann.

Handler, J.F. 1973. *The Coercive Social Worker*, Chicago, Rand McNally.

Hannah, L. 1986. *Inventing Retirement: The Development of Occupational Pensions in Britain*, Cambridge, Cambridge University Press.

Harris, J. 1977. *William Beveridge: A Biography*, Oxford, Oxford University Press.

Hatland, A. 1984. *The Future of Norwegian Social Insurance*, Oslo, INAS.

Hatland, A. 1987. *Oslotrygden – fra rikspolitisk pionaertiltak til lokal fortidslevning*, Oslo, INAS.

Heclo, H. 1973. *Modern Social Politics in Britain and Sweden*, New Haven, Conn., Yale University Press.

Hennock, E.P. 1987. *British Social Reform and German Precedents: The Case of Social Insurance, 1880–1914*, Oxford, Clarendon Press.

Higgins, J. 1981. *States of Welfare*, Oxford, Blackwell & Robertson.

Hill, M., and P. Laing. 1979. *Social Work and Money*, London, George Allen & Unwin.

Hippe, J., and A. West Pedersen. 1988. *For lang og tro tjeneste? Pensjoner i arbeidsmarkedet*, Oslo, FAFO.

Ingham, G. 1984. *Capitalism Divided: The City and Industry in British Social Development*, London, Macmillan.

International Labor Organization. 1984. *Introduction to Social Security*, Geneva.

Jackson, M.P., and B.M. Valencia. 1979. *Financial Aid through Social Work*, London, Routledge and Kegan Paul.

Jeffery, K. 1987. 'British Politics and Social Policy during the Second World War', *Historical Research*, March.

Jones, C. 1985. *Patterns of Social Policy: An Introduction to Comparative Analysis*, London, Tavistock Publications.

Jordan, B. 1974. *Poor Parents*, London, Routledge and Kegan Paul.

Jordan, B. 1976. *Freedom and the Welfare State*, London, Routledge and Kegan Paul.

Kaim-Caudle, P. 1973. *Comparative Social Policy and Social Security: A Ten Country Study*, London, Martin Robertson.

Kjønstad, A. 1987. *Norwegian Social Law*, Oslo, Norwegian University Press.

Kluge, L. 1960. 'Skolen blir til', in *Norges Kommunal og Sosialskole* (Annual Report).

Kluge, L. 1973. *Sosialhjelp før og naa*, Oslo, Fabritius.

Korpi, W. 1983. *The Democratic Class Struggle*, London, Routledge and Kegan Paul.

Kuhnle, S. 1983. *Velferdsstatens utvikling. Norge i komparativt perspektiv*, Bergen, Universitetsforlaget.

Labour Party. 1942a. *Report of the 41st Annual Labour Party Conference.*

Labour Party. 1942b. *The Labour Organiser*, No. 252, London.

Labour Party. 1943. *The Labour Organiser*, No. 255, London.

Labour Party. 1963. *New Frontiers for Social Security*, Policy Statement, National Executive Committee.

Leibfried, S., and F. Tennstedt. 1985. *Politik der Armut und die Spaltung des Sozialstaats*, Frankfurt am Main, Suhrkampf.

LO (Landsorganisasjonen i Norge) and Norsk Sjømannsforbund. 1945. *Framtidens Norge*, Stockholm.

Lorentz, E. 1974. *Arbeider-bevegelsens historie, 2. 1930–1973*, Oslo, Pax Forlag.

Lynes, T. 1962. 'National Assistance and National Prosperity', *Occasional Papers in Social Administration*, London.

Lødemel, I. 1989. *The Quest for Institutional Welfare and the Problem of the Residuum. The Case of Income Maintenance and Social Care Policies in Norway and Britain 1946 to 1966*, Ph.D. thesis, London School of Economics and Political Science.

Lødemel, I., and B. Schulte. 1992. 'Social Assistance – A Part of Social Security or the Poor law in New Disguise?', *Yearbook*, European Institute of Social Security, Leuven.

Marshall, T.H. [1965] 1985. *T.H. Marshall's Social Policy*, London, Hutchkinson and Co.

Mays, J., A. Forder, and O. Keidan. 1971. *Penelope Hall's Social Services of England and Wales*, London, Routledge and Kegan Paul.

Mishra, R. 1977. *Society and Social Policy*, London, Macmillan.

Mishra, R. 1984. *The Welfare State in Crisis: Social Thought and Social Change*, Brighton, Wheatsheaf.

Mountford, L. 1984. *The British Labour Party and the Contributory Principle of Social Insurance 1908–1931*, Ph.D. thesis, University of London.

Myrdal, Alva, and Gunnar Myrdal. [1934] 1936. *Krisen i befolkningsspørsmålet*, Oslo, Tiden.

Nervik, J.A. 1993. *Klassifisering av sosialhjelpsordningene. Hva er det viktigste sammenlikningskriteriene?*, essay, Department of Comparative Politics, University of Bergen.

Nestor, P. 1976. *Fra fattigkasser til folketrygd*, Oslo, NKSS.

Nestor, P. 1986. *Sosialpolitikken og samfunnsøkonomien*, Oslo, NKSH.

Nordby, T. 1989. *Karl Evang. En biografi*, Oslo, Aschehoug.

Ormestad, M. 1948. *De sosiale trygder. Historisk og grunn prinsipper*, Oslo, Sem og Stenersen.

Parker, J. 1965. *Local Health and Welfare Services*, London, George Allen & Unwin.

Pelling, H. 1985. *A Short History of the Labour Party*, London, Macmillan.

Pettersen, P.A. 1982. *Linjer i norsk sosialpolitikk*, Oslo, Universitetsforlaget.

Pettersen, P.A. 1987. *Pensjoner, penger og politikk*, Oslo, Universitetsforlaget.

Pimlott, B., and C. Cook. 1982. *Trade Unions in British Politics*, London, Longman.

Pinker, R. 1971. *Social Theory and Social Policy*, London, Heinemann Educational.

Pinker, R. 1979. *The Idea of Welfare*, London, Heinemann Educational.

Pinker, R. 1987. *For the Good of Others*, Times Literary Supplement.

Pinker, R. 1990. *Social Work in an Enterprise Society*, London, Routledge.

Ragin, C.C. 1994. *Constructing Social Research*, Thousand Oaks, Calif., Pine Forge Press.

Reddin, M. 1968. 'Universality versus Selectivity', in W. Robson and B. Crick (eds), *The Future of the Social Services*, London, Penguin.

Reisman, D. 1977. *Richard Titmuss: Welfare and Society*, London, Heinemann Educational.

Robson, W. (ed.). 1943. *Social Security*, London, George Allen & Unwin, for Fabian Society.

Rose, R., and P.L. Davies. 1994. *Inheritance in Public Policy: Change without Choice in Britain*, New Haven, Conn., Yale University Press.

Scheu, F.J. 1943. *British Labor and the Beveridge Plan*, New York, Island Workshop Press.

Seip, A.L. 1981. *Om velferdsstatens framvekst*, Oslo, Universitetsforlaget.

Seip, A.L. 1984. *Sosialhjelpsstaten blir til. Norsk sosialpolitikk 1740–1920*, Oslo, Gyldendal.

Seip, A.L. 1987. 'Velferdsstaten Norge', in L. Alldén et al., *Det Norske Samfunn*, Oslo, Gyldendal.

Seip, A.L. 1994. *Veiene til velferdsstaten. Norsk sosialpolitikk 1920–75*, Oslo, Gyldendal.

Seip, A.L., and H. Ibsen. 1989. 'Morsøkonomi, familieøkonomi og samfunnsøkonomi: Barnetrygden i historisk perspektiv', *Historisk tidsskrift* 4: 413–33.

Shragge, E. 1984. *Pension Policy in Britain: A Socialist Analysis*, London, Routledge and Kegan Paul.

Sinfield, A. 1978. 'Analyses in the Social Division of Welfare', *Journal of Social Policy* 7(2): 129–57.

Spicker, P. 1983a. *Stigma and Social Welfare*, Ph.D. thesis, University of London.

Spicker, P. 1983b. 'Titmuss's "The Social Division of Welfare" – A Reappraisal', *Yearbook of Social Policy*, London.

Stenersen, Ø. 1973. 'Framtidens Norge. Et ledd i planleggingsvirksomheten i eksil-LO, 1942–45', in *Etterkrigshistorie*, Vol. 4, Oslo, Universitetsforlaget.

Stephens, T. (ed.). 1943. *Problem Families: An Experiment in Social Rehabilitation*, Liverpool, C. Tinling & Co.

Stevenson, O. 1973. *Claimant or Client?*, London, George Allen & Unwin.

Stjernø, S. 1994. *Mellom krike og kapital*, Oslo, Universitetsforlaget.

Sørensen, Ø. 1991. *Solkors eller solidaritet. Høyreautoritær samfunnstenkning i Norge ca1930–1945*, Oslo, Cappelen.

Sørensen, Ø. 1993. *Verdenskrig og velferd*, Oslo, Cappelen.

Terum, L.I. 1982. *Profesjonell ekspansjon under statleg vern*, thesis (*hovedoppgave*), University of Tromsø.

Terum, L.I. 1985. *Skjønn og likebehandling*, Oslo, INAS.

Terum, L.I. 1986. *Geografisk ulikskap og nasjonale normer*, Oslo, INAS.

Terum, L.I. 1987. 'Sosialhjelp, penger eller behandling', in G. Benneche and S. Eskeland (eds), *Hvor gaar sosialomsorgen?*, Oslo, Universitetsforlaget.

Terum, L.I. 1996. *Grenser for sosialpolitisk modernisering. Om fattighjelp i velferdsstaten*, Oslo, Universitetsforlaget.

Thane, P. 1982. *The Foundations of the Welfare State*, London, Longman.

Therborn, G. 1983. *The Welfare State in State and in Class History*, symposium, Sociologisk Institut, Copenhagen.

Titmuss, R. 1950. *Problems of Social Policy*, London, HMSO.

Titmuss, R. 1974. *Social Policy*, Brian Abel-Smith and Kay Titmuss (eds), London, George Allen & Unwin.

Titmuss, R. [1968] 1979. *Commitment to Welfare*, London, George Allen & Unwin.

Titmuss, R. 1987. *The Philosophy of Welfare*, London, George Allen & Unwin.

Townsend, P. 1979. *Poverty in the United Kingdom*, London, Allen Lane.

Tutvedt, Ø. 1968. 'Sosialt arbeid – et nytt yrke', *Liv og Helse* 5: 115–19.

Tvede, O. 1983. *Sosialpolitikk i velferdsstaten. Om utformingen av sosialpolitikken i etterkrigstiden*, Department of Sociology, University of Bergen.

Webb, A. 1975. 'The Abolition of National Assistance: Policy Changes in the Administration of Assistance Benefits', in Hall et al. 1975.

West Pedersen, A. 1990. *Fagbevegelsen og folketrygden*, Oslo, FAFO.

Wilensky, H., and C. Lebaux. 1965. *Industrial Society and Social Welfare*, New York, Free Press.

Winter, J.M. (ed.). 1975. *War and Economic Development*, London, Cambridge University Press.

Zacher, H. (ed.). 1980. *Die Rolle des Beitrags in der sozialen Sicherung*, Berlin, Duncker und Humblot.

Øverbye, E. 1994. 'Convergence in Policy Outcomes: Social Security Systems in Perspective', *Journal of Public Policy* 14(2): 147–74.

Øyen, E. 1974. *Sosialomsorgen og dens forvaltere*, Bergen, Universitetsforlaget.

Index

Abel-Smith, Brian. *See* Titmuss Group
Act on Accident Insurance for Factory Workers (Norway), 39
Agrarian Party *(Bondepartiet)*, 47, 51, 53, 58, 69
'anti-social persons', 169, 170, 171
appeal (right to, in Norway), 172-74
Approved Societies (UK), 104, 107, 131
Assistance Board (UK), 211, 212, 214, 227, 233
Attlee, Clement, 88, 89, 101, 110, 122

benefit levels
  Norway, 51-52, 62, 70-73, 85
  Poor Law, 8
  social insurance (general), 32, 35-36
  UK, 95-96, 124-31
benefits: duty to repay (Norway), 174
Bevan, Aneurin, 112, 214, 232
Beveridge Report/Plan, 118-22
  contributory principle, 108-11, 136
  importance of, 257
  influence in Norway, ix, 65, 144, 145
  labour movement debate on, 100-5
  parliamentary debate on, 105-8
  party support, 114-15, 140
  social assistance scheme, 206-7, 213
  social insurance implications, 88, 259
  subsistence principle, 119-20, 122-31
  theories on, 144
  and universality, 131-34, 206
  and working women, 133
Beveridge, William
  achievements of, 257
  appointment of, 99-100, 105, 119
  welfare philosophy, 97, 108, 144, 217, 263
Bevin, Ernest, 99, 119
Blackley, William L., 40
Blehr, Otto Albert, 45, 46
Borten, Per, 75
Boyd Carpenter Plan, 136-37

cash-care: findings, 251
Castberg Child Welfare Law (Norway), 56
Chadwick, Edwin, 258
Child Care Act of 1964 (Norway), 162
Child Care Board (Norway), 195
Children Act of 1948 (UK), 230, 236
Children and Young Persons Act of 1963 (UK), 228, 237-39, 242, 244, 254
Christian Party (Norway), 69
clientele
  findings, 251, 252-56
  nature of, 202-3, 258-59
  perception of, 16, 160-71, 184-87, 190, 233-34, 252-56, 261, 271
  Poor Law, 4
  references to (Norway), 166-71
  size and composition of, 18, 153, 154, 161-66, 247, 260
Committee on Children and Young Persons (Ingleby Committee, 1960), 236-37, 244
Conservative Party (UK)
  and Beveridge Plan, 126, 128, 129
  and earnings-related benefits, 136
  and old age pension, 95, 103, 106, 107, 109, 114
  social assistance policy, 218-19, 227
  and unification of schemes, 121
Conservatives *(Høyre)*, and old age pension, 41, 43, 44, 45, 47, 49, 50, 53, 56, 62, 69, 70, 74
contributory principle. *See also* Beveridge Report/Plan; financing

vs. taxation principle, 19, 34
UK, 88, 89, 90-100, 108-11, 136, 137, 259-60
coverage
Norwegian old age pension, 48-51, 62, 85
social insurance (general), 32, 35

data (choice of), 24-26
Denmark, 32, 189, 197
Department of Social Affairs (Norway): response to 1953 proposals, 159-80
Determination of Needs Act of 1941 (UK), 212
diffusion (between UK, Norway), 64, 65, 66-67, 143-45
Disability Act (Norway), 170, 184
disability insurance. *See also* occupational insurance
Act of 1937 (Norway), 59
Disability Pension (Norway), 169-70
disabled people
Disabled Persons (Unemployment) Act of 1944 (UK), 132
social assistance dependency (UK), 131-33

earnings-related supplements, 73-75, 134, 142
Elberfeld system, 9, 193
enactment. *See* timing of enactment
explanatory factors, 16-19, 36-37

Fabian Society, 94, 99, 128, 223
decline of, 110
intellectuals, 135, 140, 264
reaction to Beveridge Report, 103-5
Family Allowance Act of 1946 (Norway), 65
Family Service Units (UK), 235, 236, 238
financing. *See also* contributory principle; taxation principle
comparison (UK, Norway), 139
Norwegian pensions, 42-48, 72-73
social insurance (general), 31-32, 33-34
UK
debate on flat-rate system, 134-37
National Health Service, 111-13
Finland, 38, 39
Folkeforsikringskomite (People's Insurance Committee), 41, 44, 56
Food Stamp Program (US), 9
France, 9, 57
Friendly Societies, 36, 91-92, 93, 111, 114, 139, 268

geographical disparities (Norway), 175-76. *See also* municipalities
George, Lloyd, 90
Gerhardsen, Einar, 75, 181, 182
Germany
Elberfeld system, 9, 193
influence on Norway, 43, 64-68
influence on UK, 93
social assistance in, 10, 253
Getz Wold, Knut, 67
Gjaerevoll, Olav, 190
Glennerster, Howard, 214, 221, 222, 223, 226
Greenwood, Arthur, 96, 103, 105-6
Griffith, James, 101, 105, 136

handmaiden model (Titmuss), 12, 14, 16, 263
Harlem, Gudmund, 182, 183-87, 188, 271
health care, 209, 229-30, 235, 241
health insurance
Norway, 39, 59, 68, 83
UK, 112-13
Health Services and Public Health Act of 1968 (UK), 243
hypothesis, 3-4, 247

Income Guarantee (UK), 220-25, 254
Independent Labour Party (UK), 94
Ingleby Committee (1960), 236-37, 244
institutional redistributive model (Titmuss), 12, 14, 15, 16, 23
Interdepartmental Committee on Social Insurance (UK), 99. *See also* Beveridge Report/Plan
International Labor Organization, 31n,

112, 145, 160
Keynes, J.M.
influence in Norway, 47, 59, 141
'Keynes-Beveridge' approach, 14, 264n
Kilbrandon Report (Scotland), 242-43

labour movement(s)
Norway. *See also* Landsorganisasjonen i Norge (LO)
influence re: old age pension, 43
power relative to Labour Party, 21, 60-61
pragmatism in, 48-49
role of, 37
UK. *See also* Trade Union Congress
debate on Beveridge Report, 100-5
wartime co-operation, 66
Labour Organiser, 102
Labour Party *(Arbeiderpartiet)*
in exile (WWII), 66-67
and labour movement, 21, 140-41
and old age pension, 42-51 passim, 55-62 passim, 67-71 passim, 73, 74, 75, 85, 86
social policy, 145, 252-53
Labour Party (UK)
and 1963 Children and Young Persons Act, 238-39
acceptance of contributory principle, 88-100, 108-11, 113-15
and Beveridge Plan, 118, 122, 123, 140, 144
and earnings-related benefits, 136
and labour movement, 21
social assistance policy, 219-25, 227, 232-33, 244, 254-55
Landsorganisasjonen i Norge (LO)
1960 pension agreement, 74
Framtidens Norge, 66, 145
power relative to Labour Party, 61, 141
Liberal Party (UK), 90, 93, 103, 104, 106
Liberals *(Venstre)*, 43-48 passim, 50, 53, 55, 58, 69, 74
Lie, Haakon, 66, 182
local authorities. *See* municipalities
Local Authority Social Services Act of 1970 (UK), 240
Local Government Act of 1929 (UK), 209
Longford group, 240, 241
LO. *See* Landsorganisasjonen i Norge (LO)
Lund, Bernt H., 188
Lynes, Tony. *See* Titmuss Group

MacDonald, Ramsay, 89n, 94, 95, 98, 99
means-test(ing)
efforts to abolish in Norway, 68-70
fear of (UK), 108-11
stigma of, 50, 107, 208, 220-21
to define social assistance, 7
types of, 172
mental health, 235
method of study, 24-26
Ministry of Social Security (UK), 225
models of welfare, 11-16, 262-65, 271
mothers' pensions/benefits (Norway), 56-58, 65, 163, 169
municipalities
central/local dimension (findings), 250
Norway
disparities, 175-76
expenditure allocation, 157-59, 164, 165
Municipal Acts of 1837, 150
pension schemes, 17, 37, 38, 44, 54-58, 62, 139, 162, 216
Poor Law administration, 192-99, 207
Report on the Reorganisation of Municipal Social Administration (1962), 194-99
social assistance obligations after 1964, 179
Social Service Departments, 199-203
UK
Local Government Act of 1929, 209
reorganisation of personal social services, 228-44
social service obligations, 207

Myrdal, Alva and Gunnar, 59

National Assistance Act of 1948 (UK), 206-24, 227, 228, 229, 231
National Assistance Board, 132, 133, 221, 230, 231-32, 236, 239
National Assistance (UK)
contrast with Norway, 207-8
development of, 208-13
and National Insurance, 109, 112-13, 117, 124-31, 142
transition to Supplementary Benefit, 216-18, 224-27
National Committee of Organised Labour on Old Age Pensions (UK), 91
National Council of Labour (UK), 99, 106
National Health Insurance (UK), 90
National Health Service Act of 1946 (UK), 229
National Health Service (UK), x, 101, 111-13, 241
National Insurance Act of 1911 (UK), 39, 91, 93, 94, 104, 114, 131, 208
National Insurance Act of 1946 (UK), 71, 88, 117, 122, 130, 132, 141, 142, 208, 259
National Insurance Act of 1959 (UK), 129
National Insurance Act of 1967 (Norway), 73-77
National Insurance (UK), 109, 112-13, 117, 124-31, 142
New Zealand, 71
Nordli, Odvar, 81
Norwegian Association of Actuaries, 44
Norwegian Association of Social Workers, 178
Norwegian Social Welfare Association, 175, 178
Nygaardsvold, Johan, 45

occupational insurance
Norway, 53, 68, 83
Act on Accident Insurance for Factory Workers, 39, 77
Disability Pension, 78-82
UK, Boyd Carpenter Plan, 136-37
old age pension(s). *See also* pensions; social security/insurance
Norway
after 1967, 75
benefit levels, 51-52, 62, 67
coverage in, 48-51, 62
development in, 38-52
financing in, 42-48
influence on Disability Pension, 80
municipal plans, 54-56, 62
Royal Commission (1885), 39
as standard for other schemes, 70, 77
universality, 68, 86-87
origins and significance of, 32
UK
1908 OAP, 88, 90, 94, 95, 114, 140
National Committee of Organised Labour on Old Age Pensions, 91
pre-World War II, 90-100
Old Age and Widows' Pension Act of 1940 (UK), 211, 232

Pacifist Service Unit (UK), 234-35
pensions. *See also* old age pension(s); social security/insurance
Norway
Disability Pension, 78-82
extensions for new groups, 77-86
Government Report (1952), 74
mothers', 56-58
Special Addition (Særtillegg), 76-77
spending on, 4, 5
UK. *See also* National Insurance
supplementation, 119-20, 122-31
People's Insurance Committee (Folkeforsikringskomite), 41, 44, 56
personal social services. See also social assistance
Norway, 192-204, 255-56
summary, 248-49, 255-56
UK, 228-44
Phillips Committee (UK), 124, 126, 127, 129, 218
policy inheritance (importance of), 17,

22, 24, 36, 59, 90, 113, 114, 139, 257-58
Political and Economic Planning (UK), 105
politicians: role of key, 20-21, 257
Poor Law(s)
of 1388 (UK), 229
of 1834 (UK), 17, 149, 191
of 1845 (Norway), 149, 174
of 1900 (Norway), 152
characteristics of, 8-11
clientele of, 4
comparison (UK, Norway), 149-51
as explanatory factor for social assistance, 17-18
influence of, 257-58, 269. *See also* policy inheritance
Norwegian social services under, 192-93, 204
reform of, 213-16
relationship to modern social sciences, 15-16
residualisation in UK, 209, 211
poverty: attitudes towards, 252-56
private welfare
Norway, 52-53
vs. public welfare, 20
'psychopaths', 169, 170, 171
Public Assistance Committees (PACs), 209, 210, 212, 227, 230
public welfare: vs. private welfare, 20

Rehabilitation Benefits (Norway), 81-82
Report on the Reorganisation of Municipal Social Administration of 1962
(Norway), 194-99
residual model (Titmuss), 12, 14, 15, 16, 23, 262

Særtillegg (Special Addition), 76-77
Scotland, 237, 242-43
Seebohm Report (UK), 240-42, 244
selectivity. *See also* benefit levels
re: Norwegian old age pension, 48-51
of social services, 269-70
vs. universality, 12-13, 32, 68, 116, 117, 127, 143, 259-60, 264-65
Seweriin, Rakel, 78, 79, 181, 182, 183, 184, 257
Smyth, J.L., 100
Snowden, Philip, 95
Sobriety Board (Norway), 183, 187, 188, 194, 195, 198
social assistance
characteristics of, 23, 24
comparative study of, 7, 11, 26
defining, 6, 7
influence of social insurance on, 18-19
nature of benefits in modern schemes, 9
Norway
changing role, 183-87, 190
departmental response to 1953 proposals, 159-80
development in, 192-99
impact on social insurance, 153-54
perception of clientele, 160-71
reform (1953 proposal), 154-59, 181-83
vs. social insurance, 13
spending on, 4, 5
summary, 248
transition from Poor Law to, 8-11
UK, 205-27. *See also* National Assistance; Supplementary Benefit
dependency, 131-33
Social Assistance Act of 1960 (Norway), 170
Social Assistance Board (Norway), 173, 176, 179, 189
Social Care Act of 1964 (Norway), 179-80, 193, 197, 199-203, 204, 214, 221, 249
Social Care Board (Norway), 194, 203, 250
social conscience theory, 15
social division of welfare (Titmuss), 265-68
social insurance. *See* social security/insurance
Social Legislation Committee

(Sosiallovkomite, 1935), 59
Social Security Act of 1966 (UK), 225-26
social security/insurance. *See also* old age pensions; pensions
benefit levels, 32, 35-36
characteristics of, 23-24
concept of, x
conclusions, 258-61
coverage (variation in), 32, 35
defined, 6, 31n
development of, 18-19, 138-45
explanatory factors for variance in, 36-37
financing, 31-32, 33-34
importance of timing for, 21-22
influence on social assistance, 18-19
Norway
extensions for new groups, 77-86
impact on assistance, 153-54
rehabilitation, 154
vs. social assistance, 13
spending on, 4, 5
summary, 141-45
variables, 31-32
Social Service Departments
Norway, 193-99, 200-3
UK, 241, 249
Social Welfare Board (Norway), 195, 200, 202
social work
Norway
impact of Social Care Act (1964), 199-203
and money, 176-79
role in, 187-88, 190, 250
UK, 236-39
Soviet Union, 71
Special Addition *(Særtillegg)*, 76-77
Standing Committee on Social Affairs (Norway), 69, 70, 71, 74
State Rehabilitation Institute (Norway), 183, 186
stigma, 80, 159, 174, 203, 223, 249, 268-70
by association, 13, 129, 225-26
of means-testing, 50, 107, 208, 220-21
of Poor Law, 54, 215
Supplementary Benefit (UK), 205, 207, 216-18, 226, 227, 254-55
Survivors' Benefits (for children, Norway), 83
Sweden, 39, 59, 74, 82, 160
Switzerland, 39

target group. *See* clientele
taxation principle. *See also* financing
vs. contributory principle, 19, 34
Norway, 44, 60, 260
Temperance Board. *See* Sobriety Board
temperance movement (Norway), 181, 182, 183, 184, 187, 188, 189
timing of enactment (importance of), 21-22, 234, 256-57
Titmuss Group, 110, 135, 136, 140, 220, 221
Titmuss, Richard
and Kilbrandon Report, 242
and Longford group, 241
models of welfare, 11-15, 23, 262-63, 264, 271
on 'poor people's services', 160, 223, 269
social division of welfare, 265-68
on welfare altruism, x
on World War II, 65, 66, 212
Townsend, Peter. See Titmuss Group
Trade Union Congress (TUC)
and Beveridge Report, 100, 106
contact with Norway, 66
and Labour Party, 61, 98-99, 110-11, 140
publications, 90, 103
rejection of contributory insurance, 93
trade union movement. *See* labour movement
Transitional Payments (UK), 98, 209-10, 211

Unemployment Assistance Board (UK), 98, 207, 210-11, 233
Unemployment Insurance Act of 1938 (Norway), 65
unemployment insurance (Norway),

68, 83
Unemployment Insurance Statutory Committee (UK), 99
universality. *See also* benefit levels
limits in Beveridge Plan, 131-34
Norway
as goal in, 49-50, 67, 68, 71
process of achieving, 86-87
re: old age pension, 48-51, 68-71
vs. selectivity, 12-13, 32, 68, 116, 117, 127, 143, 259-60, 264-65

Wales, 240, 242, 243
Webbs, the, 104, 110, 140, 191, 219, 220, 223, 224, 226, 264
White Paper on National Insurance of 1948 (Norway), 67-68, 71, 85, 145, 152
widows' benefits
Norway, 68, 83, 163, 169
UK, 130, 211, 212, 214, 215, 221, 232, 233
Wilson, Harold, 221, 224
Workers Commission (Norway), 48
workfare programmes, 9, 273
workhouse, 8, 17, 18, 108, 149-50, 186, 191
World War II (impact on Norway), 64-68
Wormdahl, Andreas, 189

Younghusband Report (1959), 222, 237

Aarvik, Egil, 189